IN THE FACE OF GOD

by Michael Horton

WORD PUBLISHING

Dallas·London·Vancouver·Melbourne

IN THE FACE OF GOD

Unless otherwise indicated, all Scripture references are from the
New King James Version of the Bible, copyright © 1979, 1980, 1982, 1990,
Thomas Nelson, Inc. Publisher. Used by permission.

Library of Congress Cataloging-in-Publication Data

Horton, Michael Scott.
   In the face of God / Michael S. Horton.
      p. cm.
   ISBN 0-8499-1302-0
   1. God—Knowableness. 2. Spiritual life—Christianity.
   I. Title.
   BT102.H65   1996
   230'.046—dc20   96-35071
                                                                        CIP

Printed in the United States of America

6 7 8 0 1 2 3 4 9 BVG 9 8 7 6 5 4 3 2

*To Dr. W. Robert Godfrey, for shouldering the burden
of being my mentor and friend with gracious equanimity.*

Heal then these waters, Lord; or bring thy flock,

Since these are troubled, to the springing rock.

Look down, great Master of the Feast! O shine,

And turn once more our water into wine!

—HENRY VAUGHAN (1622–95), "RELIGION"

ACKNOWLEDGMENTS

Special appreciation is due to the support staff at Christians United for Reformation, in affording me the opportunity to research and write this book. I am particularly grateful to Ms. Sara McReynolds for her untiring labors and thoughtful reflection, as I am to the Reverend Kim Riddlebarger and Dr. Rod Rosenbladt, my partners in crime who assisted in the critique of my manuscript. In that regard, I owe thanks to those whose work has helped shape my own thinking on this topic and who kindly took the time to review the manuscript along the way. Their names will be omitted so that the weaknesses of this work will not be imputed to them. I am also grateful to Nelson Keener, Jana Muntsinger, and the supportive team at Word.

MICHAEL HORTON, Ph.D., is the author of many books, including the Gold Medallion Award-winning *Beyond Culture Wars*, and is the publisher of *modern REFORMATION* magazine. A vice chairman of the Alliance of Confessing Evangelicals, Dr. Horton is co-pastor of Christ Reformed Church (CRC) in Placentia, California, and is currently a Research Fellow at Yale University Divinity School.

TABLE OF CONTENTS

INTRODUCTION

*"Protestants are altogether too much inclined to take things for granted.
We laugh at those on the other side of the ecclesiastical fence because
they bow and scrape and kowtow in the presence of the church. But we lack
reverence—not because we are free in the gospel, but because God is absent,
and we have no sense of his presence."*

—A.W. TOZER

G. K. Chesterton has been proved correct in his observation that when people stop believing in the true God of Scripture, it is not that they stop believing in anything, but that they now believe in anything and everything. Others have called it "credulity" and "superstition," as St. Paul did when he confronted the sophisticates in Athens: "Men of Athens, I perceive that in all things you are very religious; for as I was passing through and considering the objects of your worship, I found an altar with this inscription:

'To an unknown god'" (Acts 17:23).

Christians are faced, in every age, with the very practical question of whether they will believe in this particular God who reveals himself in history through a particular man named Jesus of Nazareth, or whether they will seek God in the idols of their culture, imagination, or works-righteousness. I wrote this book because of a growing concern that our culture is being swept into a new era not of secularism, but of superstition, and because the evidence seems to support the idea that even contemporary evangelical Christians are not sufficiently resisting the fads of our age.

I realize that some of the views I challenge are held by respected leaders who have wonderful ministries. But my convictions compel me to compare their views with what has traditionally been considered an orthodox view of Scripture.

We're no longer sinners, but seekers. We want to find a god who will not surprise us, especially a deity who comes, not "in the spirit of the day," as in paradise, to judge us for our rebellion, but one who is quite manageable, affable, and friendly—"one of the boys." Our forebears always warned us that there are two poles we must keep in tension: God's distance (i.e., transcendence), and his nearness (i.e., immanence). While the Enlightenment tended to so stress God's distance and unknowability, busying itself with nature apart from nature's Creator, Romanticism, which followed the Enlightenment, made the Creator and the creature virtually indistinguishable. The one error is Deism, the other Pantheism, and both are deeply unchristian.

Why are such distinctions important anyway? They are important because the most basic fact of biblical religion, summarized in the first Table of the Law, is that we must worship no God other than this particular God and that we must approach him only in his appointed manner. Today, we value sincerity above truth; feeling over reality. As long as people are honest, God will accept them, we reason, regardless of what they believe about him or how they intend to be (indeed, whether they even think they need to be) reconciled to him. Who is God and how can I know him? That is the question addressed in this book.

Reared in the warm environment of evangelical Christianity, I have come to appreciate more of its strengths and weaknesses in recent years. At its best, it has maintained the classic Reformation (indeed, Christian) balance between God's majesty, holiness, justice, wrath, and separateness from the sinful creature on the one hand, and God's mercy, love, freedom, and intimacy with his sinful creatures on the other. The bridge, of course, was always Christ. But we have been through a great deal over the last few hundred years, and as a result, we have sustained serious injuries.

It used to be that theological liberals were accused of getting rid of the doctrines that accent God's distance from us—doctrines such as the Creator-creature distinction, original sin, judgment, wrath, hell, and the like. All they preached was love and peace. As Yale theologian H. Richard Niebuhr caricatured the liberal perspective earlier this century, "A God without wrath brought men without sin into a kingdom without judgment through the ministrations of a Christ without a cross." Gone was anything that was offensive. After all, optimism and progress were the culture's reigning principles, and how could modern men and women understand or appreciate the relevance of such outmoded ways of thinking!

But today, these criticisms could almost equally apply to mainstream evangelical preaching, teaching, writing, worship, and evangelism. God is increasingly trivialized, as he is brought down to our level. As he goes down in our estimation, so we rise. In the end, God seems more user-friendly, more approachable, more like us, but less worth worshipping or entrusting with our eternal destinies.

What happens when we die if we have been worshiping the wrong God all this time? Will he let bygones be bygones?

I did not write this book primarily as a critique of the church, but as a readjustment of our thinking to a more biblical orientation on this most central confession of the Christian faith. It is not written merely as a doctrinal treatise, but as one long sermon. It is addressed to our heads and hearts equally, with the hope that we will all grow in both grace and knowledge. Furthermore, I did not write this book as if to settle the matter, but in an effort to provoke discussion of an issue that is sure to be unpopular among many of my brothers and sisters.

While a love for sound doctrine cannot be divorced from a personal relationship with the One about whom these truths speak, it is certain that the opposite of "dead orthodoxy" is not "living faith," but spiritual anarchy, superstition, and, in the end, paganism. For all who want to love God with both mind and heart, and who want to understand both his distance and his presence in our lives, this book will, hopefully, provide a guide. After sizing up the historical context that has placed us in this dilemma, we will turn directly to the biblical text and attempt to better appreciate the height, depth, and breadth of God's redemptive love in Christ. The goal is not only a life that is more doctrinally grounded, but one that is more eager than ever to avoid the dangers and enjoy the delights of intimacy with God.

1

⟨⟨❦⟩⟩

Too Close for Comfort

"'Am I only a God nearby,'
declares the Lord, 'and not a God far away?'"
—JEREMIAH 23:23

"It is a fearful thing to fall
into the hands of the living God."
—HEBREWS 10:31

What would you say if I told you that, according to today's pollsters and magazines, there is a groundswell of interest in spirituality? *Newsweek* has stated that more people this year will buy books on meditation, prayer, and spirituality than on sex and self-help. With angel calendars now adorning the mahogany-panelled offices of yuppies across the country, isn't this a bit of good news for a world weary of rationalism and the quenching of the spiritual?

Yes. . . . no.

Of course, it opens up tremendous possibilities for touching on religious subjects previously considered impolite. But, as the apostle Paul noted when he came to Athens, it is possible to be too spiritual or too religious. I am not concerned in this book with such sinister things as witches, ritual sacrifices, and New Age crystals. After all, Friedrich Nietzsche predicted that when the God who had been known and worshipped in Christendom is "dead," the result would be a "rain of gods," justifying G. K. Chesterton's suggestion that when people deny the biblical God it is not that they believe in nothing, but that they believe in *anything* and *everything*. My concern here is with the growing obsession

1

with the unseen world in the churches today and to point out some ways in which contemporary, Bible-believing Christians in churches across America are succumbing to the powers of superstition all around us.

First, you see the contemporary Christian obsession with superstition in its protests of Halloween, companies using strange symbols on their packaging, rock lyrics, games, and finding demons under every rock. Well-known evangelical seminaries and missions centers have become loading docks for a strange type of spiritual warfare in which territorial spirits are bound and bondage is broken through city-wide spiritual liberations. In spite of the fact that there is not a single shred of biblical support for such notions, on they go, fueled by popular fictional accounts of cities being won back from the darkness. In this scenario, the darkness does not seem to be the sort described by Scripture: spiritual death and the wrath of God (Eph. 2:1–6), but generational curses and ambiguous forms of bondage that must somehow be broken.

But in Scripture, spiritual warfare is not some metaphysical struggle with territorial spirits whom we are supposed to bind by the words of our mouths. In fact, in Ephesians chapter 6, spiritual warfare is concerned with the words of God's mouth—and not just any words, but the Word of the gospel.

Paul told the Ephesians, who were up to their garlic necklaces in superstition and magic, that Satan came to believers in order to try to destroy their faith. He would send flaming arrows of doubt, he would attempt to weaken their assurance in the forgiveness of God in Christ, he would attempt to lead them to the place where God once more became a wrathful judge to hate for his holiness and righteousness, instead of a loving Father to love because he had covered them in the holiness and righteousness of Christ.

Go back and read this famous passage on spiritual warfare, and you'll immediately discover that everything in the passage has to do with God, Christ, and salvation. It is about the gospel, not about devil-chasing or demon-binding curses.

But in every era in which the light of the gospel has been obscured and Christians have turned from the words of Scripture to feelings or images, superstition has crept in until eventually one begins hearing more about Satan than God, more about demonic forces than Christ and the gospel, more about spiritual warfare by using our own incantations (white magic, you could call it) in order to name and claim our way to happiness. As Georgia Harkness observed, "There is a difference between belief in God, which is religion, and using God, which is magic." Harkness was right; by that definition, many evangelical Christians today are practicing their own brand of witchcraft.

First, we are created in the image of God, to relate to God as a child to a father, but sin cut off that relationship. God comes to each one of us, and instead of seeing him as the fatherly source of all good, we see him as a judge who is coming to get us, sentence, and condemn us. Deep down, we know that this is what we deserve, but in our sinfulness and twistedness, we deny this. So we invent a smoke-screen. We sew fig leaves together. We think that we can appease God with our own self-made sacrifices, clothing, and offerings. But he comes to strip us of our religious opinions, images, and appeasements in order to clothe us in the perfect righteousness of Christ. The desire to escape the judgment of God by self-made and self-chosen appeasements is the root of superstition and paganism. That's why Martin Luther said, "The heart of man is empty. Man must rely on someone. But he cannot rely on God; therefore he must rely on a creature. Superstition is a pernicious emperor who rules in the world throughout the ages and whose rule the people of the world are glad to accept."

The Mystical Majority

Entertainment Weekly is not exactly the official mouthpiece of evangelical Christianity. Yet, like many secular periodicals it has a sense of the contemporary world's fascination with "spirituality." In its October 7, 1994 issue, Jeff Gordinier wrote,

> In a year when TV airwaves are aflutter with winged spirits, the bestseller lists are clogged with divine manuscripts and visions of the afterlife, and gangsta-rappers are elbowed aside on the pop charts for the hushed prayers of Benedictine monks, you don't have to look hard to find that pop culture is going gaga for spirituality. [However,] seekers of the day are apt to peel away the tough theological stuff and pluck out the most dulcet elements of faith, coming up with a soothing sampler of Judeo-Christian imagery, Eastern mediation, self-help

lingo, a vaguely conservative craving for 'virtue,' and a loopy New Age pursuit of 'peace.' This happy free-for-all, appealing to Baptists and stargazers alike, comes off more like Forest Gump's ubiquitous 'boxa chocolates' than like any real system of belief. You never know what you're going to get.

The search for the sacred continues to be hailed in evangelical and liberal circles alike, sometimes with certain qualified reservations, but often uncritically. We've adopted a marketing mentality. We're proud to see that our "product"—a faith experience—has made it into the marketplace. After all, as long as people are getting closer to God, who cares how they get there?

Duke professor William Willimon, who describes himself as "a mainline-liberal-Protestant-Methodist-type Christian," complains that evangelicals now sound like liberals. Every path the liberals once took in distorting the message of Scripture, Willimon says, the evangelicals are taking now, with psychology part of it all. Although liberals got there first, "The psychology of the gospel—reducing salvation to self-esteem, sin to maladjustment, church to group therapy, and Jesus to Dear Abby—is our chief means of perverting the biblical text."[1] To the extent that we see Christianity as a means of securing self-awareness and psychic well-being through learning secrets, we more resemble the ancient gnostics than Christians. This is a growing concern of a number of observers both inside and outside the church.

One might think that a book titled *How to Get Close to God* should begin, right out of the gate, with the answers. But one vital question has to be raised before anything else is said: Are we so sure that it is a good idea to get close to God? Suppose a friend or relative who has rarely expressed any concern for eternal matters suddenly informs you that he or she is interested in "spiritual things." Does that immediately strike you as positive? After all, isn't it better to be open to the possibility of the spiritual realm than to be a hardened skeptic?

It is not uncommon to hear, even in today's evangelical churches, that God does not really care how we come to him, just as long as we come. However, there are a number of people in Scripture who would beg to differ, offering us testimonies of a decidedly different kind. They do not tell us of how they found God through their felt needs, but of how they met Someone they did not expect. These were close encounters of the very worst kind, and before we learn the delights, we must assess the dangers of intimacy with God.

In the Garden

We know very little about the daily events in the lives of Adam and Eve, our first parents, but their experience must have been wonderful. Created in God's own image, humans were designed with the specific purpose of communion with God. Imagine creating something that could interact and relate with you on a personal level. We speak of interactive computers and even artificial intelligence, but these are merely hyperbolic metaphors. Machines may be able to follow astonishingly complex patterns of programming, but they cannot reflect, meditate, love, hate, choose, reject, or develop intimacy with their creators. Yet God created beings who could have fellowship with him.

God put Adam and Eve in charge of the creation as his underlords. "God saw all that he had made, and it was very good" (Gen. 1:31). Lavishly ornamented with every conceivable fruit and vegetable, the Garden of Eden was literally heaven on earth—God's own small-scale copy of the heavenly city. Every tree was available for the pleasure and sustenance of Adam and Eve, with the exception of one tree in the middle of the garden. From this one tree, whose fruit offered the promise of knowledge of good and evil, God commanded Adam and Eve to abstain.

God created Adam and Eve righteous, and they were entirely capable of perfectly obeying him, walking with their Creator in uninterrupted fellowship for the rest of their lives. And, in fact, there was another tree in the middle of the garden—the tree of life, from which God intended to feed Adam and Eve at the end of their probation, guaranteeing their immortality. Their eternal lives were entirely dependent on their following God's command. Unfortunately, they made a tragic choice to disobey him.

With the help of the Deceiver, Adam and Eve were drawn into the idea that if they could gain independence from God and develop their own wisdom, their own experience, their own pathways to happiness, they would actually be *like* God (Gen. 3:1–5). Not only did they want to be close to God, they wanted to *be* God! They wanted to be able to choose for themselves what to believe and how to live.

Forfeiting immortality and eternal peace with God, Adam and Eve brought themselves and the rest of humanity under the good Creator's just curse. They quickly recognized that they were now sinners—rebels against God's righteous kingdom. Ashamed, they tried to cover themselves by sewing fig leaves to hide their physical nakedness. This is the essence of spirituality, according to worldly wisdom. It is the process of patching things up, covering over guilt, despair, and disgrace. Spirituality offers self-recovery and self-help rather than confession of sin and dependence upon God alone for complete redemption.

In fact, Adam and Eve ran from God's presence: "Then the man and his wife heard the sound of the LORD God as he was walking in the garden in the cool of the day, and they hid from the LORD God among the trees in the garden. But the LORD God called to the man, 'Where are you?'" (vv. 8–9).

It was while they were in flight that God caught up with the infamous couple. How liberated were they now? Their eyes were opened, we are told (v. 7), but what did they behold? Nakedness and shame. Adam explained why he was fleeing from God's presence: "I heard you in the garden, and I was afraid because I was naked; so I hid." Some confession for a newly-discovered god to make! But, of course, Adam realized that he was not a god. In fact, now he was not even what he had been before—a faithful creature and friend of God.

Satan had lied. His program for self-discovery, self-deification, and self-fulfillment had ended in total ruin. Yet God was unwilling to allow sin and death the last word. "The LORD God made garments of skin for Adam and his wife and clothed them," (v. 21) covering them in Christ's righteousness in anticipation of his sacrifice. Even as he did this, however, God exiled them from the garden, and he posted a cherubim at the gate to bar any attempts to build heaven on earth.

The irony here is unmistakable: Adam and Eve attempted to "save" themselves from God, only to find themselves lost and miserable. Meanwhile, God himself clothed their nakedness. In spite of their high treason, God cared for them. They covered themselves with fig leaves; God made garments of skin. They ran from God; God came to them.

We are no different. Fearful of judgment, we devise new ways of dealing with our sins and consequent guilt. Our coverings may be more sophisticated, gilded with psychological or spiritual terminology, but they are still nothing more than fig leaves. We want to find "the spiritual," perhaps, but the last person we want to meet up with is the God who is always there, for he knows what we are really like and will certainly judge us. Thus, we prefer encounters with "the sacred" to encountering God himself. Sacredness is ambiguous, open, free, and boundless. God himself is a particular person—Yahweh—who holds us responsible for our sins.

When You Care Enough to Send the Very Best

Later, Adam and Eve's sons, Cain and Abel, disagreed over how to worship God:

> Now Abel kept flocks, and Cain worked the soil. In the course of time Cain brought some of the fruits of the soil as an offering to the LORD. But Abel brought fat portions from some of the firstborn of his flock. The LORD looked with favor on Abel and his offering, but on Cain and his offering he did not look with favor. So Cain was very angry, and his face was downcast. Then the LORD said to Cain, 'Why are you downcast? If you do what is right, will you not be accepted? But if you do not do what is right, sin is crouching at your door; it desires to have you, but you must master it.
>
> —GENESIS 4:1–7

When she had borne her first child, Eve thought that perhaps she had given birth to the promised Messiah. In fact, she named him Cain, which means, "Here He Is!" But Eve soon discovered that instead of Christ, she had given birth to history's first Antichrist, as Abel's murder was clearly motivated by religious persecution. The enmity God had placed between the seed of the woman and the serpent now began to play itself out in the drama of human history.

Abel believed that it was dangerous to approach God in a way that was attractive, comfortable, or reasonable to the "seeker." He offered the first-born of his flock in sacrifice, as God had commanded in anticipation of his offering of his only-begotten Son. Cain could not figure out why God would need a bloody sacrifice. Perhaps he decided to be "vulnerable" and "honest," bringing God something more personal than that which had been commanded. After all, Cain was a worker of the soil, not a keeper of flocks. Why would God not appreciate Cain's creativity and his willingness to bring something special, something unique? Whatever the rationale, Cain did not obey what God had commanded, and he was rejected by God.

These offerings were not simply a matter of divine or human whim. It was not as if God had commanded that they bring whatever they felt like on a given day. Nor was it an arbitrary choice on God's part. Even this early in redemptive history, "without the shedding of blood there is no forgiveness" (Heb. 9:22).

After the Flood, Noah sacrificed burnt offerings to the Lord and the Lord "smelled the pleasant aroma and said in his heart: 'Never again will I curse the ground because of man, even though every inclination of his heart is evil from childhood'" (Gen. 8:21). Even before the extensive sacrificial rites commanded by God in Leviticus, the principle was clearly established in the earliest days of human history: the only way into God's presence was through a sacrificed substitute, pointing to "the Lamb of God who takes away the sin of the world" (John 1:21).

Cain's jealously over Abel's acceptance by God drove him to become the first persecutor of the church, and Abel became its first martyr: "Now Cain said to his brother Abel, 'Let's go out to the field.' And while they were in the field, Cain attacked his brother Abel and killed him" (Gen. 4:8). Jesus himself held that this was a story of religious persecution, as Abel sought to worship God according to the principle of a blood-sacrifice, referring to Abel as the first prophet and apostle martyred by the proponents of false religion (Luke 11:46–51). It is interesting to note that, writing against the ancient gnostics expressly, Jude warned believers against taking "the way of Cain" (v. 11).

The presence of God in all of his holiness is devastating when we recognize our unholiness. Abel was no more acceptable to God in terms of his own righteousness than was Cain—but he knew that. This is why he offered the firstborn from his flock, as God had commanded. The bloody sacrifice was the only acceptable offering for peace with God. Like his parents, Cain sought to discover his own path to God, his own "wisdom," a way of worship that he found acceptable and appealing to his own situation. But when the true God confronted him, Cain was so filled with rage that he took it out on his orthodox sibling.

Now, in the face of another terrible sin, God's mercy was demonstrated once more. He did not execute his justice immediately, but allowed Cain to live. In fact, he placed his own mark on Cain in order to preserve his life so that he could build a city and advance culture. Civilization was no longer to be a sacred endeavor, as it had been before the Fall, but it was nevertheless important.

There was a further sign of God's mercy and his unwillingness to allow the serpent to frustrate his plans for his image-bearer: God gave Adam and Eve another son to replace Cain. This son's name was Seth, which means "Elect" or "Appointed." Seth was given in place of Abel, not Cain. The biblical text contrasts Cain's line and Seth's line at this point. While listing Cain's descendants as the founders of various branches of music, art, and craftsmanship, we read of Seth's line: "At that time men began to call on the name of the LORD" (Gen. 4:26). This was true worship—not the personal activity, creativity, opinions, or experience of fallen creatures, but calling on the name of the LORD for mercy and for grace.

God's *common* grace would lead to the creation of culture, where creativity, human wisdom and imagination, and feverish activity would advance civilization. But God's *saving* grace was reserved for Seth—"Appointed"—and his seed. Ultimately, his family line led to Jesus the Messiah, the seed of the woman who would crush Satan's head. Only because of a bloody sacrifice, received by faith alone as people called on the name of the Lord, could sinners ever again stand in the presence of a holy God. "By faith Abel offered a better sacrifice than Cain" (Heb. 11:4). Apart from that, God's presence meant disaster, judgment, and damnation.

TOWER OF POWER

Even after the Flood, humanity still insisted on repeating the original sin, searching for a pathway to deity and wisdom that avoided observance of divine commandments. Determined never again to be at God's mercy, men and women set out to build a tower that reached to the heavens. And just as Adam and Eve accepted Satan's lie that they would be *like God*, the builders of the Tower of Babel declared, "Come, let us build ourselves a city, with a tower that reaches to the heavens, so that we may make a name for ourselves. . . ." (Gen. 11:4). Nimrod was the leader of this anarchy; appropriately, his name means "We shall rebel."

Adam and Eve thought they could escape God's presence in judgment by fleeing to the forest. Now humanity assumed it could escape divine judgment by building a tower that would save them from another flood. Instead of trusting in God's name, these inhabitants of the plain of Shinar wanted to make a name for themselves. So, like Adam and Eve and Cain, they set out to solve the problem of sin through technological wit and enormous physical labor, organized by clever strategy and management. And once more God came down in judgment, this time scattering the nations and confusing their languages (v. 8).

We have seen in our own modern age a multitude of attempts at building towers reaching to heavens. We call this a secular vision, but it is intensely religious. It maintains that, by coming together in organized development, we can save the world from the curse of the Fall—from war, poverty, injustice, famine, disease, and eventually death itself. We will create life—even human life—and destroy it at will. We will be like God, knowing good and evil (or like Nietzsche, beyond good and evil).

Tragically, faith in humanity ends up—in its disenchantment with humanity—hating humanity. Faith in humanity is responsible for more wars, more devastating ecological conditions, and more genocide than any dogma of history. We have reached for the apple of autonomy only to find ourselves naked and ashamed.

WORSHIPPING THE RIGHT GOD IN THE WRONG WAY

At Mount Sinai, after God led his people out of Egyptian bondage, the law was given to Israel. God chose Israel, not because of her righteousness, but because of his free mercy (Deut. 9:4–6). No nation could own Yahweh or be owned by him apart from a formal arrangement—a covenant. It was hardly as if God was everybody's friend and they just didn't know it yet! God was the enemy of the nations, commanding Israel to drive them out of the land. He only befriended Israel by means of a covenant—through earthly means of grace (word and sacraments that foretold a coming Savior). Even Israel could not approach God on its own terms, as we see at Mount Sinai.

God instructed Moses that, as in any covenant or treaty, a mediator was needed. God did not have a "personal relationship" with each Israelite, but was the father of the nation. "You must be the people's representative before God and bring their disputes to him" (Exod. 18:19). Notice the legal, courtroom language here. The people could not relate to God directly;

they needed a lawyer, and Moses was that mediator. Finally, the people were fully assembled at the foot of the Mount. We read:

> On the morning of the third day there was thunder and lightning, with a thick cloud over the mountain, and a very loud trumpet blast. Everyone in the camp trembled. Then Moses led the people out of the camp to meet with God, and they stood at the foot of the mountain. Mount Sinai was covered with smoke, because the LORD descended on it in fire. The smoke billowed up from it like smoke from a furnace, the whole mountain trembled violently, and the sound of the trumpet grew louder and louder. Then Moses spoke and the Voice of God answered him. The LORD descended to the top of Mount Sinai and called Moses to the top of the mountain. So Moses went up and the LORD said to him, 'Go down and warn the people so they do not force their way through to see the LORD and many of them perish.'
>
> —EXODUS 19:16–22

After God delivered the Ten Commandments at the top of the mountain, Moses returned to the people below. "When the people saw the thunder and lightning and heard the trumpet and saw the mountain in smoke, they trembled with fear. They stayed at a distance and said to Moses, 'Speak to us yourself and we will listen. But do not have God speak to us or we will die'" (Exod. 20:18–19). Staying at a distance because of fear is a normal human reaction to being in the presence of God.

Gnosticism has no place for fear, as the Persian evangelist Marcion declared. In his view, the Old Testament God was insufficiently warm and friendly. A God who blew smoke and fire at people was not worth worshipping, the gnostics insisted, so they declared the Old Testament God to be bad and the New Testament God to be good.

The fact is, God reveals himself both as holy and gracious, just and merciful, in both testaments. However, the Israelites knew very well that there was a distance between themselves and God: "Go down and warn the people so they do not force their way through to see the LORD and many of them perish." These people were so conscious of the Creator-creature distinction, not to mention their own sinfulness in the presence of absolute holiness, that they did not want a direct encounter! They did not want to see or experience God in his majesty and glory. "You speak to us and we will listen, but do not have God speak to us or we will die."

11

Can we, in our day, even conceive of a God whose presence so frightens worshipers that they beg for a mediator, knowing that if they go to God directly they will perish? As it happened, the mediator came in handy. God had barely finished inscribing the Ten Commandments on the tablets before the children of Israel were dancing around a golden calf. Israel had become impatient with Moses, and therefore, with God. Why was he loitering on top of the mountain for so many days?

We must remember that God's infant nation was only recently liberated from slavery in Egypt, where the worship of foreign gods was omnipresent. And, even while the second commandment was being entrusted to Moses, the people below were breaking it. As R. Alan Coe puts it, "As later Israel wanted a human king, not the invisible divine king (1 Sam. 8:4–8), so now they want a god 'with a face,' like everybody else. The last thing that they want is to be different, by their new relationship to God: yet this is God's aim (Ex. 19:5, 6)."[2]

In actual fact, they were not worshipping a false god (a violation of the first commandment); rather, they were worshipping Yahweh falsely. Those who suggest that it does not matter how we worship God, just so long as we worship the correct God, seem to forget the second commandment: "You shall not make for yourself an idol in the form of anything in heaven above or on the earth beneath or in the waters below" (Ex. 20:4).

Before we are too hard on the Israelites, however, we must ask ourselves whether we have become so "seeker-sensitive" that we too have fallen short of true worship. Humankind wants a god we can feel, touch, see, and hear on its own terms, and this is why highly emotional religion has sold well throughout the ages. A distant God seems too irrelevant and impractical to our felt needs. We want a god who is "up close and personal," a buddy who is just as close as our locker-room pals. So when we hear the report that God has made an appearance in all his glory, to be touched, experienced, heard and seen directly, we are quick to make airline reservations and become part of the action. But wherever God is present, apart from his appointed Mediator and the means of grace (Word and sacrament), he is present only in fire, smoke, wrath, and power.

SHOW ME YOUR GLORY

A good number of praise choruses today are based upon appeals to see God's glory. The romantic nineteenth-century hymns make us sing things that simply are not true: "I come to the garden alone, while the dew is still on the roses." Suddenly the soul hears Jesus calling, "and he walks with me and he talks with me."

Or we sing, "He Touched Me." Who among us has actually been touched by God? We ask to be "baptized with fire" and to feel the fire of his presence, not realizing that this is a request for judgment (Luke 3:16–17).

Where does the Bible promise that we will feel God's touch? This is nineteenth-century Romanticism, not biblical teaching. Surely after the account at Mount Sinai, we should reassess the notion of casually entering into God's presence. Are we really sure we want to be that close to God? Before we can answer affirmatively, we must appreciate the dangers involved.

After the episode of the golden calf, God led his remnant toward the promised land. At first, Moses wanted to see God's glory. Now, on a scale—the worst end being the Fall, Cain's murder of Abel over worship, and the Tower of Babel—Moses' request does not seem all that bad. There had already been some experience with the cloud of glory (Ex. 16:10), so Moses did not want to see God's glory simply out of curiosity, but because he was God's friend. He wanted to get to know God more personally, more intimately.

It is not this desire itself that is dangerous, for God also longs for intimacy with us. But the question is, How? God's presence is his glory, and when Moses asked God to remember that Israel was his people, God replied, "'My presence will go with you, and I will give you rest'" (Exod. 33:14). It was this presence that determined Israel's destination. "Then Moses said to him, 'If your presence does not go with us, do not send us up from here. How will anyone know that you are pleased with me and with your people unless you go with us? What else will distinguish me and your people from all the other people on the face of the earth?'" (vv. 15–16).

That was a very good question. Israel had to know that they were still his chosen people, forgiven saints in spite of their great sin and rebellion. God agreed to this request. "Then Moses said, 'Now show me your glory'" (v. 18). Again, Moses was not demanding to see God according to his own sinful opinion, imagination, or experience. He was asking God to disclose himself. God's answered:

> And the LORD said, "I will cause all my goodness to pass in front
> of you, and I will proclaim my name, the LORD, in your presence. I

13

will have mercy on whom I will have mercy, and I will have compassion on whom I will have compassion.' 'But,' he said, 'you cannot see my face, for no one may see me and live.' Then the LORD said, 'There is a place near me where you may stand on a rock. When my glory passes by, I will put you in a cleft in the rock and cover you with my hand until I have passed by. Then I will remove my hand and you will see my back; but my face must not be seen.'"

—EXODUS 19–23

First, God revealed his glory to Moses in the announcement of certain doctrines: the attributes of God, namely, his goodness and sovereign freedom. It is as if he were saying, "Moses, if you want to see my glory, you must understand who I am." This could not be communicated in a moment of ecstasy, or through intense meditation and imaginative speculation. It could not be learned through a flash of experience that could not be explained in words. Quite the contrary, God insists that his glory could only be seen through words.

If one really wants to *see* God's glory, one must find it in his own revelation of himself as good and merciful. "I will have mercy on whom I will have mercy and I will have compassion on whom I will have compassion" (Rom. 9:15).

God is saying, "This is who I am, and if you want to have a personal relationship with me and experience my glory, here it is." It is not a glorious *experience* or a glorious *sight,* nor a glorious *feeling* or *idea,* but a glorious *revelation* of God himself as good and gracious. It is not something to be taken for granted, for no one has an exclusive claim to it.

Moses was granted an experience that no other sinful human being in all of human history had known or ever would know this side of heaven. Hiding Moses from the terrible brilliance of divine holiness, God covered the patriarch until his glory passed by and then removed his hand just in time for Moses to see his back. "But you cannot see my face, for no one may see me and live," God warned. (Exod. 33:20)

Moses could not see God's glory and live, because the patriarch was himself a creature, and therefore a sinner. His physical, emotional, psychological, and intellectual frame were simply too fragile to see God in all his glory. If this was true of Moses, what shall we say of those who tell us of visions with God in which he and the seer chatted informally face-to-face? If "no man can see [God] and live," the last thing any one of us should want in our present fragile state is a personal encounter with God in all his radiant glory. For sinful creatures, that is to invite a direct experience with "the consuming fire" (Heb. 12:29).

A Burning Question

Fire From Heaven, the title of Harvey Cox's survey of Pentecostalism, has been a favorite metaphor for many Christians in our day. "Fire from heaven" is a very important concept to a wide cross-section of Christians around the world who are especially interested in spiritual experience. And that makes the story of Nadab and Abihu particularly relevant. After all, it is here where the phrase "strange fire" originates. However, unlike popularized conceptions, the biblical account treats fire from heaven as a bad thing.

Nadab and Abihu were Moses's nephews and Aaron's sons and his pride and joy. They were consecrated to God's service, *summa* grads from seminary, and their whole lives were devoted to the pious worship of God as Israel's priests. One day, they decided in their great zeal to offer to the Lord a ceremony that was not commanded—"strange fire." Was God pleased? Did he appreciate the zealous creativity of his high priests?

Apparently not: "So fire came out of the presence of the LORD and consumed them, and they died before the LORD. Moses then said to Aaron, 'This is what the LORD spoke of when he said, "Among those who approach me I will show myself holy; in the sight of all the people I will be honored."'"

"Aaron remained silent" (Lev. 10:1–3). And no wonder Aaron remained silent. Imagine watching your own two sons instantly consumed in the white-hot flames of divine wrath. It was not as if they had fashioned a golden calf—as their father had done, and lived. By this time, God was close to his people and the temple was among the worshipers. Only the high priest could enter the Holy of Holies, but God had, through priestly mediation, invited his people into his presence. This nearness, however, required special attention to the observance of everything God had commanded in worship.

In this same text, God demands, "You must distinguish between the holy and the common." This is a significant statement. Mystics tend to regard everything as sacred. According to Gnosticism, the self alone, meditating on heavenly things, is just as sacred as the public worship of God through Word and sacrament. Why should one have to go to church when one can just as easily worship him through private experience and meditation?

Nadab and Abihu remind us that God did not make allowances for sincerity. "But their heart was right" was not a sufficient argument. Aaron seems to have learned his lesson about God's holiness after the sudden death of his sons. Nevertheless, God gave careful instructions to Moses after this tragic episode. "The LORD said to Moses: 'Tell your brother Aaron not to come whenever he chooses into the Most Holy Place behind the curtain in front of the atonement cover on the ark, or else he will die, because I appear in the cloud over the atonement cover'" (Lev. 16:1–2).

There was not only a holy *time* and a holy *place;* there was also a holy *way* in which Aaron the High Priest was to enter:

> This is how Aaron is to enter the sanctuary area: with a young bull for a sin offering and a ram for a burnt offering. He is to put on the sacred linen tunic, with linen undergarments next to his body; he is to tie the linen sash around him and put on the linen turban. These are sacred garments; so he must bathe himself with water before he puts them on . . . the goat chosen by lot as the scapegoat shall be presented alive before the LORD to be used for making atonement by sending it into the desert as a scapegoat . . . He is to lay both hands on the head of the live goat and confess over it all the wickedness and rebellion of the Israelites—all their sins—and put them on the goat's head. He shall send the goat away into the desert in the care of a man appointed to the task. The goat will carry on itself all their sins to a solitary place; and the man shall release it in the desert.
>
> —LEVITICUS 16: 3–4, 10, 21–22

A common thread runs through all these episodes, from Adam and Eve's fig leaves and Cain's false worship to Aaron's sons. That thread is the principle of mediation and blood-sacrifice. Any aspect of worship that attempts to take the seeker into the Holy of Holies without going through the Mediator and the sacrifice leads to judgment. Israel's faith was filled with a sense of awe and respectful distance, fearful even to spell out the divine name. This reverence stands in sharp contrast to today's "God is rad; he's my dad" informality. We must beware of scandalous familiarity with God. Perhaps we do not know him as well as we thought we did.

In God's Presence

Centuries after the time of Moses and Aaron, the Assyrian Empire was sweeping across the world in devastating conquest. Ahaz, king of Judah, turned to the Assyrian king for military defense. The result was that Israel fell to Assyria, and Judah was threatened as well. As Isaiah had prophesied, Jerusalem was spared. But the prophet warned that Judah would be carried off captive to Babylon in the future for her sins. It is in this context that Isaiah brings "woes and judgments," followed by a most unusual vision:

> In the year that King Uzziah died, I saw the Lord seated on a throne, high and exalted, and the train of his robe filled the temple. Above him were seraphs, each with six wings: With two wings they covered their faces, with two they covered their feet, and with two they were flying. And they were calling to one another: 'Holy, holy, holy is the LORD Almighty; the whole earth is full of his glory.' At the sound of their voices the doorposts and thresholds shook and the temple was filled with smoke.
>
> —ISAIAH 6:1-4

At this awesome sight the prophet was in quite a humbling predicament. Isaiah could stand up to the kings of Judah and Israel, pronounce judgment against the surrounding nations, and call his countrymen to repentance in the face of enormous opposition. But now he found himself on the other end of things: unholy, sinful, and condemned: "'Woe to *me!*' I cried. '*I* am ruined! For *I* am a man of unclean lips, and I live among a people of unclean lips, and my eyes have seen the King, the LORD Almighty'" (v. 5, emphasis added).

One encounter with God will strip even the most godly heart of any sense of personal integrity. It is easy to think that we are leading lives of righteousness before the world when we are not falling into gross public sin. However, when we are in the presence of God, we are suddenly aware of the deep depravity of our wicked hearts and affections. This encounter

17

with God, this experience of being in the divine presence, did not lead Isaiah to exalted celebration and feelings of ecstasy. It led him to utter despair.

But the good news is as wonderful as the terror: "Then one of the seraphs flew to me with a live coal in his hand, which he had taken with tongs from the altar. With it he touched my mouth and said, 'See, your guilt is taken away and your sin atoned for'" (vv. 6–7). What did Isaiah do to remove his guilt and to atone for his sin? Absolutely nothing. How could he do anything to cover over his sinfulness? Even those attempts would have been sinful acts of self-righteousness.

It was God himself who comforted Isaiah with the gospel, removing his guilt, and atoning for his sin by the work of Christ which still lay in the future of human history. God's holiness and unconditional grace are clearly exhibited throughout all Scripture. But nobody, under either the old or new administration of the covenant of grace, was allowed to come to God on his or her own terms. Even in Isaiah's vision, fear turned to laughter and joy only because God took the initiative to save him by atonement.

Then or now, the fact is, apart from the mediator, no one can stand in God's presence. The Creator of heaven and earth is not simply hoping that everyone will come to see that he really is a nice guy after all. Instead, he warns from heaven that a day of judgment is coming. This message may not satisfy the felt needs of sinful men and women, but it will satisfy divine justice and bring God glory: "Surely your wrath against men brings you praise" (v. 10).

All that we can hope for is divine mercy: "Out of the depths I cry to you, O LORD; O Lord, hear my voice. Let your ears be attentive to my cry for mercy. If you, O LORD, kept a record of sins, O Lord, who could stand? But with you there is forgiveness; therefore you are feared" (Ps. 130:1–3). That forgiveness, of course, comes to us through the life, death, and resurrection of Jesus Christ. He is the Sacrifice, and he is the Mediator.

And He Walks with Me

That old gospel song extols walking and talking with Jesus in a garden, "while the dew is still on the roses." Certainly none of us has physically done this. But the disciples did, and we have a record of many of their experiences with the Lord. While it is true that they enjoyed times of great camaraderie and friendship (Jesus was fully human as well as fully divine), there were moments when they also noted the great gulf between God and humanity. Even in the presence of Jesus, clothed in humanity, they knew that they were in the presence of the God far away (i.e., transcendent) as well as near. (See Jer. 23:23.)

Jesus called to Peter one day as the fisherman was busy trying to make his day's quota. Jesus told Peter to put the nets into the water. Peter pulled up such a full catch that the nets began to break and other fishermen had to assist him in bringing the fish on board. "When Simon Peter saw this, he fell at Jesus' knees and said, 'Go away from me, Lord; I am a sinful man!'" (Luke 5:8). Like Isaiah, in the presence of God, Peter became conscious of the gulf that separated a holy Creator from a sinful creature.

Like Peter, we all enter the Christian faith with the realization that we are not worthy of friendship with God. And yet, Jesus comforted Peter with the words, "Don't be afraid; from now on you will catch men" (v. 10). It is a sure sign that we are not enjoying the presence of the true God when we ignore that gulf and pretend that we are closer than we really are.

"Blessed are those who mourn, for they shall be comforted," Jesus would later declare in his beatitudes. Those who fail to come to terms with their sins and the distance that this creates between God and themselves will never enjoy the blessedness of being forgiven. Throughout the ministry of Jesus, there were these moments of absolute silence, moments of astonishment when men and women were suddenly conscious of being in God's presence with nothing to wear. It is only then, stripped of the fig leaves, that they—and we—can be clothed with God's sacrifice to enter into his holy presence properly and with confidence.

EATING AND DRINKING JUDGMENT

Those who explain episodes of divine fury simply cannot chalk them up to the "mean God" of the Old Testament. Divine justice, holiness, and wrath are equally revealed in the New Testament. Warning the Corinthians against "sinning against the body and blood of the Lord," Paul cautions, "For anyone who eats and drinks without recognizing the body of the Lord eats and drinks judgment on himself. That is why many of you are weak and sick, and a number of you have fallen asleep." (1 Cor. 11:27, 29).

Evidently, many Corinthians had been participating in the Supper in an irreverent and, in fact, sinful manner. Failing to comprehend this sacred meal as "a participation in the blood of Christ . . . [and] in the body of Christ" (1 Cor. 10:16), many were actually made ill, or died under divine judgment.

Some have carried this threat too far, however, using it as a source of terror for those who come to the Lord's Table as sinners. But eating and drinking "worthily" does not mean that we are required to have pure hearts and lives in order to take communion. Not only is communion available to sinners; it is available only to sinners. Eating and drinking worthily means, at least in part, that we come dressed only in the righteousness of Christ.

A day of judgment is coming, and "it is a dreadful thing to fall into the hands of the living God" (Heb. 10:31). To fall into his hands in utter despair of our own idols, our own felt needs, our own spiritual programs or pathways to God, is to find safety. But to fall into his hands in judgment is to discover eternal ruin. If we attempt to come to God on our own terms, inventing our own theology on the basis of our own personal experience or intuition, we will not find the God of mercy. We will, instead, be brought face-to-face with the God of terror, the "consuming fire," the sight of whom so terrified the Israelites that they begged that not another word be spoken.

The clear message from Genesis to Revelation is either go to hell with your own righteousness, or go to heaven with the righteousness of Christ credited to your account by faith alone. Faith in Christ is saving; faith in anything or anyone else is superstition.

In light of biblical revelation—God's own self-disclosure—we need to tread carefully, removing our shoes of speculation and emotion, for we are on holy ground. This is not meant to set the intellect against the emotions, by the way, for our idols come as easily from the speculation of our sinful minds as from the whimsical fancies of our fallen hearts.

Only when we come to God in his appointed way, through his appointed Mediator, do we find both our minds and hearts renewed. Only then can we find a genuine experience of God's goodness, grace, and intimate fatherhood. In the following chapters, we will pursue the biblical pattern for approaching God and finding intimacy with him. Let us respect the words from God's own mouth that are intended to give caution to our steps, so that we may find a warm welcome into his fellowship.

2

⊸⊷❧❦❧⊶⊷

How to Be Too Spiritual

"Self-salvation through knowledge has its own magic,
and this magic is not harmless."
—Eric Voegelin

People in other countries often accuse Americans of expressing a "greasy familiarity" with people they have met for the first time. Others find this same informality charmingly gregarious. The phrase provides a point of comparison here between our social customs and a "greasy familiarity" with God based on the belief that we have direct and immediate access to him whenever and however we want. When children in public school pray to whomever, in whatever way, God has to hear. Whenever sincere people gather in a building to worship according to their own personal tastes and opinions, God is impressed that they took the time, that they cared enough to worship. It was "real." They were "vulnerable." They got "honest before God." I call this "greasy familiarity."

While Gnosticism confuses the Creator with the creation (especially with the "divine self"), classical Christianity has always stressed the sovereignty and transcendence of God, who is distinct from, beyond, above and outside the human self. Yet, according to Yale's Harold Bloom, there is an Evangelical "creedless creed" that has at its center the belief in the "personal, subjective, experiential, and finally quite nameless." This kind of spirituality shares affinities with medieval mysticism in its search for the nameless One. It seeks a direct experience with God, the individual soul at one with God's Spirit, apart from any mediating institutions or sacraments.

It would seem that critics of modern American religion are on target in describing the entire religious landscape—New Age or liberal, evangelical or Pentecostal—as being essentially gnostic in nature. Regardless of the denomination, American religion is inward, and deeply distrustful of institutions, mediated grace, the intellect, theology, creeds, and the demand to look outside of oneself for salvation. This, of course, has enormous implications for Christian life and worship as well as theology. But there are also other cultural factors that play into today's gnostic revival.

A LIGHTNESS OF BEING

Friedrich Nietzsche (1844–1900) predicted that the "death of God"—that is, the end of any serious theological consciousness in Western society—would lead to "a rain of gods," a combination of nihilism (belief in nothing, cynical despair) and "a new Buddhism." By turning from the external—God, the world, other selves—an objective and historical atonement and resurrection—to the internal spirit, Americans have created an atmosphere of incredible "lightness," an airy, anti-material, spirit-like existence. Jackson Lears speaks of the "weightlessness" of human existence in the modern world.[1] David Wells has also made this point effectively.[2]

This is demonstrated in our modern world, where "light" technique has shoved aside "heavy" truth. Pragmatism, which is an intuitive, immediate "flash-of-insight" form of problem-solving, is valued over wisdom, an accumulated wealth of insights from the family, from the church, and from those who have long since passed from this world.

We hear "lightness" in the superficiality of our conversation, laced with the suspicion of tradition, institutions, and authority. "Lightness," or "rootlessness," is also apparent in more tangible ways, such as the replacement of neighborhoods with planned tracts of homogeneous, quickly erected, often cheaply constructed homes. These structures feature imitation marble, brick, and other "light" and inexpensive replicas of heavy materials. But there are deeper influences more directly related to the spiritual quest.

The famous sermon of Puritan William Davenport in 1684 announced,

"We have been dispatched by God and by history on an errand into the wilderness to create, on this land, a city on a hill, a light in the wilderness to all men."

Contrast Davenport's challenge with T. S. Eliot's *The Hollow Men* (1925),

> We are the hollow men
> We are the stuffed men
> Leaning together
> Headpiece filled with straw. Alas!
> Our dried voices, when
> We whisper together
> Are quiet and meaningless
> As wind in dry glass
> Or rats' feet over broken glass
> In our dry cellar[3]

Eliot goes on to speak of the human condition in terms of "shape without form, shade without colour, paralysed force, gesture without motion."

Our forebears who have long since passed into the other kingdom see us not as violent villains—that would be giving too much conviction to the modern temper. Rather, they simply, sadly, see us as "the hollow men, the stuffed men." Ours is "the dead land . . . under the twinkle of a fading star," and Eliot ends his lament with the famous announcement: "This is the way the world ends, not with a bang but a whimper."[4]

Urban humankind has been baptized into modernity, and today individuals are distinguished amidst the crowd by the series of numbers attached to their identity. University of Chicago theologian Joseph Sittler's observation concerning the effects of modernity on our physical existence could equally apply to our Christian lives:

> Contemporary humans are diminished because our roots are not as deep or as widely spread as were those of our forebears into the field, the forest, the woods. They do not touch the flowers, the animals, the daily tasks on the farm. Contemporary people, contemporary children particularly, think that hamburgers come from McDonald's. They think that Borden's makes milk and Kraft makes cheese. The closest any of them ever come to a lamb is a wool jacket. The increasing distance

from the natural world has made our vocabulary bereft of natural images, has almost stripped us of the possibility to talk of ourselves in relation to God's creation.[5]

Furthermore, modernity has obliterated time and place with the passport it gives us to the global village via CNN and the Internet. We see men and women dying on TV and pretend to be horrified, but we are not. We are dulled by access to this information, where the line between data and entertainment blurs. It is not really like being there, on the very spot where those people were shot, but it gives us the illusion that we have actually seen, heard, and touched the victims. We are not quite sure how to recognize the seam between reality and that which is beamed into our homes from satellites.

Marx may have been correct in his endorsement of Nietzsche's prediction that Christianity's decline would be followed by "a weightless period." In a mass, consumer-driven, capitalist world, declared the Communist Manifesto, "All that is solid melts into air, all that is holy is profaned." Perhaps that is, after all, what the "melting pot" of America really is: the way men and women give themselves up to become global consumers.

Marx supposed that a different economics would fill the void, but, of course, we know the rest of that story. In the end, all this has produced a light, popular culture that is mass-produced and market-driven. Unfortunately, this is not only true in greater society, but in the church as well. There the solid theological architecture has been dismantled as insufficiently "spiritual," by both liberals and pietists.

In the church we see this "lightness of being" even quite literally in church architecture. The church growth movement, unwittingly merging gnostic influences with modern marketing trends, rids churches of all of that "heavy stuff." Like the mall, the contemporary church building is designed for multi-purpose utility, not for worship. After all, if God's transcendence is no longer considered important, who needs "churchy" architecture getting in the way of the "worship experience" anyway? The designer's goal is to create an atmosphere of neutrality and comfort for the people, not to evoke a sense of divine holiness for worshipers.

Gone too are the sharp lines, rough edges, carved wood, and heavy furniture (especially the pulpit and communion table), for they cannot as easily be moved out of the way to make room on the "stage" for the performers. Like ourselves, the furniture must be mobile. The pulpit is not built permanently into the chancel, like an oak with its roots intractably clutching the earth.

This "lightness" is further served by the church growth committee's decision to get rid of the rough "masculine" edges of the architecture and to bathe the "stage" in warm mauve and turquoise light. Meanwhile, the Word has been removed, along with sacraments and discipline—the very marks of a true church. In fact, a newspaper account described a church in New Jersey that had managed to pare the service down to twenty quick minutes simply by getting rid of the sermon and the sacraments!

Most contemporary evangelical churches do not carry the idea of church growth this far, but the effects of modernity—and with it, Gnosticism—cannot be underestimated. Traditionally, the goal of the Protestant sermon was to afford an opportunity for God himself to address his people through the law and the gospel. The content, therefore, responded to a divine command: to preach the truth of God's Word and to teach the people the great doctrines of Scripture. The tone was dictated by the part of the divine address which the minister happened to be expounding.

In contemporary preaching, the goal is to meet the "felt needs" of the self. The tone is congenial, happy, informal and—above all, friendly. This approach has been described as "Church Lite," and it is this "lightness of being," this "weightlessness" of it all, that has characterized Gnosticism in every age. Every spiritual scheme that celebrates spirit over matter, soul over body, individual over community, freedom over form, subjective over objective, eternity over time, and experience over doctrine will necessarily dismantle anything of weight.

I do not believe that there is a conspiracy of a gnostic elite. Nor do I suggest that there an intentional, well thought-out renaissance of the ancient gnostic heresy in its pristine form. I am not addressing an issue espoused by a handful of powerful individuals, or a teaching that is popularly championed by movie stars and celebrity psychologists. However, something larger has crept into our Western culture like a fog, and that concerns me. I am instead attempting to explore a way of thinking that pervades the broad topography of the American intellectual, religious, and social landscape.

If one is looking for a one-to-one correspondence between the ancient gnostic heresy and contemporary manifestations, he or she will be disappointed. Like the authors who have helped me to understand the connections, I am committed to generalizations throughout this book. The "big-picture" is what I hope to bring into view, with full knowledge that many parallels will break down upon sophisticated inspection. Nonetheless, we owe it to ourselves and our Christian community to examine the situation carefully.

Narcissistic Expressivism

Alexis de Tocqueville, a French commentator, came to America in the early nineteenth century. He observed, "To escape from imposed systems" is (the Americans') goal, and "to seek by themselves and in themselves for the only reason for things, looking to results without getting entangled in the means toward them . . . So each man is narrowly shut up in himself, and from that basis makes the pretension to judge the world. . . . So the Americans have needed no books to teach them philosophic method, having found it in themselves."[6]

When this gnostic individualism and narcissism (self-worship) met nineteenth-century Romanticism and Transcendentalism, the expressive self took center-stage. After all, Emerson declared of himself, "I see all the currents of the universe being circulated through me; I am a part and parcel of God." Walt Whitman added his narcissistic anthem, "The Song of Myself." Soon Christian revival songs began to echo this self-centered preoccupation.

Then Transcendentalism met the twentieth-century therapeutic revolution, and nothing would ever be the same. We see this in its most banal form in the TV talk-show, where self-expression is the goal of everyone—from the host to the guests to the audience. Everyone believes that his or her own personal feelings are more valuable than the collective intellectual wisdom of the ages.

Again, in many ways, the church is becoming patterned on this "talk-show" approach. Recovery and self-help groups, discipleship programs and other small meetings have become more important than the worship service. We "share" our experiences or our "personal testimony," and this sharing often becomes the center of discourse. The church building itself is designed to make us comfortable. The liturgy and sermons are calculated to satisfy the self. The songs are increasingly centered around our feelings, experiences, and longings. It is not a very large step from all these to the expressivism that marks so much of contemporary "praise."

Some approaches are modest, allowing individuals to "express" themselves in their own unique way. Others push this narcissistic expressivism to the limits, insisting that the expression of joy means unplanned emotional release through laughter, roaring, clapping, dancing, or exhibiting other personal emotions. Inhibitions amount to a carnal stifling of the "spirit" (they say it stifles the Holy Spirit, but one wonders if they really mean their own spirit, which is often indistinguishable).

In this context, structured services seem to have become as passé as solid physical structures and institutions, words, sacraments, and doctrines in general. Instead, each self must be free to exhibit the ecstasy of intimate, immediate encounters with God. This follows the pattern of the culture in its obsession with creating the self rather than receiving one's identity from someone else.[7]

THE FEMINIZATION OF AMERICAN RELIGION

Calvinism is the fundamental enemy of the American religion. This is argued in nearly every recent work on the subject. Harold Bloom cites Swiss theologian Karl Barth and Presbyterian scholar J. Gresham Machen as two major antagonists of American Gnosticism. Similarly, Anne Douglas, Philip Lee, and Wade Clark Roof, flanked by a host of historians, all argue that the repudiation of Calvinism led to the feminization of religion and culture. In her latest book on New York City in the 1920s, Douglas, professor of American studies at Harvard and Columbia University, writes,

> Calvinism . . . had suffered 'the most spectacular defeat in the history of American religious life.' . . . The Calvinists' liberal nineteenth-century descendants insisted that God was less a father than a mother,. . . an 'indulgent Parent' (the term is that of the clergyman Noah Worcester), offering love, forgiveness, and nurture to all who seek Him. The Connecticut theologian Horace Bushnell, known as the 'American Schleiermacher,' explained that true religious experience meant falling back 'into God's arms,' pressed to the divine breast, 'even as a child in the bosom of its mother.'

God, Douglas says, became "well behaved, even domestic."[8] In her provocative book, *The Feminization of American Culture*, Douglas demonstrates that Calvinism was unseated by an Arminian and gnostic tidal wave that refused to believe any longer in the value of matter, the depravity of the self, helplessness in salvation, total dependence on divine sovereignty, freedom, and mercy. One glance at the nineteenth- and twentieth-century hymns will prove a shift from "Eternal Father Strong to Save" to the romantic rendezvous with Jesus in the heart's garden, to John Wimber's "Spirit Song" and, as Robert Godfrey calls it, the "God-Is-My-Girlfriend" music one often hears in contemporary Christian circles.

Surely few if any of the evangelical authors of nineteenth-century romantic hymns or contemporary praise songs would endorse radical feminism. Yet the impact of the general feminization has carried over into their compositions. Likewise, today's evangelicals are ready to attack the blatant Gnosticism of "Sophia" worship and New Age spiritualities in the mainline churches, while overlooking the subtler forms of Gnosticism that plague the evangelical world itself.

Just as Anne Douglas, herself a feminist, did not set out to make a political statement in her critique, our purpose here is not to get into the socio-political debate over women in the workplace. Personally, I am in every way favorable to non-discriminatory policies. But we must begin to recognize the ways in which Gnosticism's feminization relates to the way we view God and our relationship to him, including our worship. Feminization is, ultimately, a theological question—a biblical question.

The American Religion

A number of books have been published in recent years pointing up the "gnosticization" of American religion, including Philip Lee's *Against the Protestant Gnostics* (Oxford, 1987) and Harold Bloom's *The American Religion* (Simon and Schuster, 1992). Although Bloom, a distinguished Yale professor and the nation's leading literary critic, identifies himself as a Jewish gnostic, he provides a provocative insight into the popularization of Gnosticism.

Other studies have pointed tangentially to this same condition, such as those of professors Wade Clark Roof (University of California) and

Robert Wuthnow (Princeton University). Christopher Lasch's *The Culture of Narcissism* and Robert Bellah's *Habits of the Heart* provide similar indicators. Eric Voegelin, director of the Institute for Political Science at the University of Munich, has also argued this case and recognizes that it is not a new thesis. He cites Irenaeus, the church father who opposed Gnosticism most stridently, in the apologist's definition of the heresy: "*Gnosis* is the salvation of the inner, man. . . . *Gnosis* redeems the inner, pneumatic [spiritual] man." Voegelin shrewdly concludes, "Self-salvation through knowledge has its own magic, and this magic is not harmless."[9]

All of these writers point to the breakdown in the Reformation's orthodox stance, in both conservative and liberal camps, as opening the door to American Transcendentalism (parent of the metaphysical cults) and, finally, to the current orientation. Beyond the liberal-evangelical split, Wade Clark Roof now says we cannot discern any real differences between New Age and evangelical spirituality on a number of counts.

This new Gnosticism "celebrates experience rather than doctrine; the personal rather than the institutional; the mythic and dreamlike over the cognitive; people's religion over official religion; soft, caring images of deity over hard, impersonal images; the feminine and the androgynous over the masculine."[10] Although Roof does not make the point, these are clearly the tenets of ancient Gnosticism.

James D. Hunter observes, "The spiritual aspects of evangelical life are increasingly approached by means of and interpreted in terms of 'principles,' 'rules,' 'steps,' 'laws,' 'codes,' 'guidelines,' and the like."[11] Wade Clark Roof adds, "Salvation as a theological doctrine . . . becomes reduced to simple steps, easy procedures, and formulas for psychological rewards. The approach to religious truth changes—away from any objective grounds on which it must be judged, to a more subjective, more instrumental understanding of what it does for the believer, and how it can do what it does most efficiently."[12]

Gnosticism and the Pentecostals

Pentecostalism represents an even greater dependence on gnostic tendencies. "Just as faith healing held an important place among the medieval gnostics of southern France," Lee observes, "it has also been a significant element in the more extreme sects of Protestantism . . . The Savior God is pitted against the natural God, and before millions of television viewers the Savior God prevails."[13] Roman Catholic scholar Ronald Knox's book, *Enthusiasm* (Oxford, 1950), remains a classic study of this subject and he cites these revivals of Gnosticism in his own church as well as in Protestant sects.

In his recent work, *Fire From Heaven,* Harvard theologian Harvey Cox, who sympathizes with many of the Pentecostal groups he surveyed for his book, observes, "There is a favorite saying among Pentecostalists: 'The man with an experience is never at the mercy of the man with a doctrine.'"[14] Chronicling the enormous success of the Azusa Street Revival in 1907, Cox finds a number of affinities between Pentecostal services, Hindu mythology, and Roman Catholic folk religion— "magical realism," he calls it. The revival included trances, levitation, and ecstatic utterances as well as the visions of each other being consumed in balls of fire.[15] Like Bloom and Lee, Cox notices the affinities between Pentecostal disregard for creeds and doctrine and that of liberals, making both groups fertile soil for distinct types of gnostic spirituality. The Gnostic aversion to mediators between the pure Spirit of the self and God's Spirit is in view in Pentecostalism, which often emphasizes the Holy Spirit rather than Christ as the central figure. "It has persisted, I believe, because it represents the core of all Pentecostal conviction: that the Spirit of God needs no mediators but is available to anyone in an intense, immediate, indeed interior way."[16] Cox even notices (and celebrates) an inherent feminization of the doctrine of God in Pentecostalism.[17]

The outer edges of Pentecostalism are especially blatant in gnostic emphases, as a number of works have shown, including *The Agony of Deceit.*[18] Salvation is knowledge—"Revelation Knowledge" (Kenneth Copeland, Kenneth Hagin, Paul Crouch, and other "faith teachers" use the upper case to distinguish this from mere written revelation). The Word that truly saves is not the written text of Scripture, proclaiming Christ the Redeemer, but is rather the "Rhema" Word that is spoken directly to the human spirit by God's Spirit.

It is difficult to find a more explicit form of Gnosticism in current religious movements than in the Neopentecostal "Word of Faith" circle. No wonder Bloom writes, "Paul was arguing against Corinthian enthusiasts or gnostics, and yet I wonder why his strictures have not discouraged American Pentecostals more than they seem to have done. . . .

Pentecostalism is American shamanism." The author himself, by the way, applauds the gnostic tendency.[19]

Meanwhile, the "mind-over-matter" principles of Gnosticism, obvious in Christian Science and similar groups, are apparent in one popular Christian TV personality's "secrets" of the "invisible world." He argues, "The visible doesn't have near the power that the invisible has." Faith "brings about the control of the visible, because the invisible is infinitely more powerful than the visible."[20]

Faith in Faith Alone

God, it seems, is not the personal, sovereign "Creator of all things, visible and invisible," as the Creed says. In fact, God does not seem to be all that necessary in this scheme, as long as the initiate knows the secrets. A founder of the faith movement illustrates the point by describing what he claimed was a vision. Satan was periodically interrupting this gentleman's conversation with God. Asking God to silence the devil, God said he could not, so the "visionary" commanded Satan to be quiet. "Jesus looked at me," he wrote, "and said, 'If you hadn't done anything about that, I couldn't have.'"[21]

This teacher's booklet is suitably titled, *How to Have Faith in Your Faith,* for God is not the object of faith in this gnostic outlook. One is saved not so much by the revelation of Christ as redeemer through his blood, but by the revelation of secrets for harnessing the spiritual realm. Even prayer is not so much a means of communicating with a Deity who can change things, but a means of employing techniques that themselves secure the desired results. Or, more subtly, prayer has become therapy, a conversation with oneself more than one with a God who is distinct from oneself.

In a gnostic system, faith is a magic talisman or secret password for securing health, wealth, and happiness. In one popular charismatic's words, it is the "ability to reach into that world... across the dividing line between visible and invisible and bring forth miracles from the invisible world."[22] A renowned Korean preacher calls this invisible realm "the Fourth Dimension," and his American counterpart suggests that "God wants us to live in that world, that we would focus our attention on it, that we would understand it."[23]

No wonder, after studying the Korean pastor's Full Gospel Church in Seoul, Korea, Cox concluded that there were striking similarities between

Korean Pentecostalism and Asian shamanism.[24] Although he is no evangelical himself, and no enemy of mysticism, Cox warns Pentecostalism of "a vacuous 'cult of experience,' too much in keeping with the contemporary celebration of 'feelings,' and the endless search for new sources of arousal and exhilaration," expressing worry that "Pentecostalism could disappear into the vogue of New Age self-absorption. The popularity of health-and-wealth theology shows how quickly this could happen."[25] Their "ecstatic worship" amounts to "a kind of populist mysticism."[26]

While many Pentecostals prefer experience to theology, they have developed a theological system, and it shares many basic characteristics of Gnosticism. In fact, there really is no such thing as matter, according to one best-selling author. Everything is spirit, or what he calls "energy."[27] We follow Jesus because "he flowed with supernatural faith."[28] In other words, he shows us, teaches us, initiates us, into the secrets of the invisible world.

Even prayer is not spiritual enough, since it seems to rest on the providence of a personal God rather than on the certainty of one's own decreeing authority. "Most people ask God for a miracle," says the same author, "but many omit a key requirement—the spoken word. God has given us authority over disease, over demons, over sickness, over storms, over finances. We are to declare that authority in Jesus' name . . . We are to command the money to come to us."[29]

Geddes MacGregor, an expert on ancient Gnosticism, observes that the gnostics of the early church "claimed to possess a special kind of knowledge (*gnosis*) of the spiritual chemistry of the universe and an esoteric insight into the workings of the divine nature. These sectaries expounded wildly speculative views and indulged in fanciful and sometimes grotesque interpretations of Scripture. Some even mingled magical formulas with their teaching."[30] In that respect, there is a parallel with the advocates of the "prosperity gospel," their obsession with a secret knowledge of the way the spiritual laws operate in the invisible realm, and their view of faith as a form of magic.

A well-known religion columnist explains that Pentecostalism "is rushing into America's religious sensibilities as fire rushes into dry brush. . . . and for the same reason. Pentecostalism is the aggressive, ecstatic, humble, broken, unpretentious, celebratory, loud, rejoicing, triumphant, multiracial, purely spiritual assertion of God as Holy Spirit active upon the physical persons and cognitive souls of his beloveds. . . . "(emphasis added).[31] Our real self— "the compelling portion of our self"—is Spirit, the columnist argues. "Even the mind boggles before spirit's greater greatness and toward the hope its presence brings."[32]

The spread of Pentecostalism as a force, according to this writer, is a key indicator of where religion is headed: "That place is in the ecstatic. That place is in the elevated and celebratory state of awareness in which the self escapes its own confines in worship and joins others like itself in a universal and wordless glory."[33] While Pentecostalism may express gnostic tendencies more explicitly, it would be wrong to conclude that this is a case of "us versus them," typical of many critiques of charismatic or Pentecostal excess. We are all in this together and will have to help each other extricate ourselves from the tentacles of non-biblical world-views.

A Personal Relationship with Jesus

For those of us who were raised in fundamentalist, evangelical, or Pentecostal sects, the experience of "rebirth" comes neither through the Word of the gospel nor through the water of baptism, but through a "Spirit baptism" that does not require any prior connection to divinely-ordained means. Among many evangelicals in our day, preaching is increasingly subordinated to the "worship experience," as the worshiper communicates directly with the Spirit. Similarly, the sacraments, if given any serious place at all in worship, are often considered object lessons to stimulate the heart to feel the love of God.

The Word is primarily seen merely as an instrument for coaxing people into accepting the new birth. "Making a decision" causes the intimacy of a personal relationship with God to commence. The new birth, especially if one judges by the testimonies of converts, is not so much the result of hearing with human ears, in human words, a declaration of things that happened in human history. It is not so much the preaching of the cross, but the preaching of "my personal relationship with Jesus," the day when "Jesus came into my heart." The story we love to tell is really a story about ourselves, how we found the Lord, and how we are different people since the day we asked Jesus into our hearts.

At this point, however, in the very process of defending divine transcendence, we have to beware of denying something important to Christianity. It does not take very long for someone to notice that the Bible is a very personal book. It addresses the whole person, not merely the intellect, and it is emotionally powerful and physically demanding in response. When God either threatens judgment or promises mercy, it is not merely an idea called "humanity" that he has in mind as the recipient, but individual men, women, and children.

God sent his Son not only to redeem a people, but to redeem *me,* and to enter into personal fellowship with individuals like *me,* who were once his enemies. Reconciliation is not just a doctrine; it is the reality of a personal relationship with a holy God who has made peace through the cross. Far from opposing the exultation in the impact of the Spirit's work in our hearts, Scripture directs us to praise God for his personal activity in our lives.

Nevertheless, throughout Scripture, it is always the preaching of Christ, not of conversion and Christian experience, that is held forth as saving truth. My purpose is not to deny that personal and subjective side, but to argue that this orientation has almost entirely shoved the external and objective message of Christianity aside. Philip Lee notes,

> Whereas classical Calvinism had held that the Christian's assurance of salvation was guaranteed only through Christ and his Church, with his means of grace, now assurance could be found only in the personal experience of having been born again. This was a radical shift, for Calvin had considered any attempt to put 'conversion in the power of man himself' to be gross popery. In fact, "Rebirth in God is the exact opposite of rebirth into a new and more acceptable self, as the self-acclaimed born-again Christians would see the event.[34]

Even a reasonably sound Bible teacher who is unfamiliar with these debates can find himself unwittingly influenced by such ideas. According to one, for instance, "we meet God in the realm of our spirit."[35] Although they were believers, "many of the Corinthian Christians hadn't entered the spiritual dimension yet," leading us to wonder how a genuine Christian can be "dead in sin" and unregenerated.[36] Apparently unaware of the gnostic implications, he tells us the real reason why we still struggle with sin is that "our problem arises from living as redeemed spirits in unredeemed bodies. We desire to be delivered from these bodies of flesh so that we can enjoy the full, rich, overflowing life in the spirit."[37] We are reminded of the words of the fifteenth-century mystic, Thomas a Kempis:

34

> Learn to despise the world of outward things, and devote your-
> selves to what lies within. . . . Deep in your heart is where he [Jesus]
> likes to be. . . . Up with you, then, faithful soul, get your heart ready
> for the coming of this true Lover. . . . If you love Jesus, if you love the
> truth, if you really direct your gaze inwards . . . , then you can turn to
> God at will, lifted out of yourself by an impulse of the spirit, and rest
> in him contentedly.[38]

Similarly, a well-known evangelical seminary founder earlier this century declared,

> A Christian is a Christian because he is rightly related to Christ;
> but 'he that is spiritual' is spiritual because he is rightly related to the
> Spirit. . . . The human, at best, could be no more than the channel,
> or instrument, for the divine outflow. . . . A Spirit-filled Christian
> [is distinguished] by actualizing into celestial heart-ecstasy that which
> has been taken by faith concerning the positions and possessions in
> Christ. . . . It follows, therefore, that true leading, in this dispensa-
> tion, will be more by an inner consciousness than by outward signs.[39]

Consider a similar statement:

> We should strive to reach the Horeb height where God is re-
> vealed; and the cornerstone of all spiritual building is purity. The
> baptism of Spirit, washing the body of all the impurities of the flesh,
> signifies that the pure in heart see God and are approaching Spiritual
> Life and its demonstration.

That last quote comes to us from Mary Baker Eddy's *Science and Health*
(1915), a major text in the development of Transcendentalism's metaphysical cult of Christian Science.

My purpose is not to argue that respected evangelical Bible teachers are no different from the founders of metaphysical cults. But I want
to point out the inroads that have been made by gnostic thought, even
in our own circles where the specific tenets of Gnosticism would be, no
doubt, immediately recognized as heretical if laid out in contrast to
biblical Christianity. It is not the result of intentional error, but of reinventing a wheel that was never yet round.

FEELING FREE, FEELING BETTER

As a sort of evangelical Lourdes, a movement has spread from the Airport Vineyard in Toronto to other cities in Canada, the United States, Britain, and in many parts of the world. The much-publicized phenomena include barking, clucking like a chicken, roaring, laughing, and running "Jesus laps." Ever since January 1994, Baptists, Presbyterians, Lutherans, Methodists, and scores of non-denominational groups have been forced to take positions on whether they are for or against the "Toronto Blessing."

According to one Toronto Blessing participant, "I grew up in a sedate church that I didn't enjoy, and my profession focuses on logical thinking. Logic doesn't work with God. You have to *feel*." As Carol McGraw's *Orange County Register* article reports, "One magazine named it the city's top tourist attraction, and airlines have added extra flights to handle the 250,000 pilgrims who have come to experience the blessing."

Dismissing critics, the justification offered by Rick Wright, pastor of the Pasadena Vineyard, employs a consumer hedonism: "If you find a place that serves the best hamburgers in town, is it wrong to want one?" McGraw relates, "Believers say that during the Toronto Blessing services they are touched directly by God. Some feel as if electricity is surging through them, that they are being immersed in flames, ice, soothing oil. Thousands say this experience healed emotional, physical, and spiritual aches and pains."[40]

Ironically, while many conservative Protestants remain skeptical of such movements, mainline Protestants are increasingly open. Even Duke University Medical Center professor, Dr. Harold Koenig, says that such spiritual releases are psychologically healthy. "The manifestations are a release," he says. "They put problems in God's hands. They feel better."[41]

They feel better. In other words, these manifestations are justified, not because they are believed to be God's way of communicating with and redeeming lost sinners, but because of their cash-value in therapeutic terms. That is, of course, close to the justification that philosopher William James placed on religion, saying that the truth of a religious claim is judged in terms of "its cash-value in experiential terms." However wrong-headed his assertions, the father of philosophical pragmatism could not have summed up the typical American justification for religious beliefs and behavior more suitably.

Gnosticism's Higher Path

Gnosticism's "higher knowledge" is not found by looking outside of oneself, but by dwelling on the "inner light." It is that knowledge that one best-selling Christian author describes as "intelligence that comes from God without reliance on sight, sound, taste, touch, or smell."[42] Preaching requires sound. Reading the Scriptures requires sight. Receiving the sacraments requires taste, touch, and smell. These are the means through which God communicates with us, according to historic Christianity. But Gnosticism has always discovered a "higher" path.

The view that God speaks to us through higher means than mere words and sentences approaches the anti-intellectual mysticism of today's wider culture. Evangelical theologian Clark Pinnock asserts, "The issue God cares about is the direction of the heart, not the content of theology," and suggests that we ought to become "more spiritually Buddha-like."[43]

Again, the purpose in all of this is not to lump ancient gnostics, medieval mystics, and modern liberals and evangelicals into one indistinguishable grouping. Clearly, there are differences. Nor do I suggest that these writers are "New Agers" who should be targeted by disapproving groups. Rather, I assert that something larger than the New Age movement, modernism, and evangelical revivalism is the story behind these other stories. Harold Bloom's point is essentially undeniable: The American religion, regardless of the denominational label, is Gnosticism. It is not merely a New Age or left-leaning phenomenon. It is swallowing the culture whole, and with it, much of modern Christianity.

In Gnosticism, not only the object of faith, but the act of faith, becomes radically revised. Faith becomes magic, a technique for getting what we want by believing in it strongly enough, and by knowing the rules of the secret world. In the words of an influential missiologist and advocate of the Vineyard movement, "Empirical evidence also validates the absolute necessity of faith or whatever else you want to call it—possibility thinking or goal-setting—as a prerequisite for church growth."[44]

In Search of the Sacred

Is faith really a synonym for "possibility thinking" and "goal-setting"? Then would not everyone possess "faith"? Or is faith a unique gift from God to trust in Christ, as in biblical teaching? *The Second Helvetic Confession* (a sixteenth-century Reformed statement) declares,

> Christian faith is not an opinion or human conviction, but a most firm trust and a clear and steadfast assent of the mind, and then a most certain apprehension of the truth of God presented in the Scriptures and in the Apostles' Creed, and thus also of God himself, the greatest good, and especially of God's promise and of Christ who is the fulfillment of all promises.

The gnostic world-view is also dominated by a fascination with the dualism between light and darkness, where spiritual warfare takes on an increasingly super-spiritual preoccupation. Like some contemporary Christian novels, this popular view of spiritual warfare in which individual believers decide the outcome of battles between good angels and bad angels is too close to Manichaean Gnosticism for comfort. But this is not unique to the modern world. Abraham Kuyper, a nineteenth-century Dutch theologian and prime minister, was apparently concerned that a "Pentecostal" revival of Gnosticism was even taking place in some circles in Holland. He wrote,

> Entangled in the meshes of this Manichaean heresy . . . are those who advocate the ridiculous efforts to banish demonic influences from rooms and vacant lots. All this is foolish, unscriptural, and yet defended by believing men in our own land. O Church of Christ, wither art thou straying?[45]

IN SEARCH OF THE SACRED

The gnostic revolution has been demonstrating its elasticity in recent years in the spirituality of the "Baby Boomers" whose interest in "the sacred" has been celebrated in national periodicals. In fact, its study has become something of a cottage industry. Wade Clark Roof sampled a wide variety of "seekers," and collected their sound-bite theologies. For instance, Sonny D'Antonio, raised Roman Catholic, considers himself "a believer, but not a belonger. . . . The material parts of the church turned me off," he says.[46]

Mollie Stone, raised a Pentecostal, tried Native American spirituality, then Quakerism for its "inner peace," and is "turned on" to Alcoholics Anonymous and other recovery groups, although she is not herself an alcoholic or related to one. As for churches? "Creeds and doctrines divide people," she says.[47]

Roof observes, "The distinction between 'spirit' and 'institution' is of major importance."[48]

Although Roof does not identify Gnosticism, his studies mark undeniable parallels: "Spirit is the inner, experiential aspect of religion; institution is the outer, established form of religion. This distinction is increasingly pertinent because of the strong emphasis on self in contemporary culture and the related shift from objective to subjective ways of ordering experience."[49]

Religion is too restricting, but spirituality offers a way of "plugging into" the divine with the correct spiritual technology. We can believe anything that "works" for us, adopt any lifestyle that we find personally satisfying, and follow any teaching that lines up with our own intuition or personal experience in life. Roof explains, "As a computer programmer who happens to be an evangelical put it, without any prompting on our part: 'We all access God differently.'"[50]

Increasingly, technological terms have been transferred to theology, as if spirituality were a means of "plugging in" or "tapping" the "power" and "energy" of the spiritual world. Even the more mainstream Keswick movement, with its debt to Holiness teaching, has been criticized by Christian teachers from B. B. Warfield at the turn of the century to J. I. Packer today as engaging in "magic," because of its dependence on such language of "using God," like turning on the electricity, for one's own ends and at will.[51] Technology offers a whole new world of metaphors for gnostic emphases, such as "accessing God," and the New Age movement has done the most with this, explicitly blending science and magic.[52]

A SURVEY OF SEEKERS

Roof refers to the outer and inner worlds, the former being suspect while the latter is always respected. "Direct experience is always more trustworthy, if for no other reason than because of its 'inwardness' and 'withinness'—two qualities that have come to be much appreciated in a highly expressive, narcissistic culture."[53] But it is his surveys themselves that bear the greatest interest. Fifty-three percent of the Boomers said it was "'more important to be alone and to meditate' than to worship with others."[54] And this was as true for many evangelicals as for New Agers.

Linda is a staunch evangelical who supports causes to make America a more Christian nation. She tells us, "You don't have to go to church. I think the reason I do is because it helps me to grow. It's especially good for my family, to teach them the good and moral things."[55] In other words, the church imparts knowledge—not of sin and salvation by Christ's atonement, but offers salvation by practical techniques for Christian living.

The church that will get the "vote" of the seeker, then, is the church that offers (and delivers) more *gnosis*—saving techniques and secret formulae—than others. In fact, according to Roof's surveys, 80 percent of Americans believe "an individual should arrive at his or her own religious beliefs independent of any churches or synagogues."[56] "Respondents were asked if they agreed or disagreed with the statement, 'People have God within them, so churches aren't really necessary.' Right to the point, the question taps two views common to spiritual seekers: one, an immanent as opposed to a transcendent view of God; and two, an anti-institutional stance toward religion." The results? "Sixty percent of seekers view God in this mystical sense. . . ."[57]

The mystical seekers' spirituality "is rooted more in their own biographies and experiences than in any grand religious narrative that purports to provide answers for all times and in all places." This blends easily with secular or pagan modes of thought.[58] In Christianity, what counts is Christ's crisis experience on a Roman scaffold outside center-city Jerusalem; in Gnosticism, it is Linda's crisis experience that counts.

All of this is substantiated not only in the wider culture of "spiritual seekers," but even deep within the evangelical sub-culture. David Wells points to an important study of evangelical seminarians—tomorrow's pastors of Bible-believing churches across the country. Wells informs us that most evangelical seminarians believe "that the self is essentially innocent." A 1993 survey "seems to suggest that at the center of the lives of the participants, a vision of the self as individually discovered or created is more powerful than a vision of the self as fallen, perverse, and corrupt. This vision quite clearly has less to do with their professed theology than with their debt to their culture."[59] Perhaps this is why a majority of evangelical Christians no longer believe in such a thing as absolute truth. Of evangelical seminarians, only 26 percent believe that "long-standing doctrines are the surest guide for knowing ultimate religious truth"[60] and "64 percent reported feeling a strong need for new experiences."[61] Wells adds:

The orientation toward self is also evident in the seminarians' views concerning salvation. While 41.6 percent indicated an orthodox belief that the most important benefit of salvation was that they had been spared God's judgment because of Christ, 45.5 percent listed as the most important benefit such things as an experience of inner peace, divine power, an ability to love others, and a sense of community within the church—all benefits that are consistent with the values of a therapeutic culture.[62]

Those in the Know

The therapeutic lingo may give it a new face, but it is Gnosticism that the churches have inherited through the tributaries of German liberalism, American romanticism, and Arminian mysticism. Wells writes, "Emil Brunner has argued that the old platonic and neoplatonic thought that dominated medieval mysticism reappeared at the Enlightenment to produce ideas of universal 'interior' religion and that this vision found new life again in Protestant liberalism."[63]

If experience is most trustworthy, and the cognitive (intellectual) aspects of a religion are downplayed ("heart knowledge" over "head knowledge"), what is to keep us from another "Dark Ages" of gross superstition? Will it be higher education? Belief in ESP, astrology, and reincarnation is actually highest among college graduates.[64]

The "unknown God" of ancient Greece turns out to be not so distant from the spirituality of the nineties. As Roof puts it, the "god" of even the evangelicals is amorphous and undefined. This God is thought of in very human terms: God, as it were, is created in one's own image," and one might add, God is created in one's own experience. Even the evangelicals, Roof notes, "put a strong emphasis on the moral aspects of faith" over cognitive belief. The American religion is united in its affirmation that, "It's not so much what you believe, or which religion you follow, it's how you live.[65]

Jesus is not as much a Savior as a moral hero, teacher, and guide for the *gnostikoi*— "those in the know." "Not just dropouts, but many loyalists and returnees speak of Jesus in a way that is vague theologically, but morally uplifting. . . . Theological language seems to have given way to psychological interpretations. If there is one theme throughout that characterizes the languages of Boomer faith, it is the subjectivist character of the affirmations: 'I feel,' 'I have found,' 'I believe.'"[66]

A Means of Escape

Along with observing spiritually-questing Boomers, escape from reality is another major theme of sociologists and psychologists in our day. Television viewing habits, entertainment obsessions, small-groups and psychotherapy, end-time movements, New Age fads, the nihilistic prose of some existentialist writers, and even the banal optimism of American sentimentalists who deny the reality of sin and evil all point to the growing sense of alienation from the real world. In short, we want to escape. Even much of our worship takes on an escapist tinge when we sing, "I hear the brush of angels' wings, I see glory on each face." If we are uncomfortable in this world, we simply find our way into super-spiritual dimensions.

Some can only find comfort in this world by baptizing it with spiritual phrases. Since natural explanations seem to leave God out of the picture, everything is therefore seen as supernatural. Consequently, the most mundane human activities are spiritualized. This is why, I believe, we feel so compelled to create Christian versions of everything, why we cannot simply enjoy a secular concert, book, or piece of art.

In any age, but especially in our own, we want to be free and pure—spirits without bodies, eternal birds soaring above the restraints of time and duty, unbound by creaturely limitations including human language. Even before the advent of personal computers, direct contact with the natural world was being shut out by a lifestyle that led from a modern workplace via the freeway to our homes, perhaps after stopping off for some fast food. The village square was replaced by the mall, the neighborhood grocery by a twenty-four-hour convenience store. Such hallmarks of our age cannot be dismissed as bearing little relevance to the way we think, especially about God and ourselves.

Cyber-Spirituality

Beyond these general trends, there is a more specific sociological factor that has made us especially open to gnostic escapism from the real world. University of California professor Mark Slouka is one voice among a growing chorus of concern over just this very point. Citing a host of "technoevangelists," Slouka demonstrates how explicitly they champion the immaterial—not merely as superior to the physical, but as the replacement of the physical.

For instance, John Perry Barlow, Grateful Dead lyricist and now a computer hacker, prophesies, "When the yearning for human flesh has come to an end, what will remain?"[67] Barlow believes that Mind will be "uploaded" into the Net.[68] University of Texas at Austin professor, Michael Benedikt, believes that "cyberspace will allow us to make up for the Fall from Eden, to redeem ourselves in God's graces," as it permits us "to shed 'the ballast of materiality' . . . "[69] "Reality is death," said Benedikt, so Slouka asks, "And what would we be escaping from? Almost everything, it seemed. The Earth—grubby and all too physical. The limitations of space and time. The body—impure, treacherous, and, most annoying of all, mortal."[70]

As Slouka put it, "The literature of cyberspace . . . [is] all about salvation. The new, electronic millennium. Transcending time and space, the family and the body. Oh, and sex, too."[71] In an age of sexually transmitted disease, nearly every lustful longing will be enjoyed without physical dangers. Barlow is explicit in his ideas: "Nothing could be more disembodied than cyberspace. It's like having your everything amputated."[72] What could represent a Gnostic redemption more perfectly?

In a similar vein, Sherry Turkle, professor of the Sociology of Science at the Massachusetts Institute of Technology, wonders what will become of human identity in the midst of the cyberspace revolution. Neither Slouka nor Turkle is anti-computer, but their concerns are with the ways in which such rapid technology is changing the way we think and act. Turkle notes how the postmodern preference for subjectivity, randomness, relativism, playfulness, irony and, above all, simulation, now finds its "objects-to-think-with" in the computer.

At first, computers were used to help us relate to the real world mere tools for calculating and storing information. But today, they are increasingly used to help us escape from the real world, as tools for creating a non-material reality. Many writers, both "technoevangelists" and their critics, seem to view much of the new "Net Religion" as a form of techno-mysticism.

Where computers were at first employed as extensions of the modern way of knowing by calculating and following rules, they are now programmed in postmodern ways of knowing, breaking the rules and taking cybernauts into unexplored worlds of virtual reality. A whole generation will grow up not being able to discern the real world from virtual reality.

And at a time when we have already little contact with the real world outside our homes, offices, and cars, many will probably prefer the virtual world to the real one. Even teachers who use computers now refer to being "addicted to flux."[73]

DOES MATTER MATTER?

Despite our desire to escape from "the real world," orthodox Christianity does not encourage such departures. "God likes matter; he invented it." Attributed to C. S. Lewis, that clever aphorism summarizes yet another Christian objection to Gnosticism. As we will soon see, Platonism and Neoplatonism formed the Greek philosophical side of Gnosticism, pitting matter against spirit.

In his 1972 booklet, *The New Super Spirituality*, Francis Schaeffer argued that while the left had been taken over by transcendental mysticism, evangelical Christianity had become significantly platonic. Showing some missionary friends great works of art in Florence, Schaeffer was disappointed when they seemed to have found no pleasure at all in the paintings. It was the same tendency he saw in the negative attitude toward sexual pleasure within marriage among many Christians as well as their anti-intellectualism and legalism.[74] The obsession with the end of the world was another sign of evangelicalism's "platonic" bent.[75]

It was against this "superspirituality" that many of the sixties youths rebelled, says Schaeffer, and this was why the Christian intellectual retreat center called L'Abri earned its fame. L'Abri sounded strange to many conservative Christians, as it attempted to wrestle with the issues of culture, art, philosophy, and other forms of human endeavor. It sought to build culture constructively, because the founders of L'Abri were confident that culture was a gift of God's common grace. As further evidence of the "new platonic spirituality," Schaeffer also warned against "the new Pentecostalism" that he saw emerging, where content was pushed aside in favor of experience. "One can also see a parallel between the new Pentecostals and the liberals," he wrote.

> The liberal theologians don't believe in content or in religious truth. They are really existentialists using theological, Christian terminology. Consequently, not believing in truth, they can enter into

44

fellowship with any other experience-oriented group using religious language. . . . Questions which have been considered important enough to cause crucial differences, all the way back to the Reformation and before, now are swept under the rug. On this level too, as with the liberals, it is as though people can believe opposite things on important points of doctrine, and both can be right. Or perhaps, it is better simply to say, content does not matter as long as there are the external signs and religious emotion.[76]

If some forms of extreme fundamentalism reflect a gnostic legalism, certain forms of Pentecostal or charismatic spirituality may be guilty of gnostic antinomianism (i.e., without rules or order). By rejecting structure, form, authority, creeds, words, and by emphasizing the work of the Spirit in the individual's heart more centrally than the work of Christ in history, many "free-spirit" evangelicals run the risk of abandoning classical Christianity.

We even see these effects in our public witness. Like some medieval sects and the Muntzerite Anabaptists who, during the sixteenth century, took up arms to create a new Jerusalem, some in our day want to impose their vision of a spiritual world by sheer will and political power. Whether they follow ideologies of the left or the right, there is a hostility to culture and to institutions that often motivate such action.

Some may be driven by the ascetic side of Gnosticism, while others are motivated by its libertine side. In any case, there is within the heresy a refusal to face the realities of a fallen, sinful world and to participate in the realm of nature, unless participants see themselves as saviors who know the way back to paradise. Still others, however, refuse to be involved in the realm of nature at all, as was the case with most Anabaptists, fearing that any involvement with the world was inherently unspiritual.

Ironically, it is this super-spirituality that undermines genuine biblical piety. In Scripture we find a unity of soul and body, faith and practice, doctrine and life. Could it be that one reason for the lack of genuine discipleship and obedience among professing Christians today has something to do with the fact that we have severed the soul from the body, leading to either legalism or antinomianism? Free either to do almost nothing or almost anything, Gnosticism's twin offspring undermine, each in its own way, the unity of the human person and cannot help but produce Christians who view doctrine and life in an antagonistic relationship.

A NECESSARY RETURN TO ORTHODOXY

So far, we have seen an emerging shape to this elusive heresy of the ancient church, distinct from orthodoxy in the following preferences:

+ the subjective over the objective
+ the secret and private over the public
+ mystical experience over critical understanding
+ the feminine over the masculine
+ spirit over matter
+ eternity over time
+ direct encounters with God over events mediated by matter and history
+ spiritual techniques for gaining access to and control over the secrets of the universe
+ salvation from the body, time, institutions, and escape into a realm of pure spirit

Only Christian orthodoxy directly confronts gnostic mysticism. True Christianity negates the chief articles of Gnosticism, while replacing them with something far more meaningful than one could imagine in the ivory tower of human speculation. This is precisely Paul's argument in First Corinthians, as he wonders why the church of Corinth is tolerating the gnostics who sought to synthesize Christianity and pagan mysticism.

God's foolishness is wiser than the wisest of human speculation. And getting "close to God" without carefully defining who he is, without knowing whether he can be approached at all, and without understanding how to approach him is an immense risk. As we will discover in the pages that follow, eternity hangs in the balance.

3

⟨⟨⟨◦⟩⟩⟩

AGE OF THE SPIRIT
OR SPIRIT OF THE AGE?

"History repeats itself. It has to;
nobody listens the first time around."
—WOODY ALLEN

Some time ago I was invited to participate in a panel discussion led by an insightful Jewish interviewer well-known for his political and religious interests. Included were a Roman Catholic scholar, a mainline Protestant, and a conservative Jewish rabbi.

Representing the evangelical position, I was asked, "What is the greatest spiritual need you believe your religion fills in your life?" After clearing my throat, I replied, "An immediate relief from the guilt and tyranny of my sin, and peace with God." Now everyone else was clearing his throat, and one of the panelists—the Roman Catholic participant—quickly asked, "But surely you wouldn't deny that our other friends here, myself included, would be under God's judgment." With the "cloud of witnesses" watching from the heavenly stands, I could only nervously but confidently reply, "Apart from explicit faith in Christ as the Messiah, the sin-bearer who stood in my place under God's wrath, I would only expect to die in my sins. So, to answer your question directly, yes—apart from faith in Christ's saving work there is no hope for you." I quickly added the Good News: "But, of course, God now offers to you and to everyone the gift of eternal life before he executes his final judgment."

The conversation then immediately turned to related issues about the meaning of religion itself. Why is someone religious? "I don't know," I replied. "Without the fact of Christ's historical resurrection, I can't see much use in it." The Roman Catholic and Jewish representatives joined in suggesting, alternatively, that *spirituality* is a more helpful term, since the purpose of religion, after all, is to help people develop their inner selves. For these gracious friends, religion was about appeasing humans, not God, and reconciling broken people to themselves, not to their offended but merciful Creator.

The trouble is, I've had similar conversations with self-described evangelical Christians. Like theire secular neighbors, many professing believers find it difficult to come to terms with the historical nature of Christianity. Take it as a style, a new birth, a radical change from one way of living and feeling to another, a way of finding inner peace: None of this offends our postmodern sensitivities. But when we locate Christianity's message—upon which it either stands or falls—on a life lived, surrendered, and taken back up again in our world and history, it is impossible to avoid making precise theological statements that offend our hearers, and sometimes even us ourselves.

But this postmodern situation is similar in many ways to the world in which the early Christians struggled. While Rome would easily have tolerated religious pluralism (i.e., belief in many gods) as a crossroads for the far-flung empire, it was the exclusivity and particularity of concrete claims that led the Christians to their deaths with the cry, "*Christos Kyrios!*" (Christ is Lord.) Meanwhile, there were always those who knew how to "spin" religion toward the "cultured despisers" of their day. They were the gnostics, and their curious elixir of Christianity and pagan religion threatened to poison the emerging church.

The New Gnosticism

"Heresy" is a big word, one that has plagued the Christian world since the time of the apostles. Heresy continues to be the result of ignorance among God's people. Few people seem to discern truth from error in today's culture. Perhaps this is why Jesus asked, "When the Son of Man comes, will he really find faith on the earth?" (Luke 18:8). St. Paul also warned Timothy, "In the last days men will be lovers of themselves . . . " (2 Tim. 3:1). These days, a narcissistic preoccupation with self corrupts all areas of life.

It is not as if our day is unique in that sense, but the modern Christian world is certainly characterized by a human-centered orientation and a forgetfulness of sound doctrine.

Among the heresies that plagued the struggling Christian community of the first few centuries, nothing was more devastating than Gnosticism. In fact, Gnosticism is as old as Satan's lie: "You shall be as gods." Contemporary American religion, whether liberal or conservative, evangelical or New Age, Mormon or Pentecostal, represents a revival of at least some aspects of that ancient heresy. The early church struggled to hold fast to basic Christian beliefs and practices (including spirituality) at a time when the "seeker-driven" approaches of their day insisted that they become more sensitive to the needs of an audience that found Christian doctrine alien.

Some things never change. In a *Los Angeles Magazine* article titled, "God For Sale," Kathleen Neumeyer wrote, "It is no surprise that when today's affluent young professionals return to church, they want to do it only on their own terms—what's amazing is how far the churches are going to oblige."[1]

Many of today's believers live like the Israelites in the Book of Judges: "In those days there was no king in Israel; everyone did what was right in his own eyes" (Judg. 21:25). In fact, one advocate of market-driven approaches to church growth writes, "This is what marketing the church is all about: providing our product [which he describes as 'relationships'] as a solution to people's felt need." "It is critical," he says, "that we keep in mind a fundamental principle of Christian communication: the audience, not the message, is sovereign."[2]

A *Newsweek* article describes today's churches: "They have developed a 'pick and choose' Christianity in which individuals take what they want . . . and pass over what does not fit their spiritual goals. What many have left behind is a pervasive sense of sin."[3] In the place of the sin-and-grace emphasis of Scripture, a variety of self-help cures attempt to make Christianity into a spirituality that will appeal to seekers. But as the quest for "spirituality" supplants Christian truth, one wonders if the salt has lost its savor.

St. Paul called the gnostic prophets "super-apostles" who apparently knew more than even God himself did. They were able to "see" into the heavenly secrets and offer techniques for escaping earthly existence. "Timothy," Paul warned, "guard what has been entrusted to you. Avoid the profane chatter and contradictions of what is falsely called knowledge; by professing it some have missed the mark as regards the faith" (2 Tim. 6:20). "We demolish arguments and every pretension that sets itself up against the knowledge of God" (2 Cor. 10:5).

The "super-apostles" preached a different gospel and a different spirit. "For such men are false apostles, deceitful workmen, masquerading as apostles of Christ. And no wonder, for Satan himself masquerades as an angel of light" (2 Cor. 11:13). That particular reference specifically refers to the gnostic emphasis on the angel of light versus the angel of darkness.

What Was "Gnosticism"?

Not far beneath the surface of much of the New Testament, especially in the Gospel of John and in the Epistles, is a running polemic against what most orthodox commentators agree was one of the most dangerous heresies in church history. According to one of its early opponents, St. Clement of Alexandria, Gnosticism (from the Greek word *gnosis,* meaning "knowledge") consisted of the knowledge "of who we were or where we were placed, whither we hasten, from what we are redeemed, what birth is, and what rebirth."[4] Knowledge of these secrets provided the key to redemption.

Furthermore, the gnostic sects were divided between libertines and ascetics. The former indulged in orgies, because they viewed moral rules as material fetters on the free spirit. The latter imposed strict restrictions. Both behaviors were rooted in disrespect for the human body. While the former sought to escape the "prison-house" of the body by self-indulgence, the latter sought to transcend physical existence by punishing or severely restricting it.

We see an example of the libertine gnostics in Corinth, where "free" worship led to disorder, confusion, and sexual license. This was so common that church discipline had vanished, and people were even getting drunk at communion. Meanwhile, an example of the ascetic brand of Gnosticism was found in Colossae, where Paul explains the cross as the final victory over sin and evil, concluding, "So let no one judge you in food or in drink, or regarding a festival or a new moon or sabbaths, which are a shadow of things to come, but the substance is Christ." The apostle's next words strike at the heart of the gnostic ascetics:

> Let no one cheat you of your reward, taking delight in false humility and worship of angels, intruding into those things which he has not seen, vainly puffed up by his fleshly mind, and not holding fast to the Head, from whom all the body, nourished and knit together by joints and ligaments, grows with the increase that is from God. Therefore, if you died with Christ from the basic principles of the world, why, as though living in the world, do you subject yourselves to regulations— 'Do not touch, do not taste, do not handle,' which all concern things which perish with the using—according to the commandments and doctrines of men? These things indeed have an appearance of wisdom in self-imposed religion, false humility, and neglect of the body, but are of no value against the indulgence of the flesh.
>
> —COLOSSIANS 2:18–23, NKJV

Few heresies that have perpetually haunted the halls of Christendom find their champions explicitly refuted in the biblical text itself. So it is a rather serious business to say that the chief heresy that occupied the attention of New Testament writers now influences modern culture, including liberal and evangelical Protestantism. Exploring this issue will require us to do a bit of historical homework, but it will also provide us with a necessary framework for analyzing contemporary spirituality and determining whether our approach to spirituality is genuinely biblical, or whether it is simply a replay of prior infidelities.

GNOSTICISM: THE ORIGINAL RECIPE

Gnosticism can be described in two ways: as an intentional rediscovery of the gnostic texts, or as an unconscious affinity with certain gnostic tendencies. Many secularists who have rediscovered "spirituality" are explicit champions of the former. The discovery of the Nag Hammadi literature and the scrolls of Qumran (Dead Sea Scrolls) in 1947 led to a flurry of academic fascination with ancient gnostic texts and their relation to the early Christian community.

The mood of the day, preferring experience to doctrine, has become fertile soil for such fascination to evolve from a quest for scholarship into a personal interest in esoteric spiritualities. I often browse in secular bookstores in the "religion" or "philosophy" sections. Among books about the

Bible, there are a number of handy references written by people who purport to have found "lost" biblical texts, often referred to as "the gnostic Gospels."

It's interesting that these are called "lost" texts, even though these writings have long been "found", and Christians have been aware of them for centuries. They were not lost at all, but were excluded from the canon of accepted biblical books on the basis of their lack of authenticity. Now, a number of feminists, mystics, and theological liberals have embraced explicit forms of ancient Gnosticism, mediated through the Jewish and Christian mystical tradition, Transcendentalism, and spiritualism, all sharing affinities with the New Age movement.[5]

Of course, modern evangelicals are not doing anything equivalent to New Age channeling; nor are they writing liturgies to Sophia. But the culture's gnostic undercurrent is deeply felt in even the most unlikely places. In fact, the revival of Gnosticism in our day has far more to do with the influence of nineteenth-century Romanticism and evangelical Revivalism than with the discovery of the Nag Hammadi documents, Elaine Pagels, and the so-called gnostic gospels. The gnostic revival to which we are directing our attention is much larger in its influence, sweeping the entire culture, from science and politics, as Eric Voegelin has pointed out, to art and religion.[6] The following are some of the chief characteristics of ancient Gnosticism:

1. "Cut-and-Paste" Spirituality

Scholars agree that Gnosticism was an eclectic religion, taking bits and pieces from Christianity and popular culture (especially Greek mysticism) and blending them together in a practical scheme. Since it was inherently opposed to systematic and orderly ways of thinking, Gnosticism could appeal to a wide cross-section of first-century "seekers." It was a hodge-podge of spirituality.

Philip Lee observes, "Gnostic syncretism . . . believes everything in general for the purpose of avoiding a belief in something in particular. In the case of Christian Gnosticism, what is being avoided is the particularity of the gospel, that which is a 'stumbling block to Jews and folly to Gentiles.'"[7]

We recall Paul in the Athens Areopagus, where "people did nothing but discuss the latest ideas" (Acts 17:21). There the apostle announced to his audience that they were superstitious. It isn't difficult to imagine an evangelist going to Harvard today and remarking, "As I looked at the kiosks and read the week's events, I noticed that you are very superstitious." The very subjects that one might find in a secular university environment today—"hot topics" in spirituality—were popular in Paul's day, especially among those who sought to blend Greek paganism and Christianity.

2. Individualist and Subjective

While gnostic writings are extremely esoteric and mystical, they exhibit an obvious thread of individualism and an inward focus which is generally characteristic of mysticism. As in Greek Platonism, the subject (the knower) has priority over the object (the known), and the path to spirituality is through inwardness, meditation, and self-realization. Gnostics believed that whatever happened to them in their own private experience was the final court of appeal.

By contrast, Christianity maintained that God had chosen individuals to form a community, sent Christ to redeem that community, and sends the Holy Spirit to unite the whole church to Christ. The church confesses its faith in what God did in history, not in one's own private experience. By looking outside rather than inside ourselves, we are brought into a saving union with Christ. The apostles and the early defenders of the faith knew nothing of an "inner light" or "divine spark" in the soul, a spark that could be fanned into a flame if given half the chance. Rather, said Paul, "You were dead in trespasses and sins . . . and by nature children of wrath" (Eph. 2:1, 5). Salvation, in the biblical sense, comes from without, not from within.

3. God's Nearness Over His Distance

Theologians refer to two poles: God's transcendence, meaning his distance from his creatures because of his holiness and greatness, and God's immanence, referring to his nearness and relatedness to his creatures. The ancient gnostics so emphasized God's immanence that they came to believe that God was actually a part of them. Their spirit was the "divine spark" that related directly to God. As one scholar explains, "The self is the indwelling of God."[8] In our day, Matthew Fox, repeating the warning of self-described gnostic psychologist C. J. Jung, expresses this sentiment well: "One way to kill the soul is to worship a God outside you."[9]

In fact, while one must beware of reductionism, the obsession with the psychic or spiritual aspect of the self is infused with gnostic overtones.

Modern psychology frequently mingles magic and science in a modern equivalent of medieval alchemy, so that the line between science and New Age mysticism is often thin indeed.

In gnostic literature, the relationship between "God" and the self is often described in romantic, even erotic language. The early church resisted this tendency to blur the distinction between creature and Creator, arguing for the biblical teaching that God is unapproachable by sinful human beings. While Scripture promises believers a personal relationship with God because of Christ, if there is to be a saving relationship with God, it must be God who takes action to find and redeem the lost.

4. Spirit Over Matter

The Greek and gnostic world-view is dualistic. It divides the world into matter (evil) and spirit (good). Evil, suffering, illness, and death are all attributed to the existence of matter. The Fall was not from innocence to rebellion (as in the biblical account), but from pure spirit to physical bodies. Imprisoned in a material world, the self is alienated from its true home. This theme of a war between light and darkness, spirit and matter, the divine within and the world outside, and the sense of alienation, despair, loneliness, and abandonment in the physical world is the recurring key to understanding Gnosticism.[10] It is popularly referred to in our day as "mind over matter."

The supposed battle between matter and spirit led gnostics to a rejection of Christ's incarnation. How could God become flesh if flesh was inherently evil? Jesus only *appeared* to have a physical body, they insisted. That is why they earned the nickname "Docetists," from the Greek verb meaning "to appear."

This belief also affected the Christian doctrine of the Resurrection. How could our salvation be won by the resurrection of the Redeemer's flesh? Furthermore, how could the resurrection of *our* flesh be considered "redemption"? It was the spirit's release from the "prison-house" of the body, not its eternal "incarceration," that gnostics considered truly redemptive. Redemption came from the soul's ascent from earthly to heavenly existence, not from God's descent from heaven to earth in a physical body.

A number of the Anabaptist sects at the time of the Reformation also seemed to share this dualistic outlook, viewing this world as inherently evil and incapable of being what Calvin called "the theater of God's glory." Salvation meant escape from the body and from the physical world, and the inheritance of a purely spiritual existence. In fact, Menno Simons (founder of the Mennonites) and John Calvin were locked in intense debate because Simons argued that Christ only "appeared" to have a real human body.[11] Menno Simons contended Jesus's earthly body was "heavenly," not earthly, and this the Reformers correctly recognized as Docetism.

It was this same heresy that St. John had in mind when he warned, "Many false prophets have gone out into the world," offering the following test: "This is how you can recognize the Spirit of God: Every spirit that acknowledges that Jesus Christ has come *in the flesh* is from God, but every spirit who does not acknowledge Jesus is not from God. This is the spirit of antichrist, which you have heard is coming and even now is already in the world" (1 John 4:1–3, emphasis added).

Related to this spirit-versus-matter orientation is the perfectionist character of Gnosticism. By transcending the earthly realm, mystics believed that they were climbing a ladder of spiritual perfection, freeing themselves from this world. Following Plotinus (205–270), a Greek philosopher, some of these writers argued that everything emanates from The One (God). Like a light-bulb, The One sends its emanation of light out, and the further one gets from the source, the darker his or her existence. That which is spirit is closer to the light, and that which is material is the most distant. It was this theory of emanation that became the basis for medieval mysticism's images of climbing a stairway of perfection, ascending the mountain within the soul to find the inner light.

5. Anti-institutional Orientation

Associated with matter and the physical imprisonment of the self, Gnosticism views institutions as spiritual enemies. The "Outside God" and the "Outside Church" are enemies of the soul, directing the self away from one's own inner experience, toward other people and to formal structures of authority, creeds, doctrines, rituals, and sacraments. Anything that makes God distant or somehow external to oneself is considered unspiritual. This leads to a hostility against forms, structures, institutions, and a sense of responsibility to the world.

St. Ignatius of Antioch (d. 110 A.D.) charged, "They have no concern for love, none for the widow, the orphan, the afflicted, the prisoner, the hungry, the thirsty. They stay away from the Eucharist and prayer."[12] But from the gnostics' perspective, why would they need these ecclesiastical rituals and relationships? They were the "spiritual ones." This did not mean that they did not form communities, but their communities were ascetic sects that served to nurture individuals. Within them were practiced experiential rather than liturgical and doctrinal forms of public worship. In their view, spirituality was best nurtured in private, not in public.

Throughout church history, the gnostic impulse that guided the sects of the Middle Ages, the radical wing of the Reformation, the Quakers, and the scores of cults and sects of America, has led to a rejection of the authority of the institutional church. Often led by charismatic leaders who claim to be privy to divine revelations, these groups are suspicious of the checks and balances that formal structures place on free spirits. They glory in their rebellion against traditional church teachings and structures. Their views were reflected, though indirectly, in liberated hosts of the sixties and in the New Agers of the present day.

By contrast, the early church, appealing especially to the New Testament epistles, directed believers to commit themselves to the church officers who had charge over them. They were exhorted to follow the doctrine and practice laid down by Christ and his apostles in Scripture, and upheld, explained, and defended by those whom God had placed as shepherds in his church (Heb. 13:17).

6. Anti-sacramental

Closely related to its suspicion of created matter and the institutional church is Gnosticism's disregard for sacraments. They believe that the spiritual self enjoys a direct and immediate relationship with God's Spirit, and that knowledge comes through a secret revelation of a mystical character. Therefore the introduction of material "means of grace"—the printed word (accessible to everyone), water (in baptism) and bread and wine (the Eucharist) actually become impediments to real fellowship with God. Where is the Spirit working directly and immediately? That is what the gnostic wants to know. Preaching is merely human speech—too unspiritual and unspectacular, as are the earthly elements of water, bread, and wine. How could salvation be mediated through matter?

Just as Menno Simons thought it was beneath God to actually become human, earthly flesh, gnostic sects throughout history have suspected that it is equally beneath God to require other common earthly elements for communion with him. Furthermore, the *gnosis* (revelation knowledge) is based on the idea that only a few really know the secrets. Christianity's emphasis on Word and sacrament—available to anyone who can listen, read, or eat—challenges this private, spiritual elitism. Their "inner light" doctrine led the Quakers, like the ancient gnostics before them and the transcendentalists like Emerson after them, to reject the sacraments of baptism and the Lord's Supper altogether.

7. Anti-historical

Philip Lee notes, "gnostic 'knowledge' is unrelated in any vital sense either to nature or to history."[13] As spirit is opposed to matter and individual inwardness is opposed to an institutional church, eternity is opposed to time. Salvation for the gnostic is redemption from the body, from institutions, and from the grinding process of history into which the pure self is mercilessly "thrown."

In biblical religion, God not only created the world (material as well as spiritual) and pronounced it good, but he unfolded his salvation through matter and history. In Christianity, redemption does not take place in a super-spiritual sphere above real human history, but within it. Gnosticism, however, emphasizes instead the self's personal, direct encounter with God here and now and has little or no place for the historical events of God's saving activity. Whatever has happened in the past is unrelated to the Spirit's direct activity in one's life today.

8. Suspicion of the Old Testament

Biblical religion focuses on God's personal involvement with the world in creation and redemption, beginning with the bloody sacrifices that anticipated the Messiah. In light of this, Gnosticism harbors a deep distrust of the Old Testament God. In fact, two gnostic sects appear in this connection. Marcion (d. 160 A.D.) rejected the Old Testament entirely on the basis that it represented a wrathful Judge who created matter and imprisoned souls in history, while the New Testament God (Jesus) was the God of Love. The Creator-God (Old Testament) and the Redeemer-God (New Testament) were viewed as opposites in Marcionism. In addition to the Old Testament, Luke's Gospel and Paul's epistles underwent radical revisions.

A century later, Mani, a Persian evangelist whose ideas spread quickly to the West and were embraced by St. Augustine before his conversion, founded the powerful sect of Manichaeism. Once again, it was deeply dualistic (spirit vs. matter, etc.) and championed salvation chiefly in terms of secret knowledge of the principles for overcoming the world, nature, and history through spiritual ascent. Again, nature had to be overcome by Spirit.

9. Feminist Theology

Ancient Gnosticism, as we have seen, divided the world into spirit and matter as if into columns of "good" and "bad." Feminine characteristics—love, freedom, affirmation, nurture—were placed in the "good" column. Those of masculinity—justice, law, wrath, strength—were associated with evil.

All this sharply contrasts with the Christian God who, in both testaments, is good, gracious, loving, and saving as well as just, holy, and sovereign. *Sophia*, the Greek word for "wisdom" (after the goddess of wisdom), became the deity of many gnostics. Reflecting a preference for feminine imagery, the thirteenth-century mystic Meister Eckhart wrote, "What does God do all day long? God gives birth. From all eternity God lies on a maternity bed giving birth." This image is replete in mystical literature.

"Ancient Gnosticism," Lee writes, "loathed the patriarchal and authoritarian qualities of official Christianity. From the gnostic point of view, the structure and discipline of the Church stifled the spirit."[14] The antipathy toward the natural order was reflected in the gnostic celebration of the "androgynous self."[15] While the body may be either male or female, the spirit is "free."

Contemporary feminist theologians have made a great deal out of the gnostic literature at this point. One example is the collection of essays edited by Karen L. King, *Images of the Feminine in Gnosticism* (Fortress, 1988). As we shall see in the pages that follow, the much-publicized "Re-Imagining Conference," where mainline Protestant feminists launched liturgies to Sophia that amounted to celebrations of lesbianism, was explicit in its Gnosticism and rejected the cross as a male religion of violence.

It is interesting to see that these same convictions are evident in the works of nineteenth-century romantic writers, poets, and artists. For instance, Nathaniel Hawthorne's characters are often distinguished by the negative traits of the masculine and the material, and by the positive characteristics of the feminine and spiritual. The pre-Raphaelite painters often depict subjects (especially angels) that are neither male nor female. Is it more than coincidental that these androgynous angelic images are presently making a comeback, even in Christian circles? There are those who find it offensive to think of Jesus as a male, with all the physical and emotional characteristics that go with that sexual identity. Gnostics, new and old alike, have been put off by the suggestion that God not only became human, but became a man.

10. Anti-intellectual

"Gnosticism" comes from the Greek word "knowledge." But we must beware of defining knowledge in our own terms. Lee observes:

> The difference between orthodox knowledge and gnostic knowledge has been described as the difference between open revelation and secret revelation. Although it is true for both faiths that the Holy Spirit is at work to open the eyes of the believer that he may know the truth, within orthodox thought the Holy Spirit's work takes place in the presence of, and in terms of, given historical data and within the context of the Holy Catholic Church. Thus, in the Apostles' Creed, the article affirming belief in the Holy Spirit is securely nestled between belief in the person and work of Jesus Christ and a willingness to learn from the Holy Catholic Church.[16]

Gnostic "knowledge" is not only anti-historical and subjective; it is also anti-intellectual and immediate. This is why St. Irenaeus called it "pseudo-knowledge" and Paul told Timothy it was "knowledge falsely called" (1 Tim. 6:20). Gnosticism preferred what we often call "heart knowledge" to "head knowledge," although Christianity knew no such dichotomy.

Geddes MacGregor observes, "All human thought, notably philosophical and religious thought, has two indispensable components: the speculative and the critical. The former is the imaginative, creative element, the latter the logical and analytical."[17] This is an important point for, as MacGreggor points out, Gnosticism represents the former tendency, while the orthodoxy against which Gnosticism reacts closely follows a written text and analyzes everything else in the light of the Bible's revealed truths.

Those who enjoy speculating and creatively imagining what God is like will probably be impatient with doctrines and rituals. Although not all aspects of medieval mysticism can be described as full-fledged Gnosticism, the Reformation was a revolt against the medieval triumph of the speculative over the critical, the mystical over the textual. It is, again, more than coincidental that, in our day, the same people who attack Christian orthodoxy as patriarchal are those who add such shibboleths as "logocentric" (word-centered) and "propositional" to their list of complaints. While feminine spirituality is creative, whimsical, and playful, orthodoxy is perceived as excessively logical, absolute, and restrictive.

T. P. van Baaren summarizes the characteristics of ancient Gnosticism. "Gnosis," he writes, "is not primarily intellectual," but chiefly mystical, intuitive and immediate. The gnostic knows what he knows by a flash of sudden revelation, a burning in the bosom, or an inexplicable "inner light." Furthermore, "*gnosis* is related to certain ways of understanding time and space," rejecting or down-playing the importance of real time and place, since existence is primarily concerned with the spiritual and non-material. "Gnosis is essentially secret, not available to all comers."

In other words, one has to know the "keys" to understanding the principles of the invisible world. "Sacred writings such as the Bible are interpreted allegorically. Where the question arises, there is a tendency to disparage or downgrade the Old Testament." As for the physical creation, van Baaren states that for the gnostic, "The world is regarded with pessimism," brought into being or ruled by evil beings. "Man is a mixture of spiritual and material components. The spiritual ones are the cause of his longing to return to God."[18]

In a way that is strikingly familiar to those who were raised with the famous biblical annotations of C. I. Scofield and other writers, van Baaren observes another central characteristic of Gnosticism: "Human beings are of three kinds: (i) those who possess full *gnosis* (the pneumatics) and are therefore capable of full salvation; (ii) those who have faith and have a limited capacity for salvation; (iii) those who are wholly absorbed by the cares of the world and are consequently incapable of salvation. . . . The mind-matter dualism generally leads to a severely ascetical manner of life, though it can also lead to a libertinism that is the very opposite."

Accordingly, van Baaren concludes, "Gnosticism is a religion of revolt" against institutional forms of religion, while it "appeals to the desire to belong to an elite." Much like modern liberalism, Gnosticism had no place for the Christian belief in Christ's deity and humanity united in one person: "Where the question arises, the tendency to distinguish sharply between Christ as 'heavenly Saviour' and 'the man Jesus' is prominent. Hence the docetism [denial of Christ's true humanity] that was a popular outlook in first-century Christian thought."

In addition, Christ is not so much the Redeemer by his saving work, but by his example. Because he overcame his earthly existence, we can learn how to conquer as well. Finally, "Salvation consists in the complete emancipation of the spiritual from the physical. This is expressed in the myth of 'the ascent of the soul.'"[19] Already we should begin to see some striking, and perhaps even uncomfortable, parallels to our own day and its view of spirituality.

GNOSTICISM TODAY

Giovanni Filoramo, a respected Italian historian of Gnosticism, asks, "Are we witnessing a rediscovery of *gnosis*? To judge from the many indications that may be found collectively or singly in contemporary culture, the answer would seem to be 'yes.'"[20] In every period of crisis and a loss of meaning, the tendencies toward esoteric speculation and mystical spirituality become increasingly attractive. This is especially true, Filoramo says, in a culture that has an unquenchable thirst for the novel. This we share with the first century Greeks.[21]

T. Roszak explains why this new way of knowing seems attractive to us in this particular time and place:

> We are in for an interlude during which an increasing number of people in urban-industrial society will take their bearings in life from the *I Ching* and the signs of the zodiac, from yoga and strange contemporary versions of shamanic tradition. The question for a communal reality assumes the shape of a massive salvage operation, reaching out in many unlikely directions. I think it is the greatest adventure of our age and far more humanly valuable than the 'race for space.' It is the reclamation and renewal of the old *gnosis*.[22]

After two world wars, Westerners became disillusioned with the grand scheme of turning this world into paradise restored. Like Romanticism's reaction against the cold sterility of the Enlightenment's rationalism, whether Unitarian or orthodox, we are witnessing a new call to go inside for the winter. Neither classic liberalism nor Protestant orthodoxy is attractive to today's "Boomers," who want to avoid religion in favor of spirituality.

Our historical situation has a lot to do with this turn of events. While the chronically depressed Dane Soren Kierkegaard, in his reaction against the Enlightenment and a dead, formalistic state church, helped to sow the seeds of discontent, it was the disillusionment that followed the so-called "Gay Nineties" that brought such optimism to a halt for many. Then when "the war to end all wars" was merely followed by another brutal conflict that massively destroyed lives and cities in Western Europe, Albert Camus, Jean-Paul Sartre, Franz Kafka, and Andre Malraux poured their energies into lamenting despair and alienation. The theme of humanity being "thrown" into the world, imprisoned in evil material structures and institutions, became prominent in American universities.

The legacy of Hegel, who believed that history was the evolution of matter into spirit, was carried on by Nietzsche and was executed by Hitler and Stalin. Expressing the sentiments of his hero, Friedrich Nietzsche, Nikos Kazantzakis wrote, "It is not God who will save us—it is we who will save God, by battling, by creating, and by transmuting matter into spirit."[23] Attracted by and indebted to Buddhism, Kazantzakis, reared in Greek Orthodoxy, is typical of the blending of Christian images and Eastern mysticism that is far more important in the long run than any New Age craze. Although the sixties gave rise to popular New Age trends, this attraction to Eastern religious and philosophical world-views actually emerged in the modern age, especially with the triumph of German and American romanticism.

Popular Existentialism blended with an older Transcendentalism, which had always seething just beneath the surface of the American consciousness, to produce a post-war generation of "seekers," ripe for gnostic spirituality. As we understand that Transcendentalism, we come to see how modern evangelicalism and liberalism represent sister "denominations" in what Yale literary critic Harold Bloom calls "The American religion."

EVANGELICALS, LIBERALS, AND ROMANTICS

Mysticism has a long tradition within Christianity. Although it developed out of the same influences and centers as Gnosticism itself, it was deemed acceptable even by some who had opposed the heresy. The "ladder of spiritual ascent," and the dualism between spirit and matter, inwardness, and related themes remind us that the difference is a matter of degree. In a sympathetic treatment, titled, *Mysticism in the Wesleyan Tradition* (Zondervan 1989), United Methodist theologian Robert G. Tuttle, Jr. traces the influence Greek and Roman Catholic mysticism had on John Wesley.

Various Holiness groups emerged in America in the nineteenth century. Through them, evangelicalism was heavily influenced by a form of spirituality that was considered by many during that century, especially at Princeton Seminary, to be a rival to the historic Christianity recovered in the Reformation. The very popular Keswick movement, also known by the phrases, "Higher Life" and "Victorious Christian Life," carried a heavy gnostic, mystical, and perfectionist strain into mainstream evangelicalism by the end of the nineteenth century.[24] We will specifically discuss this movement in a later chapter.

The gnostic view of the person as body, soul, and spirit was given new life, as best-selling writers argued that the "fleshly man" was the believer who was bound to his body and human passions, while the "spiritual man" was victorious.[25] It must be pointed out that by mentioning such evangelical stalwarts, my intention is not to mark them out as heretics. One seminary founder, for instance, was an ally in the battle for orthodox Christianity on many fronts. However, the currents of Gnosticism can affect even the most alert fundamentalist.

There were other influences, especially trends in the wider culture, that contributed to the gnostic awakening in America. A New Age mystic or mainline liberal feminist will surely express convictions that would have been regarded by most Christian writers as nothing short of the occult. But there is some irony in the extent to which certain limited connections with a larger gnostic framework are shared. Just as the medieval church was unwittingly shaped by Greek platonic and neoplatonic influences, modern American Christianity, both liberal and evangelical, is shaped by Romanticism—itself a revival of Greek and gnostic influences.

One popular romantic, Ralph Waldo Emerson (1803–82), resigned his Boston Unitarian pastorate in 1832 because he could no longer accept institutional religion and refused to serve "communion." (Since Unitarians, rejecting Christ's deity with its related truths, do not have a genuine communion, it is difficult to regard this as a major departure.) After all, Emerson said, he was himself a spark of God and enjoyed direct access without an incarnate Mediator, or the impediments of physical sacraments. At Harvard, Emerson declared that orthodox Christianity was dead, and the only way forward was to recover the "spiritual" dimension of religion.

Henry David Thoreau (1817–62) was closely associated with Emerson and other "transcendentalists," as many of the American romantics were now being called. One source defines Transcendentalism as "an optimistic, mystic and naturalistic state of mind rather than a system of thought," which had "a wide influence on American literature, philosophy, and religion. Based on English Romanticism (Coleridge, Wordsworth, Carlyle) and German philosophical idealism, it found Calvinistic orthodoxy too harsh and Unitarian liberalism too arid. It emphasized individual experience as sacred, unique, and authoritative."[26] We do not have the space to cite other authors extensively. Suffice it to say that as orthodoxy was rejected among American thinkers and the only other option was liberalism, the romantics turned inward.

The revivalists seemed to parallel this trend. Even their moral and social activism took on the flavor of romantic zeal for making the holy interior self a foundation for a new Jerusalem in America. The sense of alienation among the romantic writers is apparent in Nathaniel Hawthorne: "Taking no root, I soon weary of any soil in which I may be temporarily deposited. The same impatience I may feel, or conceive of, as regards this earthly life."[27]

If this feeling was true in the early nineteenth century, it is certainly exacerbated by the influences of modernity: the rootlessness precipitated by rapid travel, mobility, displacement of families, technological advances that tend to dehumanize existence. As for the gnostic preoccupation with spirit and the eternal over matter and time, Emerson declared, "I am to invite men drenched in Time to recover themselves and come out of time, and taste their native immortal air."[28]

Like the ancient gnostics who, according to St. Ignatius, did not bother themselves with the physical needs of this world, Emerson's spiritual arrogance knew no bounds, in the face of slavery: "I have quite other slaves to free than those Negroes, to wit, imprisoned spirits. . . . " "They have," he said, "no other watchman, or lover, or defender, but I."[29] In fact, while many evangelical sects were setting dates for the Apocalypse (in their great desire to escape this world), Emerson's Gnosticism took a different direction: "The end of the world will not affect me; I can live without it."[30] Just as ancient Gnosticism was divided into two camps: the licentious and the ascetic, many of the romantics tended toward moral libertinism, while revivalism represented severe restrictions on the body and moral action.

A LOOK AT THE REVIVALISTS

Concurrent with the romantics, we do not have to look very far to see the influence of the revival movement on nineteenth-century Protestantism. The revivalist evangelicals wanted to escape from this world by a personal experience of being "born again" and through successive experiences: A "second blessing" or a "rededication" would revive the soul in its flight toward Deity and "full surrender." Doctrine was considered an encumbrance, as were creeds, liturgies and sacraments, and the anti-intellectual strain of Gnosticism reared its ugly head.

In orthodox Christianity, grace redeems the world; in Gnosticism, grace redeems the self from nature. Grace did not save nature, but provided a way of escape from it. At the same time, "the liberals," according to Philip Lee, "made ample room for nature on their stage by moving grace into the wings. There remained in both camps a gnostic separation of Creation from Redemption."[31]

Popular evangelist Charles Finney reflected a number of gnostic tendencies in his rejection of creeds, confessions, church authority, liturgy, divine sovereignty, and the unimportance of sacraments. We also see it in his mystical perfectionism, which was closely related to the sects that were spawned in western New York, a strip of territory nicknamed "the psychic highway."[32] Again, none of these dependencies on Gnosticism is direct, and Charles Finney was, if anything, eclectic in his make-up.

During this period, hymns shifted from their objective focus on God's character and his saving work in Christ to the individual believer's subjective experience of God. Preaching also turned from the objective emphasis on God's saving work in Christ to techniques for self-improvement which were psychologically and morally conceived.

Romanticism brought enormous changes to the Protestant landscape, especially in Germany and America. Theology (the study of God) was shoved aside in favor of psychology (the study of the self) in the wider culture. Meanwhile, popular evangelical religion also shifted to the experience, wants, longings, and motives of the heart. So it is not too wide of the mark to regard Romanticism in general, and revivalism in particular, as America's "Counter-Reformation."

The Protestant Reformation had recovered the preached Word, as the severity of God's judgment (law) and the sweetness of his grace (gospel) were clearly set forth. But during the romantic period, the law and the gospel underwent serious revision in evangelical preaching. Considered too offensive for the brittle, immortal, and innocent "self," the law was not suitable for preaching unless it could be shown that it was somehow beneficial for personal transformation—in other words, as therapy. Divine commands had to be seen as attainable and reasonable principles for self-enhancement and universal love.

Meanwhile, damnation was entirely out of place as a purpose for the law—or for any sociable discourse. Similarly, the gospel, hardly distinguishable now from the gnostic "law," became a secret formula *(gnosis)* for rebirth, self-realization, and the personal unmediated experience with the Divine. This was equally true for liberals and evangelicals, Unitarians and revivalists, as well as for the many gnostic cults that were born in this environment (Christian Science, Unity, Adventism, etc.), however differently each may have stated it.

Horace Bushnell marks the departure from an evangelical Calvinism to an evangelical Romanticism: "My heart wants the Father; my heart wants the Son; my heart wants the Holy Ghost. . . . My heart says the Bible has a Trinity for me, and I mean to hold by my heart. I am glad a man can do it when there is no other mooring."[33] Beliefs became subordinate to feelings.

Part of this shift may be attributed to the rise of Pietism (from the word "piety"). Born in reaction to what it perceived to be an arid, heartless orthodoxy in the Reformation churches of Europe, Pietism, and Romanticism shared certain affinities for subjective religion. Friederich Schleiermacher, the father of modern liberalism, considered himself both a pietist and a romantic.

When evangelicals sing hymns such as, "He Lives," with the line, "You ask me how I know he lives? He lives within my heart," they have little trouble accommodating Schleiermacher's insistence that the essence of Christianity is "the feeling of absolute dependence." And when evangelicals eschew creeds, doctrines, liturgies, and sacraments over personal experience, how can they quibble with the liberal Adolf von Harnack, who believed that "the authentically spiritual is composed of those things that are inward, spontaneous and ethical as opposed to the outward, organized, ceremonial, and dogmatic"?[34] In fact, Harnack echoes the ancient heretics in his "modern" declaration that "It is by self-conquest that a man is freed from the tyranny of matter."[35]

Thus Gnosticism becomes the tie that binds not only liberals and evangelicals, but romantics of all stripes with their roots in nineteenth-century American religion. This includes the Mormons, who ask potential converts to accept their teachings on the basis of the missionary's "testimony," which they call "a burning in the bosom." This experience is honored, regardless of the historical and doctrinal contradictions of Mormon teaching.

But now we turn our attention from the negative—our accommodation to the spirit of the age—to the biblical initiaiton to intimacy with God on his terms.

4

JACOB'S LADDER

We are climbing, climbing, climbing,
Jacob's ladder, ladder, ladder. . . .

Do you remember singing that popular old Sunday school song? As you hum the familiar melody, you may even find yourself inadvertently making the hand-motions, climbing a make-believe ladder to heaven. Meanwhile, you're probably wondering what "Jacob's Ladder" has to do with Gnosticism.

The fact is, *climbing* is one of the leading metaphors for attaining spirituality, from medieval mysticism to the New Age. By ascending from matter to spirit, the gnostic believes he will finally attain union with the divine. Gnosticism encourages us, in its various forms, to set the spirit free to climb a ladder of emotion, meditation, or self-effort in order to escape the material world.

Whether we're evangelical, Roman Catholic, or New Age, techniques abound in the supermarket of spirituality, offering new heights of self-fulfillment and nearness to the divine. The spirituality of the medieval church was similarly reliant on ladder-climbing. Recalling his life as a devoted and scrupulous monk, Martin Luther called attempts to climb into God's presence a "theology of glory." Against this brand of spirituality, the Reformer called for a return to the "theology of the cross," which he found clearly laid out in Scripture.

The ancient church apologists, in their opposition to Gnosticism and related heresies, defended the Incarnation as God's descent to us rather than our ascent to him. The Protestant Reformers recovered this emphasis. And we, too, need to renew our appreciation for this essential principle of biblical spirituality.

A New Look at an Old Story

After swindling his brother Esau out of his inheritance of the Abrahamic blessing as the eldest son, Jacob fled for greener—and safer—pastures. How is it that Jacob became one of the patriarchs through whom the promise and the reality of the Messiah came to us? Why is Yahweh called "the God of Abraham, Isaac, and Jacob" instead of the God of Abraham, Isaac, and Esau? Was it because Jacob was more clever, and God was "stuck" with his promise to accept whomever Abraham blessed as heir to the promise? Actually, the opposite is true. In his defense of predestination and God's freedom to choose whomever he will to be saved, the apostle Paul explains,

> Yet, before the twins were born or had done anything good or bad—in order that God's purpose in election might stand: not by works but by him who calls—who was told, "The older will serve the younger." Just as it is written: "Jacob I loved, but Esau I hated." What then shall we say? Is God unjust? Not at all! For he says to Moses, "I will have mercy on whom I have mercy, and I will have compassion on whom I have compassion." It does not, therefore, depend on man's desire or effort, but on God's mercy.
>
> —ROMANS 9:11–16

Although Jacob used cunning and deceit to obtain the inheritance, God was working out his purpose in history through Jacob's sin. God has never left the outcome of salvation up to us, either individually or corporately. Graciously, he has chosen his heirs of salvation. And amazingly, not even our most grievous sins can stand in the way of his plan. Let's take a closer look at the story of Jacob in Genesis 28, and at the history of spiritual ladders.

STAIRWAYS TO HEAVEN

Fleeing his brother, Jacob set out for Haran. Much like the Egyptian pyramids or the Aztec or Mayan temples of Central and South America, the Mesopotamian ziggurats, with their stairway leading to the small altar or shrine at the top, dotted the landscape of Jacob's travels. Some of these ancient ziggurats have been at least partially preserved, and we can learn a lot about their use from their inscriptions. For instance, common names were, "House of God," "Gate of Heaven," and "Portal to Eternity."

As night fell, Jacob stopped to sleep and experienced his famous dream. "He had a dream in which he saw a stairway resting on the earth, with its top reaching to heaven, and the angels of God were ascending and descending on it" (v. 12). From the top of the stairway—usually the spot on which the pagan sacrifices were offered—God descended and renewed his covenant of mercy with Jacob and his spiritual descendants. "All peoples on earth will be blessed through you and your offspring," he tells him (v. 14). Angels were ascending and descending as attendants of God.

How could Jacob have grasped God's infinite mercy? Not only had God saved him, but he was going to bring the Messiah to the nations through him: nations he could not have even remotely imagined, either because of physical or historical distance—such as China, Ethiopia, the islands of the Pacific, the Aztec culture, the United States—would recognize the name of Jacob, patriarch and ancestor of the Savior of the world. "All peoples on earth will be blessed through you and your offspring," God said in the dream, referring, of course, to the Messiah, the Seed promised to Eve.

God further promised never to let Jacob out of his sight. He promised always to protect him, guide him, and bring him back to the land "until I have done what I have promised you" (v. 15). "When Jacob awoke from his sleep, he thought, 'Surely the LORD is in this place, and I was not aware of it.' He was afraid and said, 'How awesome is this place! This is none other than the house of God; this is the gate of heaven'" (vv. 16–17).

Jacob's first reaction was one of fear. We ought always to suspect the vision-seer who is happy and carefree in the presence of God. When he tells you of the informal, "chatty" nature of the conversation, remember that the universal response of everyone in Scripture who received a dream or vision from the Lord was one of terror and great distress. Jacob had simply chosen a common piece of land for a night's sleep, but suddenly it has become holy ground, not unlike the ground surrounding the burning bush in Moses' encounter with God. Instead of the pagan ziggurats off in the distance, where people climbed their way into the presence of the gods through sacrifices and spiritual zeal, this spot was truly "the house of God; this is the gate of heaven."

Behold the Lamb of God!

Contrary to the venerable Sunday school song, "Jacob's Ladder", nowhere in the dream is Jacob climbing the stairway. Instead, God himself descends to Jacob, addressing him as angels ascend and descend. In fact, Jacob is not even involved in the conversation! He is fast asleep while God is doing all the talking, making all the promises. Jacob does not even have a bit part in this scene. One is struck by the number of times God says, "I will. . . . " It is God's promises that have real currency, not ours. It was not the promises Jacob was willing to make—for God knew then as we know now that Jacob was not a promise-keeper.

Jacob named the otherwise common plot of ground on which he had fallen asleep, *Bet'El*, meaning, "The House of God." It was here, with angels ascending and descending, that God revealed to Jacob his promise that salvation and blessing would come through Jacob's offspring. Centuries passed. Generations of Jewish mothers prayed that they would give birth to the Messiah; fathers dreamed that the messianic promise would be fulfilled in their day. Finally, so many centuries later, the country fell under Roman control, and many despaired that Messiah would ever appear.

Then one day, while John the Baptist was baptizing in the Jordan, a thirty-year-old carpenter appeared. John "saw Jesus coming toward him," He declared to the crowd, "'Look, the Lamb of God, who takes away the sin of the world!'" (John 1:29). The next day, John the Baptist repeated his declaration, as Jesus passed: "Look, the Lamb of God!" (v. 36). On hearing this, Andrew (Simon Peter's brother), and another disciple became the first followers of Jesus Christ.

The day after John's glad announcement, something quite interesting happened. Jesus called Philip to follow him. Philip, in turn, went to Nathaniel and announced, "We have found the one Moses wrote about in the Law, and about whom the prophets also wrote—Jesus of Nazareth, the son of Joseph."

Nathaniel was unimpressed with the credentials thus far: "Nazareth! Can anything good come from there?" But when Jesus prophetically informed Nathaniel of what he had been doing before they'd arrived, a skeptic became a convert. "Rabbi, you are the Son of God; you are the King of Israel."

Jesus replied, "I tell you the truth, you shall see heaven open, and the angels of God ascending and descending on the Son of Man" (John 1:51).

Jesus was announcing that *he* was Jacob's Ladder! He is "Bet' El," "The House of God," the "Gate of Heaven," the "Portal Between Heaven and Earth." Is there a meeting place, a point of contact, a portal from this world to eternity and from humanity to God? Yes. These were precisely the images that Jesus applied to himself throughout his ministry: "I am the Way, the Truth, and the Life. No one comes to the Father except through me" (John 14:6); "I tell you the truth, I am the gate for the sheep. . . . I am the gate; whoever enters through me will be saved" (John 10:7, 9).

Jesus is the ziggurat, the temple-tower, the stairway from heaven to earth (Matt. 12:6).

UP THE DOWN STAIRCASE

One of my favorite childhood challenges was trying to run up the "down" escalator, racing toward the next floor against all odds. I never once succeeded, and the more energy I put into each attempt, the less progress I seemed to make. In my present condition of physical fitness, I am rather pleased simply to make it from one floor to another by using the correct escalator. But I'm old enough now to understand that Christianity is like that "down" escalator. Every other religion and variety of spirituality is concentrated on the soul's ascent to God, the gods, or "things spiritual." But Christianity insists that these are all dead-ends—or worse, ends that lead to death.

This is completely alien to some of our contemporaries, who lump Christianity together with "spirituality" in general, imagining that any ladder to heaven will do. In actual fact, true Christianity is more nervous about "seekers of spirituality" and stairways to God than the most ardent atheist.

No one understood the dangers of such things better than a legalistic monk in the sixteenth century. Martin Luther had devoted his energies to spiritual ascent until he could climb no longer. In retrospect, he said that there were three "ladders" devoted saints sought to climb in order to experience nearness to God: the ladder of mysticism, the ladder of merit, and the ladder of speculation. He eventually came to despair of them all.

Above all, the monk ascended by mysticism. Stanford's Lewis Spitz describes this late medieval mysticism in terms that remind one of contemporary approaches to "spirituality." "Mysticism is based on the assumption that the ultimate nature of reality or the divine essence may be known by the mystic through immediate apprehension, insight, or intuition."[1]

The mystic believes that God cannot be known chiefly through normal channels of thought. In other words, he is so far beyond the individual's understanding that even the Bible's teaching falls short of truly unveiling him to our eyes. Mystics refer to this as the "ineffable quality" of God, the inexplicable glory and wonder of his majesty. But this inability to put words to God's essence does not put the mystic off; rather, it seems to justify a short-cut. Instead of trying to understand God exclusively through the study of Scripture and theology, the mystic is convinced of a higher sort of knowledge. Like the ancient gnostics in this respect, modern mystics believe that "heart-knowledge," or personal experience with God, is more reliable than "head-knowledge," or correct beliefs about God. Spitz explains,

> Within the Western Christian tradition all mystics agree that true beatitude consists of union with God and that this union is attained through ecstatic contemplation. The nature of this contemplation is love, and this love is made possible by a life of discipline and order regulated to that end. Certain general concepts important for later mysticism developed during the early Middle Ages. . . . The first of these was the body-soul dichotomy. . . . The second concept was perfectionism. . . . The life of monastic renunciation in flight from the world was the most promising way to attain perfection. . . . The third concept was that of love, seen as a ground of reference above reason. Since the religious experience transcends reason and ordinary vocabulary used in propositional statements, the need to resort to symbolism was early recognized.[2]

Steps Toward Spirituality

Even Roman Catholic historian Joseph Lortz and Cardinal Joseph Ratzinger point out that by the late Middle Ages the mystical tradition had become remarkably subjective. The entire focus was turned inward to the progress of the individual soul toward God and spiritual perfection.[3] The whole of the monk's life was taken up in striving toward the goal of experiencing God directly in his pure essence, as he really is in himself.

Various levels marked the way to this mystical encounter. First, the monk concentrated on confession of sin. By recalling his misdeeds and naming them, he believed he was removing the obstacles of true fellowship and closeness with God.

Second, he would move on to purgation. At this level, he might follow some prescribed form of penance, where he would "purge" his sinful affections, desires, and actions by performing a series of duties. This might require an additional hour or two of "devotions" or it might mean that he would fast, denying his body its physical, earthly pleasures.

The third level would involve contemplation, and emptying himself in order to be filled with the Spirit. At this stage, the monk would meditate on God, perhaps by focusing on his love and beauty, trying to imagine his glory with "the inner eye of the soul."[4]

Finally, if sins were confessed, the soul was purged, and meditation was focused, the individual could experience "illumination"—the Spirit enlightening the spiritual understanding. This would result in the experience of "union" with God, or what Thomas Aquinas and others called the "beatific vision"—the sight of God in his beauty, majesty, glory, and love.

In our first chapter, we followed the historical influences of Gnosticism and we mentioned Platonism. Plato, a giant of Greek philosophy, contrasted the heavenly realm with the material realm. He claimed that the former was real, and in some sense permeated with divinity, while the latter was essentially flawed simply because it was material. The eternal or heavenly realm was, therefore, vastly superior and could be reached by deep meditation and avoidance of worldly pursuits.

MYSTICAL VOICES FROM THE PAST

A revival of Plato's philosophy, led by the third-century philosopher Plotinus, was even more extreme and was exploited by the gnostics. This school, called Neoplatonism, became the most important influence throughout the Middle Ages, providing part of the rationale for monasticism and mysticism. Curiously, the medieval church mercilessly uprooted entire communities of gnostic sects that proliferated throughout Europe, committing adherents to the Inquisition. Yet these sects differed from medieval spirituality only in degree.

One of the startling discoveries of the Renaissance involved Dionysius the Areopagite. He was a mystic whose work more than any other shaped Western spirituality. Rather than being a disciple of the apostle Paul (as the medieval church maintained), it was revealed that he was actually a sixth-century figure with deeply neoplatonic (i.e., gnostic) sympathies. But by this time, it was too late: the Pseudo-Areopagite had already shaped centuries of spirituality. As one reads him today, it is difficult to distinguish his work from various New Age or metaphysical texts.

Proponents of neoplatonic mysticism within the official church argued that the spirit, which was one with God, was imprisoned in the material body. The monk's duty was to escape worldly constraints—the body, time, history—in order to experience a personal, individual, subjective encounter with God. The thirteenth-century German mystic, Meister Eckhart, taught that every soul was a "divine spark," and his neoplatonic Gnosticism led him finally into pantheism, the belief that God is part of everyone. Spitz reminds us, "The central religious experience is the mysterious birth of God in the soul."[5] Being "born again" was more important than any other biblical teaching, and Eckhart pushed it beyond the limits of Christian teaching. Spitz summarizes this idea:

> The mystical way begins with negation, a mental purgative, an emptying of the soul of every created thing, of all images. In this state of emptiness one is overwhelmed by a feeling of despair—the dark night of the soul, as the Spanish mystic St. John of the Cross was later to call it. At that moment, when one feels that one is farthest from God, there occurs the birth of God in the soul. The divine spark (scintilla) in man leaps across the chasm and experiences momentary union with God. The traditional dogmas of sin, grace, the incarnation in Christ fade into the background in this context, and pantheistic tendencies are truly in evidence.[6]

Sounding strikingly familiar to those of us who have been raised on the publishing and preaching that goes on under the banner of contemporary Christianity, including evangelicalism, the following quote from this seminal mystic's work demonstrates the parallels to our own day:

> God is foolishly in love with us; it seems that He has forgotten heaven and earth and happiness and deity; His entire business seems

to be with me alone, to give me everything to comfort me; He gives it to me suddenly, He gives it to me wholly, He gives it to me perfect, He gives it all the time, and He gives it to all creatures. . . . Know then that God is bound to act, to pour Himself out [into thee] as soon as ever He shall find thee ready. . . . Finding thee ready, He is obliged to act, to overflow into thee. . . . The instant spirit is ready, God enters without hesitation or delay. Thou needest not seek Him here or there, He is no further off than the door of thy heart; there He stands lingering, awaiting whoever is ready to open and let him in. He waits more patiently than thou for thee to open to Him.[7]

Many New Agers and self-proclaimed gnostics and mystics of our day would happily regard themselves as heirs to Meister Eckhart. However, most evangelical Christians would be surprised to see how closely their spirituality concurs with his late medieval mysticism. Eckhart's is a ladder leading to heaven by emptying oneself, being filled by the Spirit, and attaining "the higher life," "full surrender," "victory," or similar ecstatic experiences with God directly. Its focus is inward, on the rebirth of the soul. While the parallels between Eckhart's mysticism and various contemporary evangelical trends break down at important points, the connections in terms of an over-arching spiritual world-view cannot be denied. We should also note that for his gnostic tendencies, especially his pantheism, Eckhart was condemned for heresy.

FROM TRANSCENDENCE TO IMMANENCE

It bears repeating that there are two opposite poles toward which we swing in pendulum-like fashion when we are not anchored to God's self-revelation in Scripture. The first is to over-emphasize divine distance (transcendence), dismissing the reality of God from our lives altogether, even if we believe in his existence on paper. Deism represents this tendency, along with the secularism that follows in its wake.

The opposite extreme is to over-emphasize divine nearness (immanence) so that we regard everything as divine or part of the divine. Everything is viewed as a miracle, and every person is believed to have a "divine spark" as part of his or her inner self (spirit). Pantheism represents this tendency, along with the mysticism and magic that follow in its wake.

In his *Screwtape Letters,* C. S. Lewis has Satan advising his apprentice to turn people into scientist-magicians—that is, into people who deny the reality of God's existence and the miraculous resurrection of Christ, and yet spend evenings conducting seances in order to communicate with the deceased. Today's New Age movement champions this approach, just as medieval alchemists and pantheistic mystics before them.

Johann Tauler (1300–1361), another German mystic, tried to avoid Eckhart's pantheism, but argued that mysticism was "practical," useful in preparing believers for good works and a life of consecration to the Lord. Later, Thomas a Kempis (1380–1471), author of the ever-popular *Imitation of Christ,* emphasized a practical rather than doctrinal approach to Christianity, believing that Christianity was above all else a religion of love and a personal relationship with God based on the believer's imitation of Christ's life.

Not all mystics, of course, were pantheists or gnostics. However, their spirituality was often characterized by these tendencies. They seemed less concerned about understanding God as he had revealed himself in words and in the historical events surrounding the person and work of Jesus Christ than about the inward motions of Christ. As Spitz pointed out above, the themes of sin and redemption were often pushed aside in favor of more psychological concepts. As we've seen, these mystics had a profound influence on the young Martin Luther.

EMBRACED BY THE CROSS

Luther was raised in the Christian school movement of the day, called the Brethren of the Common Life. This group attempted to merge German mysticism and the simple life of the apostles in the Book of Acts. Out of this background, Luther entered the monastery at Erfurt. Lest we react too strongly against the mystical tradition, it must be understood that the medieval church was a bureaucratic institution that had separated the average believer from access to God. There was a seemingly endless list of go-betweens, from the Virgin Mary and the saints to the local priest who dispensed God's saving grace through the sacraments, most of which were withheld from the laity. The distance between God and the sinner seemed vast, a Grand Canyon that could not be crossed by the average believer. Therefore, it is no surprise that the offer of a direct, personal, and immediate encounter with God through individual experience was attractive.

No one ever wanted to get close to God more than Martin Luther. And he eventually despaired of the possibility. In his reading of Scripture, Luther discovered that God demanded absolute righteousness, yet that all people were born sinful and were incapable of attaining this righteousness. Were all people therefore to be condemned? God's absolute justice and holiness required it, according to Scripture.

Then why all of this climbing? Why all of these attempts to "find God"? Luther soon realized that the God at the top of the staircase would not be the "beatific vision," the God of forgiving mercy who "lets bygones be bygones." He would be, instead, "the consuming fire." While most mystics promised that an encounter with God would lead to salvation, Luther could not escape the truth that it would lead him to damnation. It was out of this experience with God that Luther discovered that he had been trying to climb up the "down" staircase.

This awareness, inspired by Scripture, led Luther to define two radically different religions: a theology of glory and a theology of the cross. Everything he had known had been a theology of glory, an attempt to see "God in the nude," as Luther put it, an attempt to experience God directly as he is in all of his majesty. Luther knew the texts that we considered in our second chapter. He knew that God was good, but that humans were not. He also recognized that God was not, as Eckhart suggested, standing at the heart's door, waiting patiently to enter. He was a judge, intending to execute his wrath.

If this is the case, then, how can a sinner ever come to know God's salvation? How can a sinner know God as a loving father rather than as a wrathful judge? The only way, Luther discovered from Scripture, was through the theology of the cross. As Walther von Loewenich points out, the word of the cross was not merely one topic of conversation among many, but was quite literally the crux of the whole Christian message and every subject was to turn on its meaning.[8] "The theologian of glory sees God everywhere present," says von Loewenich, but for Luther, "God can be found only in suffering and the cross."[9] Did Isaiah not declare, "Truly you are a God who hides himself, O God and Savior of Israel" (Isa. 45:15)?

Both Martin Luther and John Calvin opposed the theology of glory with a theology of God's own self-revelation. This is why *sola Scriptura*— "only Scripture," one of the Reformation's battle-cries—was so important. The Christian is to find God only as he has revealed himself in Scripture, not through direct experience, nor as one deduces things about his nature from that which is visible. Unlike the theology of glory, where the pious and zealous climbers find God through their own experience, "surrender," meditation, and ecstasy, the theology of the cross points to the zeal of God, who descends to sinful humanity by becoming one of us. The cross is a real event in human history. It is not a private spiritual experience. The cross is God's chosen method of saving sinners and bringing them into his family.

While paganism in all of its forms is concerned with human ascent, Christianity is concerned with divine descent. The Reformers learned from the biblical writers the radical nature of human depravity: "There is no one righteous, no not even one" (Rom. 3:10). Gone is the ladder of merit.

"There is no one who understands" (v. 11). Gone is the ladder of speculation.

"There is no one who seeks God" (v. 11). Gone is the ladder of mysticism.

All attempts to find God through one's own activity, opinions, or experience are forms of "the works of the Law," and Paul concludes this section of Romans, chapter 3 with this judgment: "Now we know that whatever the law says, it says to those who are under the law, so that every mouth may be silenced and the whole world held accountable to God. Therefore no one will be declared righteous in his sight by observing the law; rather, through the law we become conscious of sin" (vv. 19–20).

In Luther's day, on one side stood the Church of Rome, with its bureaucracy of pious mediators between God and sinners. On the other stood the mystics, with their direct access to a God who would only consume them for presuming to enter his presence on their own terms. In the middle stood the cross, with John the Baptist pointing to the Messiah as "the Lamb of God who takes away the sin of the world," and the "one God and one mediator between God and men, the man Christ Jesus" (1 Tim. 2:5).

WISDOM AND FOOLISHNESS

But this theology of the cross is, as Paul confessed, "foolishness to those who are perishing" (1 Cor. 1:18). Why is this so? It is not because the claims for the historical crucifixion and resurrection of Christ are without foundation. Nor does the cross contradict the plain facts. Rather, it is because it contradicts human reason and self-confidence.

Part of our sinful inheritance is the belief that we can approach God just as we are, that he is waiting to embrace us in the arms of his love, regardless of our sinfulness. If we simply show an interest in him and try to do our best, follow the basic principles of spirituality and morality, we can expect to find a welcoming God at the end of it all. This is the pagan heart's expectation.

Paul says that the Greek finds the theology of the cross foolish because he is looking for "wisdom"—which, in essence, amount to the ladders of speculation, merit, and mysticism. The Jew finds it foolish because he is too busy looking for signs and wonders. Everyone is trying to climb into God's presence to gain a glimpse of "God in the nude," and seeking to find him through every avenue but the cross. "Jews demand miraculous signs and Greeks look for wisdom, but we preach Christ crucified: a stumbling block to Jews and foolishness to Gentiles, but to those whom God has called, both Jews and Greeks, Christ the power of God and the wisdom of God. For the foolishness of God is wiser than man's wisdom, and the weakness of God is stronger than man's strength" (vv. 22–25).

Worldly wisdom—especially Greek philosophy that opposes spirit to matter—is put off by the idea of salvation by God becoming flesh, suffering in this world, and saving sinners through the symbol of the greatest humiliation. Imagine a committee inventing a new religion, settling on the electric chair as its universal symbol. This is precisely what the cross represented to the ancient world.

Defeat, humiliation, despair tell the story of the crucifixion—the very antithesis to worldly expectations. And yet it was in this event that God disclosed himself for all to see. From the perspective of unbelief, there could not have been a darker moment. But from the vista of faith, a new world was being born—a new age of God's kingdom, the dawn of salvation.

Alister McGrath explains Luther's discovery of the Bible's "theology of the cross." First and foremost, it is a theology of revelation rather than speculation.[10] God does not wait for us to find him (for that would be forever), but instead he finds us. Even before he came in the flesh, he came to the patriarchs and prophets through his spoken and written Word. This was not human discovery, but divine self-disclosure.

"I AND THE FATHER ARE ONE"

When Philip, in John 14:5–10, asked Jesus to show him the Father, Luther tells us that the disciple is a theologian of glory at this point.[11] It was just

81

after Jesus had explained that he was the way, truth, and life—the only way to the Father. Simply echoing the cry of the average heart, Philip asks, "Lord, show us the Father and that will be enough for us." Is this not what the mystic requests?

Here, Jesus is treated as a gnostic revealer, knower, a guide, an inside agent who has special access to the "beatific vision," who can somehow lead his disciples into it. In reality, Jesus seems exasperated by Philip's demand: "Don't you know me, Philip, even after I have been among you such a long time? Anyone who has seen me has seen the Father. How can you say, 'Show us the Father?' Don't you believe that I am in the Father, and that the Father is in me? The words I say to you are not just my own." How astonishing to hear from the mouth of our Lord himself the words to Philip, "Anyone who has seen me has seen the Father!"

To seek God apart from Christ is devastating, for Christ is God. It is not only devastating because Christ provides information about God or because he was closer to God than the rest of us, but because he is God in person! Outside of Christ, there is no accurate knowledge of God or of his salvation. Outside of Christ's cross, there is no true knowledge of what God was doing in the person and work of Christ. In fact, outside of Christ and his cross, the Bible itself is a closed book, as Jesus made clear to the Pharisees who prided themselves on their Bible-knowledge (John 5:39).

WISDOM: HUMAN AND DIVINE

It is not by imitating his life, nor by following his teachings, nor by experiencing his power, but by trusting in his cross that sinners find God to be a friend rather than a judge. God's glory, his majesty, his "nakedness," which so enticed the mystic, is clothed in the humanity of Christ. His power is revealed in the weakness of crucifixion.

But this is not where the contradictions between heavenly wisdom and earthly wisdom end. Luther wrote that God is always "condemning what men choose, and choosing what men condemn."[12] Human reasoning says that people should be rewarded for seeking God. Divine wisdom condemns the "merit" of such striving.

Human reasoning takes for granted the belief that when someone does something good, out of love and concern for God and others, it should be rewarded. Heavenly wisdom judges the best works of our hands and the best motives, intentions, and desires of our of our hearts worthy only of eternal death (Isa. 64:6; Jer. 17:9).

Human reasoning believes that bad things happen to bad people and good things happen to good people; that heaven awaits those who deserve it and hell awaits those who do not. God's wisdom declares that all of us, being sinners by nature and by choice, deserve condemnation and are only accepted by divine mercy.

We all remember choosing up teams as children. The captain of each team selected the most talented candidates until the last doleful player was at last adopted, albeit regretfully, by the captain who got stuck with him. This is natural, for we all want a winning team.

But God's way is "upside-down." As Paul unfolds the theology of the cross in 1 Corinthians 1, he concludes, "But God chose the foolish things of the world to shame the wise; God chose the weak things of the world to shame the strong. He chose the lowly things of this world and the despised things—and the things that are not—to nullify the things that are, so that no one may boast before him" (vv. 27–29). In other words, God chose the "losers" in the eyes of the world—those who were never chosen by the world's team captains. Sports may differ from religion, but what both share is this basic theme of the human heart: choose the winners.

God has chosen the losers. That is why, when he became flesh, he preferred the company of publicans and sinners to Pharisees and Sadducees. Understand the cross, Paul says, and you understand God. Not only does God choose those who are least worthy in the eyes of the world; his way of saving them is equally "weak" and "foolish." Flying in the face of human nature's standard of merit, the gospel is offensive to those who are perishing. They are, interestingly enough, usually the last people to think of themselves as perishing.

It is, therefore, only in the cross where the despairing sinner finds relief from the curse and wrath of God. It is not by looking within, but by looking outside of oneself and one's own experience, to the sight of Christ crucified, that the trembling heart can find peace with God. The advocate of orthodoxy in the face of modern liberalism, J. Gresham Machen, declared,

> If you want health for your souls, and if you want to be the instruments of bringing health to others, do not turn your gaze forever within, as though you could find Christ there. Nay, turn your gaze away from

your own miserable experiences, away from your own sin, to the Lord Jesus Christ as he is offered to us in the gospel. . . . It is the same old story, my friends—the same old story of the natural man. Men are trying today, as they have always been trying, to save themselves—to save themselves by their own act of surrender, by the excellence of their own faith, by mystic experiences of their own lives. But it is all in vain. Not that way is peace with God to be obtained. It is to be obtained only in the old, old way—by attention to something that was done once for all long ago, and by acceptance of the living Savior who there, once for all, brought redemption for our sin.[13]

In the "hiddenness" of God, we find the ultimate revelation. It is through God's brilliant foolishness and his Herculean weakness that we are reconciled. As Luther stated in a sermon, "Man hides his own things, in order to conceal them; God hides his own things, in order to reveal them."[14] Where we expect to find mercy (through our attempts to find, appease, and experience God), we find only wrath. And where we expect to find wrath (the cross, where God's judgment is on display), we find mercy. Thus, it is that "the foolishness of God is wiser than man's wisdom, and the weakness of God is stronger than man's strength" (1 Cor. 1:25).

LOOKING FOR LOVE IN ALL THE WRONG PLACES

The mystic, whether ancient or modern, is right to seek love. And what greater love can one find than God's? And yet, "There is a way that seems right to a man, but in the end it leads to death" (Prov. 14:12). The apostle Paul understood the motives of his fellow-Jews, for he had himself been a religious leader among them and a persecutor of the church. He knew that they could not fathom God's "down escalator." He wrote:

> Brothers, my heart's desire and prayer to God for the Israelites is that they may be saved. For I can testify about them that they are zealous for God, but their zeal is not based on knowledge. Since they did not know the righteousness that comes from God and sought to establish their own, they did not submit to God's righteousness. Christ is the end of the law so that there may be righteousness for everyone who believes. . . . But the righteousness that is by faith says: "Do not

say in your heart, 'Who will ascend into heaven?'"(that is, to bring Christ down), or 'Who will descend into the deep?'" (that is, to bring Christ up from the dead). But what does it say? "The word is near you it is in your mouth and in your heart," that is, the word of faith we are proclaiming. . . .

—ROMANS 10:1–8

Scripture declares that zeal for spiritual things can be the very thing that keeps us from eternal life. Rather than building on the Rock of Christ, it is so easy for us to build our relationship with God on the shifting sands of our own experience, effort, devotion, "surrender," "yieldedness," or our ideas of what God is like. All these things attempt to establish our own righteousness, instead of accepting the righteousness that is a gift from God through faith alone.

We do not have to traverse the heights or depths of spirituality in order to find God. Why not? Because God is already in our hearts? Because he is known in our own personal experience? No, Paul goes on to say, it is because "The word is near you; it is in your mouth and in your heart."

Everything in the Bible can be distinguished into two categories: "law" and "gospel." The law does not save us; it condemns us. It does not encourage us in our attempts to become acceptable before God, but fills our hearts with dread. While that part of God's Word to us is essential for driving us to Christ, it is the other Word from God that Paul has in mind here. This is the gospel: "That is, the word of faith we are proclaiming: That if you confess with your mouth, 'Jesus is Lord,' and believe in your heart that God raised him from the dead, you will be saved" (v. 9).

5

⟨⊰❈⊱⟩

WHO MAY ASCEND
THE HILL OF THE LORD?

*"... even if we could make the climb, we would be arrested
for trespassing instead of welcomed into God's presence."*

Fire and ladders are familiar mystical symbols. There is also another image that captivates the ecstatic soul: the hill or mountain. We find it in John of the Cross's *The Ascent of Mount Carmel.* In Walter Hilton's *The Scale of Perfection.* In Jane Lead's *The Ascent to the Mount of Vision.*

This imagery takes its cue, at least in part, from Psalm 24: "Who may ascend the hill of the LORD? Who may stand in his holy place? He who has clean hands and a pure heart, who does not lift up his soul to an idol or swear by what is false." Not long ago, I heard a sermon on this text. Like so many teachings I recall from my youth, this message exhorted us all to make sure that we have clean hands and a pure heart, so that we too may ascend the hill of the Lord.

Mystics have always found this a key passage. It appears to justify the process of turning within in order to purge oneself of impurity through contemplation, confession, purgation, illumination and, finally, union with God. One contemporary Christian writer, after quoting this passage, counsels,

> We cannot even find the hill of the Lord, much less ascend it,
> if there is deceit in us. If we say, 'We want to see You, Lord,' He

responds, 'Then let Me cleanse your hearts, for only the pure in heart behold Me' (see Matt. 5:8). If we would abide in the holy place, we must dwell in integrity—even when a lie might seem to save us. To rise toward God is to increasingly enter a furnace of truth where falsehood is purged from our souls. Each ascending step upon the hill of God is a thrusting of our souls toward greater transparency—toward a more perfect view into the motives of our hearts.[1]

Is this really the point of the passage? We have already seen how Jacob's ladder has been misinterpreted, with man climbing toward God instead of God descending toward man. Is it possible that we have done the same thing with "the hill of the Lord"?

If we read beyond the two verses cited above, we would immediately recognize that the person in view is Christ: "Lift up your heads, O you gates; be lifted up, you ancient doors, that the King of glory may come in. Who is this King of glory? The LORD strong and mighty, the LORD mighty in battle. Lift up your heads, O you gates; lift them up, you ancient doors, that the King of glory may come in. Who is he, this King of glory? The LORD Almighty—he is the King of glory" (vv. 7–10). This psalm is not about us, but about God and his victory over sin and death. It is an Ascension Psalm.

The language here is rich in imagery, as the "heads" or posts at the top of the mountain, where the royal castle firmly sits, are commanded to be raised to make way for the entrance of the victorious King. The King of glory is the ascended Lord:

> The Son is the radiance of God's glory and the exact representation of his being, sustaining all things by his powerful word. After he had provided purification for sins, he sat down at the right hand of the Majesty in heaven So he became as much superior to the angels as the name he has inherited is superior to theirs.
>
> —HEBREWS 1:3–4

The writer to the Hebrews does not say that after we have purified ourselves, purged our thoughts, affections, and behavior, and ascended the hill, we finally gained victory and saw God face-to-face in his holy place. Rather, after Christ "had provided purification for sins, he sat down at the right hand of the Majesty in heaven." It is Christ's purification, his battle against the forces of darkness, his triumph over sin and death, that saves us. He is the only one who ever lived as a man here on earth about whom it could honestly be said, "He indeed had clean hands and a pure heart."

As for the rest of us, Jeremiah says, "The heart is deceitful above all things and desperately wicked" (Jer. 17:9). God declares, through Jeremiah, "Although you wash yourself with soda and use an abundance of soap, the stain of your guilt is still before me" (Jer. 2:23).

Sin has so stained the human heart that even the best works of the finest Christians in this life are "like filthy rags" (Isa. 64:6). We require Christ's intercession and merit to cover the guilt that clings to our heartiest efforts and most noble intentions. If "there is no one righteous, no not even one" (Rom. 3:10), surely it is impossible for any one of us to ascend the hill of the Lord. If we were to stand in his holy place, we would perish.

We only conceive of these spiritual backpacking trips because we think that we are capable of making the journey. We would never even set out to climb the mountain if we knew that we cannot survive the steep ascent. And even if we could make the climb, we would be arrested for trespassing instead of welcomed into God's presence. How can we ever hope to stand in his holy place? If our hands are not clean and our heart is not pure, is judgment not certain?

CLOTHED WITH CHRIST

It bears repeating that we are made right with God because Christ is our substitute. He lived a perfect life in our place, died to atone for our sins, and was raised not only for himself, but for us—guaranteeing our justification, sanctification, glorification, and the redemption of our bodies. This is how Jesus Christ fulfills his mission—not merely by showing the way, but by *being* the Way. He saves us fully and finally, and leaves no room for us to say, "Ah, yes. But I did do that one good thing."

If we cannot cleanse our hands or purify our hearts, is there any hope? Two of our Lord's parables answer this question, and they both concern clothing—to be specific, a robe.

When he told the now-famous parable of the prodigal son, tax collectors and "sinners" were gathered around the feet of Jesus, while the religious leaders looked on, muttering, "This man welcomes sinners and eats with them" (Luke 15:2). In the parable, Jesus describes a man who had two sons, the younger one squandering his inheritance on wild living in a far country, while the elder son kept his post on the estate.

Finally, the junior son came to his senses and returned, willing to be demoted from the status of son to that of a mere servant. "But while he was still a long way off," our Lord says, "his father saw him and was filled with compassion for him; he ran to his son, threw his arms around him and kissed him." Apparently deaf to his son's pleas for being accepted merely as a servant, the father ordered, "Quick! Bring the best robe and put it on him" (v. 22). A fattened calf was prepared and there was dancing into the night. "For this son of mine was dead and is alive again; he was lost and is found" (v. 24).

Next, Jesus offers us the parable of the wedding banquet, to which those with written invitations refused to come. So the king, the groom's father, sent his servants to the street corners to bring in the riffraff, "both good and bad," resulting in the filling of the banquet hall for his son's wedding.

"But when the king came in to see the guests, he noticed a man there who was not wearing wedding clothes. 'Friend,' he asked, 'how did you get in here without wedding clothes?' The man was speechless. Then the king told the attendants, 'Tie him hand and foot, and throw him outside, into the darkness, where there will be weeping and gnashing of teeth.' For many are invited, but few are chosen" (Matt. 22:1–14).

In this parable of the wedding feast, Jesus is warning us that whether Jew or Gentile, we must be properly clothed if we are to be able to attend the feast. Coming off of the streets, we are hardly dressed appropriately for a royal banquet in honor of the Son's marriage to his Bride, the Church.

The haunting question, "How did you get in here without wedding clothes?" may strike us as an unusually demanding request for someone as cheerfully compassionate as this king. Yet, it is he himself who provides the garments. Those who insist on remaining in their own street clothes have only themselves to blame for refusing such royal generosity. Their self-constructed "fig leaves" will not cover their guilt.

THE BRIDE OF CHRIST

The image of wedding garments is found throughout Scripture. Isaiah reminds Israel that the nation's captivity is not due to any weakness on

God's part, "but your iniquities have separated you from your God; your sins have hidden his face from you, so that he will not hear" (Isa. 59:1–2). Whenever Israel attempts, like Adam, to cover herself with her own self-righteousness, God mocks the vain attire: "Their cobwebs are useless for clothing; they cannot cover themselves with what they make" (v. 6).

Later, Isaiah represents redeemed Israel when he cries out, "I delight greatly in the LORD; my soul rejoices in my God. For he has clothed me with garments of salvation and arrayed me in a robe of righteousness, as a bridegroom adorns his head like a priest, and as a bride adorns herself with her jewels" (61:10).

The bride of Christ has been won at great cost, by the price of the husband's own blood (1 Pet. 1:18–19). This is why one of God's names happens to be, "THE LORD OUR RIGHTEOUSNESS" (Jer. 23:6). He does not merely direct us in the paths of righteousness, giving us a map to the mountaintop city or even by only leading us to it. Rather, he presents us holy and without blame before the Father (Eph. 1:4).

According to our Lord's parable, it is not as if we are unwanted trespassers now, but invited guests, chosen and accepted by God and dressed in his own righteousness. He is our righteousness. This is why Paul declared, "It is because of him that you are in Christ Jesus, who has become for us wisdom from God—that is, our righteousness, holiness, and redemption. Therefore, as it is written: 'Let him who boasts boast in the Lord'" (1 Cor. 1:30–31).

GARBED IN RIGHTEOUSNESS

The prophet Zechariah received a revelation in which Joshua the high priest was standing before the angel of the LORD, with "Satan standing at his right side to accuse him" (3:1). We read the following report of this vision:

> The LORD said to Satan, 'The LORD rebuke you, Satan! The LORD, who has chosen Jerusalem, rebuke you! Is not this man a burning stick snatched from the fire?' Now Joshua was dressed in filthy clothes as he stood before the angel. The angel said to those who were standing before him, 'Take off his filthy clothes.' Then he said to Joshua, 'See, I have taken away your sin, and I will put rich garments on you.' Then I said, 'Put a clean turban on his head.' So they put a clean turban on his head and clothed him, while the angel of the LORD stood by (vv. 3–5).

This scene is rich with courtroom intrigue. The angel of the LORD (a frequent reference to Christ in the Old Testament) is the "Perry Mason" of the story, defending his client against the accusations of the prosecuting attorney. No one has to wonder for long the identity of that prosecutor: Satan is called "the accuser of the brethren" (Rev. 12:10).

But once Joshua is stripped of his unrighteousness and clothed in perfect holiness, he is instantly impervious to Satan's accusations. Bluster all he will, with documentation of case after case of flagrant violation of God's commands, Joshua stood clothed in perfect righteousness, "while the angel of the LORD stood by."

When finally we reach the end of the story (which is really just the beginning), we see a sea of saints dressed in God's best linen:

> After this I looked and there before me was a great multitude that no one could count, from every nation, tribe, people, and language, standing before the throne and in front of the Lamb. They were wearing white robes and were holding palm branches in their hands. And they cried in a loud voice, 'Salvation belongs to our God, who sits on the throne, and to the Lamb'. . . . Then one of the elders asked me, 'These in white robes—who are they, and where did they come from?' I answered, 'Sir, you know.' And he said, 'These are they who have come out of the great tribulation; they have washed their robes and made them white in the blood of the Lamb.'
>
> —REVELATION 7:9–14

St. John comforts believers in the face of their great tribulation and persecution by depicting them in heavenly attire. Condemned by the world, they stand before God holy and without blame because they are robed in Christ's righteousness. But only those who are justified by grace alone, through faith alone, because of Christ alone, are dressed in such finery. Only one robe is allowed in God's holy place, a robe that makes its wearers appear holy and perfectly blameless before him.

CLEAN HANDS AND A PURE HEART

This is the only way can we be said to have clean hands and a pure heart before God, as we are robed in Christ's righteousness. His hands and heart are substituted for our own. Even as Christians, even at our best, we remain sinful. In fact, it was not our sins that Isaiah had in mind, but our good works, when he said, "Our righteousness is like filthy garments" (Isa. 61:6).

The good news, therefore, is that someone has ascended the hill of the Lord in our place. His victory has secured our safe entrance to that high and holy place:

> In bringing many sons to glory, it was fitting for God, for whom and through whom everything exists, should make the author of their salvation perfect through suffering. Both the one who makes men holy and those who are made holy are of the same family. So Jesus is not ashamed to call them brothers. He says, 'I will declare your name to my brothers; in the presence of the congregation I will sing your praises.' And again, 'I will put my trust in him.' And again he says, 'Here am I, and the children God has given me.' Since the children have flesh and blood, he too shared in their humanity so that by his death he might destroy death—that is, the devil—and free those who all their lives were held in slavery by the fear of death.
>
> —Hebrews 2:10–15

Like the poor man who refused the host's wedding garment, it will be a dreadful day when so many receive the news that they are to be tied up and thrown into outer darkness.

"But I served the Lord and supported his work my whole life."

"This can't be true: I've had so many direct encounters and experiences with God! He lives in my heart!"

"I have followed the steps to victory over my sins and circumstances: How could I be condemned?"

"But I was a defender of family values and virtue, an ardent opponent of secular humanism in society."

None of these responses will change the verdict. Those with white robes are welcomed, while those dressed in their own attire are judged.

The good news, of course, is that nobody is excluded from the invitation, however sinful and ruined. God delights in robing people off the street in his wedding garments, turning servants into sons, and making them co-heirs with his own Son. Poet William Cowper (1741–1800) expressed this good news in the following ascription of praise and confession:

My God, how perfect are thy ways!
But mine polluted are;
Sin twines itself about my praise,
And slides into my pray'r.
When I would speak what thou has done
To save me from my sin,
I cannot make Thy mercies known
But self-applause creeps in.
This heart, a fountain of vile thoughts,
How does it overflow,
While self upon the surface floats
Still bubbling from below!
Let others in the gaudy dress
Of fancied merit shine;
The Lord shall be my righteousness;
The Lord forever mine.

Where can we look for help in ascending the hill of the Lord? It is only by Christ's ascension that we are carried into the heavenlies, where we are seated with Christ (Eph. 2:6). This is not something to be achieved, but to be received. It is the true righteousness that comes by faith, not the false sense of righteousness that comes by works.

ARRAYED FOR BATTLE: SPIRITUAL WARFARE

Unfortunately, even the "heavenlies" take on an unbiblical meaning in today's world. Part of today's new spirituality is a concentrated emphasis on the invisible world. As we've seen, many evangelical leaders have argued that the believer somehow controls what happens by understanding the secrets of the spiritual dimension. This gnostic tendency is certainly not mitigated by the interest in "power encounters," "spiritual mapping," "generational curses," and fictional accounts of warfare in which Christians decide the outcome of the battle in the heavenlies.

In Harvey Cox's sympathetic study of Pentecostal groups, he was especially struck by this emphasis. About one best-selling novel, he writes, "one sometimes gets the impression that the human beings are little more than puppets tugged and jerked by transcendental forces." Cox compares such books to "the old movie, *The Invasion of the Body Snatchers,* with a few themes from *The Exorcist* and Bram Stoker's *Dracula* thrown in."[2]

It is not so much a piece of fiction, and its storyline is rather inconsequential, Cox argues. "It is about cosmology," that is, a view of the structure and laws of the universe. "It is a geography and gazetteer of the angelic and demonic domains. As I read it I had the curious impression that I was back in graduate school studying some of the Jewish apocalyptic documents we analyzed to help us understand the prehistory of the New Testament, such as First Enoch or Baruch or some of the scrolls from the Dead Sea."[3]

By the way, those particular documents have had a large hand in the revival of interest in such gnostic texts, and Cox sees some affinities at this point not only with this fictional genre, but with the scads of non-fiction books in this genre. Even Cox, who is not particularly sympathetic to my own theological position, expressed discomfort over the popularity of C. Peter Wagner and so many others who engage in cosmic speculations.[4] He cites C. S. Lewis on this point, from The Screwtape *Letters.* Lewis writes,

> There are two equal and opposite errors into which our race can
> fall about the devils. One is to disbelieve in their existence. The other
> is to believe and to feel an excessive and unhealthy interest in them.
> They themselves are equally pleased by both errors, and hail a materi-
> alist and a magician with the same delight.[5]

It is no exaggeration to notice that today's cosmological fiction emphasis bears resemblance to the metaphysical dualism of the gnostic sects, in their contest between the good god and the bad god. Zoroastrianism was a sixth-century B.C. Persian religion that launched astrology and magic, and influenced the mysticism within both Judaism and Christianity. It taught that everything revolves around a cosmic, metaphysical battle between the good spirit Ahura Mazda and the evil spirit Angra Mainyu. The Manichaean gnostics of the early Christian era were also prone to this sort of world-view.

In opposition to this, Christianity teaches the sovereignty of God over "all things, visible and invisible." As Creator of everything and sustainer of everything, God has predestined everything that comes to pass for his own ends and not even Satan can thwart his purposes (Dan. 4:34–39). Satan is not a rival deity, but a fallen angel who is already judged, dethroned by Christ's triumph over the grave.

It is that battle, won through the Resurrection, that stands at the center of Christian teaching, not the believers' patrols, searching for demons in their bunkers. Furthermore, God has promised to bring the whole material creation into the enjoyment of redemption at the end of history. The Christian neither despairs of that hope in the face of demonic evil, nor attempts to take it upon himself to cast Satan into the lake of fire. It is generally agreed by scholars that Jude was written to warn the Christians against Gnosticism, as they are called to "contend for the faith that was once for all entrusted to the saints" (v. 3). These mystics, Jude warns,

> . . . reject authority and slander celestial beings. But even the archangel Michael, when he was disputing with the devil about the body of Moses, did not dare to bring a slanderous accusation against him, but said, 'The Lord rebuke you!' Yet these men speak abusively against whatever they do not understand; and what things they do understand by instinct, like unreasoning animals—these are the very things that destroy them. Woe to them!

These super-apostles are "clouds without rain, blown along by the wind" and "wild waves upon the sea, foaming up their shame; wandering stars, for whom blackest darkness has been reserved forever" (vv. 8–13). All those engaged in demonic duels should be put off by this warning, especially when they explicitly rebuke Satan and his demons by "the authority of the believer," instead of settling for the less auspicious, "The Lord rebuke you!"

What then is spiritual warfare and how are we to engage in it according to Scripture? The most famous "spiritual warfare" passage is Ephesians, chapter 6, which picks up on the imagery of Isaiah 59:17: "He put on righteousness as his breastplate, and the helmet of salvation on his head; he put on the garments of vengeance and wrapped himself in zeal as in a cloak." This is how the Lord went into battle when he became flesh and overcame temptation, the prince of darkness, death, and hell. But in Ephesians, Paul applies this same attire to believers:

> Finally, be strong in the Lord and in his mighty power. Put on the full armor of God so that you can take your stand against the devil's schemes. For our struggle is not against flesh and blood, but against the rulers, against the authorities, against the powers of this dark world

and against the spiritual forces of evil in the heavenly realms. Therefore put on the full armor of God, so that when the day of evil comes,
you may be able to stand your ground, and after you have done everything, to stand. Stand firm, then, with the belt of truth buckled around
your waist, with the breastplate of righteousness in place, and with
your feet fitted with the readiness that comes from the gospel of peace.
In addition to all this, take up the shield of faith, with which you can
extinguish all the flaming arrows of the evil one. Take the helmet of
salvation and the sword of the Spirit, which is the word of God.

—EPHESIANS 6:10–17

Once again we are identified with Christ. He wore the full armor of
God and secured victory by his own power. Whatever warfare we endure
on earth, the outcome has already been determined by our conquering
general. We do not fight in order to save ourselves, but in order to persevere in the faith in which we are already securely established. And we are
not left with our own weapons or armor, but with the same armor that
won Christ's victory in the first place. He clothes us with his victory, with
his righteousness, with his truth, with his gospel, and his salvation. His
Word protects us from Satan's designs.

That approach may not be as exciting as the theology of glory, which
reads a passage like this one as if it were a *Star Wars* script. It is, however,
sufficient to keep us from dying on the battlefield. If spiritual warfare were
really concerned with "taking back" territory and goods stolen by the devil,
in terms of "naming and claiming" the salvation of loved ones or automo-
biles, we would be the saviors.

Instead, we are wearing borrowed armor. And it is alien armor—pro-
tective gear that is not our own. Furthermore, there is nothing here about
territorial spirits whose activity can actually be "mapped" by specially gifted
prophets—that has more to do with superstition and magic than with
Christianity. Folk religion always finds a way of deifying and demonizing
"spirits of the forest" or "spirits of the cities." Nor does this passage tell us
how to get rid of so-called "generational curses"—that is, the attribution of
demonic activity to genetic or hereditary problems.

There is not the slightest hint of such superstitious tendencies in
this key passage on spiritual warfare. In fact, Satan most likely uses
such diversions to distract us from the real battle, which Paul is anxious to
set in our view. In this passage, the apostle warns that Satan's approach in

spiritual warfare is to undermine the believer's and the church's confidence in the gospel and in the Word.

TRUE ARMOR, REAL VICTORY

The first article of armor is the belt of truth. Doctrine and theology get in the way of most spiritual warfare programs these days. Those of us who question gnostic tendencies are often simply dismissed as "witch-hunters" who are dividing the body of Christ. But Paul leads off his list of defenses with truth.

If we do not know what we believe and why we believe it, we will eventually be taken as prisoners of war. If we rely on experience, Satan can always convince us that we are either too good to require an external act of salvation, or that we are too sinful to be capable of redemption by God. My own experience often lies to me. Sometimes it tells me that I am righteous, when I am not; other times, it condemns me and leads me to conclude that I have finally out-sinned God's mercy. Truth comes to us in such moments and anchors us on the Rock of Ages. God's Truth is objective, and therefore reliable.

The second article of armor is the breastplate of righteousness. When Satan the accuser comes to prosecute his case against me in the heavenly court, where do I take shelter? In my piety? In my resolutions to "surrender all?" In the depth of my desire to live for the Lord and be a good witness? Do I look within, to God's work in my life, or to the change in my heart?

What we need when Satan comes to undermine our faith is perfect righteousness, the kind of righteousness that will overthrow his case against us. This, as we have already seen, is found only in Christ—"The LORD Our Righteousness" (Jer. 23:6), the LORD Mighty in Battle whom God has made "our righteousness, holiness and redemption" (1 Cor. 1:30).

Paul goes on in his description of armor to "feet fitted with readiness that comes from the gospel of peace" (v. 15). Why are we prepared to serve God? Not because of our own resolve or dedication, but because of the Good News of the gospel itself. We are only prepared for a life of spiritual battle if we are "confident of this, that he who began a good work in [us] will carry it on to completion until the day of Christ Jesus" (Phil. 1:6) and that "there is therefore now no condemnation to those who are in Christ Jesus" (Rom. 8:1).

"In addition to all this, take up the shield of faith, with which you can extinguish all the flaming arrows of the evil one" (Eph. 6:16). In the theology of glory, faith is a human work. It is the "one thing" that I did to save me. Some will even go so far as to say that it is the believer's power to command things from the invisible realm to appear in the visible. However, Paul saw it differently. He wrote that this faith is "not of yourselves; it is the gift of God" (Eph. 2:8).

Faith is the knowledge of what God has done for us in Christ, the confidence that this is a true, historical fact, and the assurance that, by this saving work of Christ in history, we are accepted before God apart from anything that we have done. This is why God gives us the sacraments of baptism and the Lord's Supper to confirm our faith in his gospel and to seal us in its promises.

The apostle concludes with "the helmet of salvation and the sword of the Spirit, which is the Word of God" (v. 17). The helmet of salvation is simply another way of saying what he has already said: The objective, finished work of Christ for sinners as the only basis for living the Christian life and for answering the accusations of Satan.

Our sword is the Word of God because, once again, we need something outside of ourselves to constantly mediate God's assurance of pardon. If we were to rely on our inner experience or progress in sanctification, our changed lives, or our feelings, our conscience would immediately pronounce us guilty. But God's Word stands outside of us, directing our attention to Christ and his saving work. Those who rely on their own subjective feelings will be easily swallowed up in despair. But the Word contradicts our reason, our experience, and our consciences whenever we are assaulted by fears, sins, and doubts.

Everything in Paul's list of armor is objective rather than subjective, external rather than internal, Christ-centered rather than self-centered. God's armor has to do with the Word, the gospel, justification and truth— not with binding demons of addiction or setting up face-offs between the forces of darkness and the forces of light through signs and wonders.

The great issue of this battle is a contest for truth and faith in Christ against error and unbelief. For many engaged in spiritual warfare programs today, the Word is often down-played in favor of the Spirit's direct revelation and activity apart from the Scriptures. Truth and the doctrines of salvation are often regarded as "hair-splitting" academic debates that have little relevance for the real battles. Satan, it would appear, has gained a tremendous foot-hold in this spiritual battle by drawing us off course through decoys.

If we will recover this biblical idea of spiritual warfare and accept the armor that God has offered for our battles, we may see genuine awakening in our time. We will not find it through elaborate strategies for "victory" and the filling of the Spirit. Nor will be achieve it by programming the Spirit into "revival" because we fulfilled the conditions, fasted, and held successful prayer summits "calling down power."

Awakening will only come through the Word of the gospel, the announcement of our free justification in Christ. It will only come if we give up on our efforts at ascending the hill of the Lord. It will only come when we rest our whole confidence on the ascended King, who at this very moment intercedes at God's right hand on our behalf.

6

⋘⋗◦⋖⋙

THEY TOUCHED GOD

*"The truth is anchored not in what happened inside a person,
but in what happened in the ancient land of Israel two thousand years ago."*

Heaven came down and glory filled my soul!" Like "Jacob's Ladder," "Heaven Came Down" is another familiar chorus that many of us recall singing in churches. But what do the words really mean? Are we saying that we have experienced God directly, by the descent of heaven itself into our hearts? Do we really mean that his glory filled our souls? These questions take on a new significance, once we've considered how dangerous it can be for heaven to come down upon sinful creatures. And it is equally risky to be present when divine glory falls. The only way that particular sentiment can have a biblical foundation is if "heaven" is Jesus Christ, and the "glory" that floods our souls is the sovereign mercy of God offered through him.

Fortunately for us, heaven did come down in the person of Christ, the servant of the Lord, fulfilling all of the Old Testament hopes and dreams of entering into a personal relationship with God. All of our Christian spirituality flows out of this supreme self-revelation of God. It is in Christ, and Christ alone, that we are able to enjoy intimate fellowship with God. In him, we see God's merciful "backside."

We have already surveyed some of the key events in biblical history

101

where God's transcendence—his distance from humankind—is clearly evident. In this chapter, we will appeal to several of these same events in order to show how, in Christ, God becomes "up close and personal."

How Heaven Came Down

When Adam reached for a "higher wisdom" and a "higher knowledge" than God's revealed Word, he found himself naked and ashamed. In panic, he fled from God's presence. Being close to God when one is conscious of one's sinfulness and rebellion is a little like being a husband in bed with his wife immediately after committing adultery. There is something deeply disturbing about the presence of the other person, something that makes one look for the nearest exit. That is precisely what Adam tried to do. Problem is, God is everywhere. He tracked Adam down, confronted him with his guilt, and announced his verdict of condemnation.

But God the judge was also God the redeemer. Even in this early stage in redemptive history, he promised a Messiah (Gen. 3:15), and clothed both Adam and Eve in the skins of sacrificial animals. In reality, it was God's Messiah whose bloody sacrifice covered Adam and his believing posterity in the righteousness of God, even before Jesus' actual appearance in history. And it was with this Messiah in mind that Isaiah so many centuries later would declare in anticipation,

> But he was pierced for our transgressions, he was crushed for our iniquities; the punishment that brought us peace was upon him, and by his wounds we are healed. . . . Yet it was the LORD's will to crush him and cause him to suffer, and though the LORD makes his life a guilt offering, he will see his offspring and prolong his days, and the will of the LORD will prosper in his hand. . . . For he bore the sin of many, and made intercession for the transgressors."
>
> —ISAIAH 53:4–12

The apostle Paul contrasts the first Adam with Christ, whom he calls the second Adam: "For just as through the disobedience of the one man the many were made sinners, so also through the obedience of the one man the many will be made righteous" (Rom. 5:19).

Unlike the first Adam, Christ obeyed his Father. When the serpent came to offer him glory, together with all of the kingdoms of the world, the second Adam fasted instead of eating the forbidden fruit. And rather than listening to vain promises of a "higher knowledge," the second Adam answered the serpent, "It is written: 'Man does not live on bread alone, but on every word that comes from the mouth of God'" (Matt. 4:4).

Pitting God's Word against Satan's appeals to his felt needs, Jesus Christ obeyed in our place, so that his life of perfect conformity to God's will is credited to every believer. We who shared in Adam's judgment now participate together in Christ's righteousness. Only in this way can we come close to God without fear of judgment, for we are wearing the righteousness of Christ instead of the fig leaves of our own pretensions.

A CRY OF FORGIVENESS

As we've seen, Cain brought an offering to the Lord that was not the one he had commanded. Foreshadowing the cross of Christ, humanity was required to bring the sacrifice of the first of the flock, just as Jesus was the firstborn of the Father. Instead, Cain sought his own path to God, his own form of worship, and was rejected by God.

But now the story becomes even more poignant. When God approached Cain after the murder of Abel, the Lord declared, "Listen! Your brother's blood cries out to me from the ground" (Gen. 4:10). Yet as tender as that cry was to God's ears, we are invited "to Jesus the mediator of a new covenant, and to the sprinkled blood that speaks a better word than the blood of Abel" (Heb. 12:24). While Abel's blood cried out for vengeance, the blood of Jesus cried out for forgiveness. In response, God cared enough to send his only-begotten Son. For us to devise any other way to God—despite the best of intentions—is to invite God's wrath (John 3:18).

The Tower of Babel was a similarly human attempt to scale the heights of achievement, to flee divine wrath, and to find safety in numbers. It, too, was met with divine judgment. Just as men were building their way to God in salvation, God descended in judgment. His Holy Spirit confused their languages and scattered the nations.

However, when the Word became flesh and redeemed his people, the Spirit descended once more upon the nations, and this time the effect was quite different. As the first Christians were gathered in the upper room during the Feast of Pentecost, with men and women from the scattered nations present in Jerusalem, the Holy Spirit fell in grace instead of judgment. Rather than confusing the languages, he united them as each person heard the gospel in his own tongue (Acts 2:1 ff.).

Then there was the story of the Israelites at the foot of Mount Sinai, warned not to "force their way to see the LORD and many of them perish" (Exod. 19:21). The sight of fire and smoke, flashes of lightning and peals of thunder terrified the Israelites so that they kept their distance. Far from forcing their way into God's presence, they demanded a mediator. Moses pleaded their case before Yahweh, just as he spoke the very word of Yahweh to the people.

And yet, as great as Moses was in his role of mediator—even willing to substitute himself for Israel when God threatened to destroy the nation—he, too, was a sinful creature. Even Moses needed a mediator. Of Christ, the writer to the Hebrews declares,

> He was faithful to the one who appointed him, just as Moses was faithful in all God's house. Jesus has been found worthy of greater honor than Moses, just as the builder of a house has greater honor than the house itself. . . . Moses was faithful as a servant in all God's house, testifying to what would be said in the future. But Christ is faithful as a son over God's house. And we are his house, if we hold on to our courage and the hope of which we boast.
>
> —HEBREWS 3:1–6

THE WORD BECAME FLESH

When Moses cried out for the vision of divine glory, he was told, "No one may see me and live" (Exod. 33:20). Sheltering Moses behind a rock, with his hand covering the prophet's face, God allowed his glory to pass by. How much more are we to cry out concerning Jesus, "Rock of Ages cleft for me! Let me hide myself in thee."

It remains true that no one can see the divine face and live. However, "the Word became flesh and made his dwelling among us" (John 1:14). In Greek, the phrase is, "He pitched his tent among us." The tabernacle moved with the children of Israel as the divine presence led them through the wilderness. In a similar sense, God "tabernacled" or "pitched his tent" among us in the person of Jesus Christ.

During Jesus' time, the Pharisees had been trying to climb the stairway of heaven by their own legalistic righteousness. If devotion to moral rigor, rules, techniques, and spiritual exercises could have raised anyone to Paradise, surely these men would have been among the most advanced. Nevertheless, Jesus was not impressed. "No one has seen the Father except the one who is from God," said Jesus. "Only he has seen the Father" (John 6:46). "You do not know me or my Father," he told them.

The self-righteous Pharisees were confident that they were in God's good graces because they had, in their estimation, conformed to the divine requirements. "Once more Jesus said to them, 'I am going away, and you will look for me, and you will die in your sin. Where I go, you cannot come" (v. 21).

That kind of talk is certainly not very "seeker-friendly!" Where is the modern-day God, begging people to keep him company, to accept his love and to be a part of his family? Jesus says, in effect, "If you do not go to the Father through me as the Son, you will die in your sin. And if you die in your sin, you cannot enter the Holy of Holies and find rest for your souls."

"SHOW US THE FATHER"

According to recent surveys, nearly everybody in America believes in the existence of hell, but only 11 percent fear the possibility of going there.[1] We assume that we have the "right" to enter into God's presence. The suggestion that we are born into this world as enemies of God and slaves of our own sinful hearts is quite offensive. This is especially true of those of us who are confident in our own righteousness, spiritual devotion, or religious pedigree. When the Jews again insisted that Abraham was their father, Jesus replied, "You are doing the things your own father does." Unfortunately for them, it was not Abraham he had in mind as their father.

"'We are not illegitimate children,' they answered. 'The only Father we have is God himself'" (v. 41).

Think of the difficulty of Jesus' confrontation here. He is speaking to those who are his own flesh and blood, the chosen people of Israel. If anyone had a personal relationship with God, surely it was these devoted zealots. In fact, they cannot conceive of the possibility of not being God's children.

> Jesus said to them, 'If God were your Father, you would love me, for I came from God and now am here. I have not come on my own, but he sent me. Why is my language not clear to you? Because you are unable to hear what I say. You belong to your father, the devil, and you want to carry out your father's desire. . . .' The reason that you do not hear is that you do not belong to God."
>
> —John 6:42–47

In a startling declaration that left no doubts in the religious leaders' minds as to his meaning, Jesus announced, "I and the Father are one" (John 10:30).

It was not enough for those seeking "power encounters" and a theology of glory to see Jesus—God made flesh. Flesh and bone were too natural, too human, too earthly, to excite their emotions. And yet, what could have been more moving than being able to touch the very God, whose face, up until then, no one had been able to see and live?

The Image of God

I am convinced that the principal reason for the second commandment—that is, the prohibition of any physical representation of God—is because only Christ is "the image [icon] of the invisible God" (Col. 1:15). Just as the Israelites were bored by "dead orthodoxy," while Moses was having all the fun being in the presence of God, we are often bored without immediate encounters and experiences with God in his glory. So, like the Israelites, we create a physical representation of God. Out of our imaginations, we mold golden calves.

Through mysticism, speculative ideas, and the works of our own hands, we carve idols of the true God so that we can experience him here and now. But when God became physical, he was not a golden calf. He was not like the idols of the nations. He was so fully human, in fact, that his own brothers by blood, raised together in the same family, did not believe in him until he was well into his ministry—at least thirty years of age (John 7:5).

> He was in the world, and though the world was made through him, the world did not recognize him. He came to that which was his own, but his own did not receive him. Yet to all who received him, to

those who believed in his name, he gave the right to become children of God—children born not of natural descent, nor of human decision or a husband's will, but born of God.

—JOHN 1:12–13

Just as Moses asked to see God's glory and Philip asked Jesus to show him the Father, we seek to experience God directly. And we need a mediator just as surely as did Israel. God gave us the only mediator who could redeem sinners from the curse of the Law by his own obedience and sinless sacrifice. "For the law was given through Moses; grace and truth came through Jesus Christ. No one has ever seen God, but God the One and Only, who is at the Father's side, has made him known" (John 1:18). To know God is to know Christ. But to know God outside of Christ is to know him as a judge and destroyer.

THE FIRE IN THE FIREPLACE

The resurgence of classic mysticism is powerful in our day and, given modern materialism, this is understandable. Modernity has shriveled the soul, leaving us with the numbing sense that we are little more than machines, a complex but accidental bundle of neurons and chemicals that stimulate brain waves in predictable patterns. No wonder there is a reaction in the culture, a rebellion against psychological or scientific determinism. The New Age movement attracts rebels with a cause, but they are rushing in where angels—one of their major obsessions—fear to tread.

In the physical person of Christ, we find the fire in the fireplace, kept from destroying sinful flesh through the gentleness of the baby in the manger; through the kindness of the man who healed the blind, preached good news to the poor, and reconciled prostitutes to God; through the compassion of One who wept at Lazarus' tomb and gave himself up to crucifixion for our salvation. It is because he was baptized with fire that the writer to the Hebrews could assure believers,

You have not come to a mountain that . . . is burning with fire; to darkness, gloom and storm; to a trumpet blast or to such a voice speaking words that those who heard it begged that no further word be spoken to them. . . . The sight was so terrifying to them that Moses said, 'I am trembling with fear.' But you have come to Mount Zion, to the heavenly Jerusalem, the city of the living God. . . . You have come to God, the judge of all men . . . , to Jesus the mediator of a new covenant, and to the sprinkled blood that speaks a better word than the blood of Abel."

—HEBREWS 12:18–24

God was terribly severe in these Old Testament ceremonial laws. Or was he? Has anything really changed? Of course, the ceremonies—being shadows of the reality which was to come—have been fulfilled and are therefore no longer in force. And yet, the reality to which these shadows pointed is just as true for us as it was for the Israelites.

Like Aaron, we cannot enter the most holy place of God's presence whenever we choose and however we choose. We must enter with the precious blood of Christ, bathed in the waters of baptism and adorned in the white linen of Christ's righteousness. God is still just as holy, just as insistent on being approached in the manner in which he has commanded. Christ is the only way to the Father; access to God is through his blood and righteousness alone.

Our Second Adam fasted instead of feasting. He ignored the serpent's invitation to glory by interposing God's Word. And his resistance to Satan is credited to us as if we were there with him in the wilderness of temptation, just as we were there with Adam in his disobedience. Every victory over doubt, temptation, despair, and compromise is credited to each believer. We are not only saved by Christ's death, but by his thirty-three years of perfect conformity to God's will in heart, soul, mind, and strength.

This means that there really was and is only one truly devoted "victorious Christian," and he devotes us to God by imputing to us his obedience in life and in death: "For their sakes I sanctify myself, that they may be truly sanctified" (John 17:19).

This once more underscores the "down" escalator thrust of the gospel: God coming down to rescue sinners. Salvation is not gained by the ascent of sinful creatures through greater heights of devotion, ecstasy, or commitment; it amounts to the descent of God in mercy. It is Christ's commitment, his devotion, his obedience, his fervor, his relationship with God that secure our salvation. Because he is devoted to God and all that belongs to him is devoted to God, we too belong to God and will never be devoted to destruction. The author of Hebrews writes,

Since the children have flesh and blood, he too shared in their humanity so that by his death he might destroy him who holds the power of death—that is, the devil—and free those who all their lives were held in slavery by their fear of death. For surely it is not angels he helps, but Abraham's descendants. For this reason he had to be made like his brothers in every way, in order that he might become a merciful and faithful high priest in service to God, and that he might make atonement for the sins of the people. Because he himself suffered when he was tempted, he is able to help those who are being tempted.

—HEBREWS 2:14-18

CAN GOD DWELL WITH MAN?

How can we comprehend the magnitude of this announcement, "The Word became flesh and 'tabernacled' among us" (John 1:14)? Blinding light, unapproachable glory, were veiled in human nature. The same God whose very presence could bring disaster to sinful creatures was practically indistinguishable from his friends and relatives. None of us really knows what might have been the effect of God coming to earth in all of his glory. While God's "hiddenness," as we see Christ's full humanity, left contemporaries with the sense that Jesus was no more than a man, it was infinitely better than unveiled glory.

Just a decade ago, a thick cloud of anxiety was hanging over the individual and collective psyche of Soviet and American citizens. It was the fear that at any moment tempers could flare and nuclear weapons would be launched. Annihilation would surely follow a diabolical exchange in which there could be no winners. Even the utter destruction of the major metropolitan areas of the West would not be the end of the misery, because a nuclear winter would then leave the creatureless topography barren and grotesquely deformed.

This threat of nuclear devastation provides an apt analogy. If God were to "disrobe" (to use Luther's image of "the naked God"), and show us his glory and power, his majesty and splendor, the winds of fire would sweep across the blue planet. Leaving death and destruction in its wake, this appearance of God would not bring hope, but ruin.

Woe to you who long for the day of the LORD! Why do you long for the day of the LORD? That day will be darkness, not light. It will be as though a man fled from a lion only to meet a bear, as though he entered his house and rested his hand on the wall only to have a snake bite him. Will not the day of the LORD be darkness, and not light—pitch-dark, without a ray of brightness?

—AMOS 5:18–20

Paul tells us that the Word of God holds together the atoms of the universe (Col. 1:17), and Peter reminds us, "But the day of the Lord will come like a thief. The heavens will disappear with a roar; the elements will be destroyed by fire, and the earth and everything in it will be laid bare" (2 Pet. 3:7–10). John Milton said it well:

> With such a horrid clang
> As on Mount Sinai rang
> While the red fire and smoldering clouds outbrake;
> The aged Earth, aghast
> With terror of that blast,
> Shall from the surface to the centre shake,
> When at the world's last session
> The dreadful Judge in middle air
> shall spread his throne.
>
> "ON THE MORNING OF CHRIST'S NATIVITY,"
> THE HYMN, STANZA 17

THE ROBED GOD

In his first advent, God comes to us fully robed, concealing his glory and power in our humanity. "No man can see me and live," God told Moses. And yet, the disciples gave the following report, as they were battling the gnostics: "That which was from the beginning, which we have heard, which we have *seen with our eyes*, which we have *looked at* and *our hands have touched*—this we proclaim concerning the Word of life" (1 John 1:1, emphasis added).

No doubt Jesus and his disciples enjoyed a deeply personal friendship, telling stories, recalling memories of weddings, funerals, and reunions with friends and family together. The same God whose voice shook Mount Sinai and sent fear into the hearts of their distant ancestors was now con-

110

versing with his companions in familiar terms. They touched God and lived to tell about it.

As we have already discovered, Gnosticism finds this concept utterly offensive. Too spiritual to appreciate material, physical, earthly "stuff," Gnosticism cannot swallow the idea that God became flesh, that he was experienced not in the internal emotions and ecstatic moments within the soul, but in the normal, ordinary events of daily human existence. Furthermore, they do not want to be saved by someone proclaiming these historical acts of God-in-the-flesh, as John says here, but by accessing through their own efforts some spiritual secrets for their personal employment.

Gnostics want to know God within their own hearts. The disciples reported that the way they came to know God was outside their own hearts, outside their own experience and their inner spiritual world, in the particularities of real human events and activities. These events were true, not because of the experience of the disciples. They were true, no matter what radical change their reality made in the disciples' lives, no matter what meaning, hope, and sense of purpose they provided.

That is not to say that these historical events and the reality to which they pointed do not lead to magnificent experiences, emotional rapture, and changed lives. But this is not what makes them either true or useful. They are true because they happened in history, and things that happen in history are not just true for direct participants. They are true for everyone.

THE CASE OF THE HISTORICAL JESUS

The claims of the disciples are not made on the level of psychology, anthropology, morality, sociology, marketing, or even—at least initially—theology. They are historical claims. The eye-witnesses do not tell us about private experiences that they had, encouraging us to experience the same things: "You ask me how I know he lives? He lives within my heart." Nor are their claims based on the relevance of the events: "Jesus changed my life and he can change yours too."

The disciples' witness, unlike much of what we hear in Christian circles, was more like legal testimony than a pitch for a product or an interview on a talk-show. The court was to make its judgment, not on the basis of the psychological or moral impact of these experiences, but on the basis of whether or not these events which the eye-witnesses reported actually took place.

The gnostic sees historicity as a distraction, turning us away from the inward, spiritual dimension of religion, attaching us to things that are external to our own personal experience. They are correct to see it in those terms. "Look," the gnostic pleads, "the real issue isn't whether these things reported in the Bible actually happened in this world. What really matters is the 'moral to the story,' the meaning and hope that these spiritual, heavenly ideas represent."

This is not the case. Christianity is an objective religion with subjective application, not a subjective religion with a few objective "givens" upon which people of all faiths can agree. Its truth is anchored not in what happens inside a person, but in what happened in the ancient land of Israel two thousand years ago.

However, this is not to say that there is no experience of God, and this is the second point one must make about John's striking announcement (1 John 1:1). The eye-witnesses of Jesus' life, death, and resurrection were bursting with experiences. How can one read the gospels and come away without being deeply affected by the emotional impact of God's life intersecting directly and physically with the lives of human beings?

A contemporary American woman may be correct in suggesting that the Battle of Waterloo is irrelevant to her daily life, but she cannot say that the events surrounding this Jewish rabbi are similarly trivial to her own experience. That is because of the magnitude of the event. The Battle of Waterloo is important, especially in the history of war and diplomacy. But the life, death, and resurrection of Jesus Christ are all saving events for us today. If Jesus died, but was not raised, that is not only significant for historians, it is crucial for every one of us. In a familiar passage, the apostle Paul relates,

> And if Christ has not been raised, our preaching is useless and so is your faith. More than that, we are found to be false witnesses about God, for we have testified about God that he raised Christ from the dead. . . . And if Christ has not been raised, your faith is futile; you are still in your sins. Then those also who have fallen asleep in Christ are lost. If only for this life we have hope in Christ, we are to be pitied more than all men.
>
> —1 CORINTHIANS 15:15–19

Paul stated that Christianity cannot go on without the Resurrection— an historical event. To be sure, the eye-witnesses experienced the God-Man, but it was because this God-Man had found them in their world, not vice versa. He confronted them, as he had confronted Adam and Eve after their sin in the Garden of Eden. This profound meeting between the offended Creator and the offending sinner nearly two thousand years ago still brings confrontation and crisis in the lives of multitudes from every nation and language.

Because God's saving work in Christ changed his relation to the world (from judgment to redemption), individual men, women, and children this very day are invited to enter into the benefits of sonship to God. Because of this event, we are no longer strangers in relation to God, thrown into a vast cosmic machine from which we must escape. Having taken on human nature, the Divine Son has secured the redemption of matter, whether animate or inanimate (Rom. 8:19–23). Because of him, it is good to be human again, good to be in the world.

THE CHRIST OF CHRISTMAS

Let us put this in practical terms. Every year, Christmas rolls around whether we like it or not, and it is a wonderful time for many people. Homecomings, warm moments with the generations bundled to sing carols, gift-giving, twinkling lights: it is a picture-perfect scene. But that is not the only side of Christmas. For others, the holidays bring about tremendous anxiety, depression, and disappointment.

It is those who struggle with the Advent season who especially need the message of Christmas: Emmanuel, God with Us. The psalmist lamented that there is no guarantee that believers will be happier, healthier, or wealthier than their unbelieving neighbors. In fact, he said, it seems that all the unbelievers he knows are doing well, while he is suffering. Isn't there some injustice in that? He writes, "My feet had almost slipped; I had nearly lost my foothold. For I envied the arrogant when I saw the prosperity of the wicked. They have no struggles; their bodies are healthy and strong. . . . Surely in vain have I kept my heart pure; in vain have I washed my hands in innocence." But then he realizes the transitory nature of earthly happiness, and the eternal view of things once again restores his balance.

Still, the question hits a wide cross section of people not only at Christmas, but the year-round: Where is God when life hurts? The very Christmas message answers with power. Just as the human race was groaning under the burden of its sin and guilt, God was dispatching his Son on a voyage across the great heavenly expanse, to enter time, to lay aside the glory of his divine person, to become a zygote in the womb of a simple, poor virgin daughter of Israel.

In the person of Christ, the eternal meets time; the One who owns the entire universe becomes poor; the God who is incapable of experiencing human passions becomes a laughing, weeping, threatening, comforting Man among us. Emmanuel, God with Us, is one of our Lord's most salutary biblical names. By coming to us, he was able to empathize with us.

THE EMPATHETIC CHRIST

There are two words we use describing the way we involve ourselves with other people's problems. One word is *sympathy*. It comes from the Greek words for "feeling" and "together." *Sympathy* is my feelings agreeing with those of another person. The other word is *empathy*, from the Greek words for "in" and "feeling." *Empathy* is not only to agree with another person in feeling, but to actually see that person's experience through his or her eyes. Someone who is well-provided for materially may sympathize with a home-less person, but only those who have once shared in the condition of homelessness can actually empathize with such an individual.

A person without children may be able to sympathize with a couple's recent loss of a child to a disease, but only other parents will really be able to empathize.

In the same way, God is spoken of in Scripture as though he had emotions. I say "as though," because God is not subject to human emotions. Whenever we read that God was angry or wept, grieved or laughed, these are called anthropomorphisms; that is, words that God uses to describe himself in ways we will understand. God does not really have wings; he doesn't really have arms or legs. He is a spirit, without parts or passions. These expressions are "baby talk."

But after that still night in Bethlehem nearly two thousand years ago, these anthropomorphic expressions were turned to reality. Now we observe, in the apostolic reports, God in the flesh, actually experiencing emotion, pain, suffering, and human pleasure. In the past, God had spoken through the prophets, but as the writer to the Hebrews announced, "now he has spoken to us in these last days through his own Son."

If God had been formed in Mary's virgin womb without a fully human nature, Mary could not have survived the experience. If God the Son had not clothed himself in flesh, his glory would have instantly turned Pharisee and fisherman alike to ash. But instead, prostitutes approach him, thieves repent, and sinners eat with him. Here we see God playing the bartender at a wedding reception (John 2:3) and screaming in outrage over the unnatural horror of death (John 11:38–44).

Gnostics read these texts in utter disgust. First, Jesus was affirming the goodness of creation by turning water into wine at a party. This is hardly the ascetic spirituality that characterized gnostic abhorrence of the world. Further, for the gnostic, death was terrific because it meant the escape of the spirit from the prison-house of the body. It was hardly something to lament! The resurrection of the body was, for the gnostic, hell rather than heaven. Such sentiment is not unfamiliar to those of us who recall funerals in which mourners were encouraged to celebrate the unfettering of the spirit from the prison-house of the body.

"He who eats my flesh and drinks my blood has eternal life," Jesus declared in John 6 to the bewilderment of his audience. What a crude, earthy religion! Saved by eating someone's flesh and drinking someone's blood? Such a metaphor could only have been calculated to provoke John's Greek audience.

All these flesh-and-blood incidents affirm the humanity of Jesus. They refute any teaching that he was God but not man; spiritual but not really physical. But he also revealed to his disciples that he was more than man. And he did it in a dramatic and unforgettable way.

A GLIMPSE OF HIS GLORY

A strange thing happened on a mountain before Jesus went to the cross. Taking Peter, John, and James, Jesus began to pray:

> As he prayed, the appearance of his face was altered, and his robe became white and glistening. And behold, two men talked with him, who were Moses and Elijah, who appeared in glory and spoke of his death which he was about to accomplish at Jerusalem. But Peter and those with him were heavy with sleep; and when they were fully awake, they saw his glory and the two men who stood with him. Then it happened, as they were parting from him, that Peter said to Jesus,

'Master, it is good for us to be here; and let us make three tabernacles: one for you, one for Moses, and one for Elijah'—not knowing what he said. While he was saying this, a cloud came and overshadowed them; and they were fearful as they entered the cloud. And a voice came out of the cloud, saying, 'This is My beloved Son. Hear him!' When the voice had ceased, Jesus was found alone. But they kept quiet, and told no one in those days any of the things they had seen.

—Luke 9:28–36

Representing the entire Old Testament, the law, and the prophets, Moses and Elijah were given the privilege of a conversation with the incarnate Word. The face upon which Moses could not look in his mortal frame was now beheld in the cloud of God's presence. Peter and the others saw Christ's glory for a brief moment, and immediately Peter wanted to set up a permanent place to enjoy this encounter. Interestingly, Luke records that Peter made the suggestion, "not knowing what he said," for this display was not intended to provoke curiosity or excitement. Jesus was discussing his cross, not his glory, with the patriarchs.

The ancient gnostics did not have to deal with relating the historical visitation of God in flesh to their present experience. They would have had no difficulty singing about walking and talking in a garden with someone no longer physically present, because for them powerful encounters "in the spirit" were all that really mattered. The glory was there, even apart from—perhaps even especially apart from—the physical presence of Jesus.

But orthodox Christians have to face this dilemma head-on. Christ is no longer physically present with us and is now seated at the Father's right hand, interceding for sinners. In what sense can he be said to continue to relate personally to our lives here and now? It is that question that we will turn to in our next chapter.

7

THE COST OF INTIMACY

"Look to the blood-stained cross, with flies and splinters,
with angry mockers, with the Father forsaking the Son."

S t. Paul established the Church of Corinth on the truth of the gospel and
the message of the cross. But before long, traveling salesmen invaded his
territory, trying to persuade people to incorporate Greek mysticism and
magic into Christianity. Theirs was a form of gnostic spirituality. Like contemporary "cafeteria-style" seekers, the Corinthians were open to a wide
range of doctrinal perspectives, so long as they could be judged by their
practical utility. In response, Paul wrote,

> For if someone comes to you and preaches a Jesus other than the
> Jesus we preached, or if you receive a different spirit from the one you
> received, or a different gospel from the one you accepted, you put up
> with it easily enough . . . but I do not think I am in the least inferior
> to those 'super-apostles.'"
>
> —2 CORINTHIANS 11:4-5

Those "super-apostles" presented themselves as wiser than Paul, because they knew how to appeal to the felt needs of pagan seekers. They
offered Christianity as a way of attaining the same "higher knowledge" of

the spiritual realm that Greek mysticism sought (1 Cor. 1:18–21). Meanwhile, they also emphasized signs and wonders (v. 22).

The pagans wanted "how-to" principles and spiritual power, with the promise of close encounters with the "naked God" and divine fire falling from heaven. The gnostics were there to make the sale. Paul's Gospel, it seems, was too foolish and weak to compete in the marketplace of smorgasbord spirituality. Even the disciples had been so obsessed with seeing Christ's glory that they had been unable to comprehend the meaning of the cross until after the Resurrection. Now these super-apostles made it easy to find "salvation" through something more exciting and less offensive than death by crucifixion.

If religion or spirituality is described in terms of the movement of human beings toward God, what is needed most is a great moral example— a hero, a strategist, and spiritual coach. We need someone to look up to, a role model like the Greek and Roman gods who were little more than glorified Olympian athletes, conquering generals, and beauty queens. A theology of glory and a gospel of health, wealth, and happiness and unending "victory" require celebrities, patterned on the "Great Celebrity," and we have seen what this had done to create a worldly evangelical subculture: "Who will be the greatest in your kingdom?" we still ask Jesus.

If, however, religion is seen as the movement of a gracious and sovereign God toward fallen and helpless sinners, what is needed is a Savior, a Redeemer—a sacrificial, substitutionary atonement. It all depends on how one views the problem. Dysfunction requires recovery; success is the answer to unhappiness, and self-esteem is the solution to failure. If we are not settled on what it is that leaves us in the lurch—the "big problem" that plagues us all—then we will never be agreed on the nature of salvation. And, though it is no longer popular to say so, that "big problem" is, in a word, *sin.*

CHRISTIANITY WITHOUT A CROSS?

That's not what Gnosticism maintains, however. Gnostics believe that humankind's problem is two-fold. First, we are innocent spirits who have been thrown into a world of fleshly and material evil and are trying to escape our earthly, time-bound, body-bound existence. Second, we lack sufficient know-how about the way the spiritual realm operates. If we could only figure out the "rules of the road" or have someone reveal them to us, we could make our way back home.

In our modern world, we have experts in philosophy, science, morality, psychology, and politics claiming to possess the saving knowledge we lack. We also have evangelists of cyberspace proclaiming a gospel of knowledge: by having access to an unlimited stream of data, we can create a pure, clean, pleasant, and care-free world that avoids messy involvement with the material world.

The pursuit of salvation through know-how has even helped engineer a massive pragmatism in the evangelical world. Among those more "spiritually" inclined, this means discovering principles of spiritual victory over violence, poverty, sickness, and depression that are built in or encoded into the universe. They must simply be discovered by the spiritual technicians (i.e., the *gnostikoi*—those in the know) and passed on to the rest of us.

The secular roots of this ideology and its influences on evangelical church life should not be underestimated. The idea is that if we can figure out how to end suffering, war, and poverty, we can save the world. Evil comes in the form of institutions such as government, schools, churches, and homes, and in this way matter—external structures—imprison and corrupt the innocent self. Salvation, therefore, must come in the form of liberating the self to free expression—unbounded and unrestricted freedom to overthrow custom, tradition, and institutional authority.

In more liberal cultural circles, this has emerged as a sort of 1960s radicalism. In more conservative, even Christian circles, it has led to a rebellion against creeds, rituals, corporate dimensions of faith, and church authority. In either case, the self is sent on a private quest for freedom and spiritual "well-being," offered in different versions by both liberals and conservatives. For liberals, it is radical politics; for conservatives it is pop-psychology (and conservative politics).

Liberal Protestants accommodate the Christian message to make the academy happy, given whatever latest intellectual fashion happens to be in vogue. Meanwhile, evangelical Protestants accommodate the Christian message to suit the marketplace. The "product" has to sell, so both liberal and evangelical Protestants pare off the offense of the cross in order to reach the largest possible market-share.

At the controversial 1993 "Re-Imagining" Conference in Minneapolis, representatives of the mainline Protestant churches gathered to worship "Sophia" rather than Jesus. *Newsweek* magazine reported, "Jesus was never invoked. But his death in atonement for the sins of man—the meaning of the cross—was dismissed by one theologian as the grotesque product of the male imagination," reminding us of ancient Gnosticism's feminism and its critique of the theology of the cross as a male invention. "'I don't think we need folks hanging on crosses and blood dripping and weird stuff,' said the Rev. Dolores Williams, who teaches at Union Theological Seminary in New York."[1]

All this has a history to it, not only in ancient Gnosticism, but in its modern revival. During the romanticism of the last century, God was increasingly seen as a feminine spirit who simply wanted to nurture the self, love the self, and satisfy the soul's deepest longings for intimacy. A relational theology, shaped by psychological rather than theological concepts, eventually replaced the theology of the cross. The notion of God's wrath against sin, requiring the execution of his own Son as a sin-bearing sacrifice, had become too harsh and unbecoming of a good God. Once again, the so-called "Bad God" of the Old Testament was sent into the ring against the "Good God" of the New Testament, and the supposedly nicer God won.

Conservatives honestly and courageously cried out against this extreme form of explicit gnostic ideology. Yet the same cultural currents that produced the "Re-Imagining" Conference, even in evangelical churches, tone down the preaching of the cross in favor of more psychologically relevant inspirational talks that speak to our feelings. This is so because the whole culture is awash in a sea of romanticism, not because evangelicals are being influenced directly by the same people who are shaping liberal and radical Protestantism. A parallel sentiment runs through the mystical tradition, evidenced in the comment of English mystic Julian of Norwich (1342–1420). Referring to God as both Lord and Mother, Julian denied that God was ever wrathful:

> I saw truly that our Lord was never wroth [angry], nor ever shall be. For he is God: good, life, truth, love, peace. . . . What is the mercy and forgiveness of God? For by the teaching I had before, I understood that the mercy of God should be the forgiveness of his wrath after the time that we have sinned. . . . But howsoever I might behold and desire, I could in no wise see this point in all the showing. . . . For I saw no manner of wrath in God, neither for short time nor for long.[2]

The concept of eternal judgment follows the same fate as God's more troubling attributes. How, critics ask, could final punishment reform wayward sons and daughters? The emphasis on love in our culture (The Beatles' "All We Need Is Love" comes to mind) has rendered many of our churches effete in their understanding of the deep depravity of the human heart. It mitigates the necessary justice of God in punishing sin and evil wherever it exists in heaven and earth. More recently, a so-called "megashift" is taking place in evangelical theology, from the classic theory of a substitutionary atonement to a more relational approach. The mainline Protestant encyclopedia, *The Westminster Dictionary of Christian Theology*, explains how nineteenth- and early twentieth-century liberal theology experienced this "megashift":

> The most important new factor influencing views of the nature of the atonement was the increasing sense of the autonomy of the individual and the significance of interpersonal relationships. Philosophers had already directed attention to the individual: thinking and feeling and constrained by moral demands. Now the question began to arise: How could atonement be viewed in the context of familiar human feelings and relationships?[3]

Today, this relational emphasis dominates much of evangelical reflection. Concepts such as wrath and propitiation are often set aside in favor of more "seeker-friendly" concepts.[4] How, then, are we to understand the message of the cross? Must we, like the super-apostles who brought Gnosticism to the early church, get rid of the offense, and turn Christianity into a more likable religion?

THE PRICE FOR OUR INTIMACY WITH GOD

Yale theologian H. Richard Niebuhr offered a pithy summary of liberalism's message when he characterized it in the following terms: "A God without wrath brought men without sin into a kingdom without judgment through the ministrations of a Christ without a cross."[5] But, as evangelicals, we can no longer throw stones, judging by the information we find in Christian bookstores and receive in many churches.

What do we believe? Do we think that people are born into the world enemies of God, under divine judgment? Or that they are born into the world friends of God who simply do not yet know him? If we insist on the latter, there really is no price for intimacy with God, since there is no wrath to be assuaged, no satisfaction of justice to be made, and no atonement to be offered in order to enter into a relationship with God. All that is necessary is spiritual information. However, as we have seen in Scripture, God does not tolerate our curious "seeking" for intimacy with him. He is holy and distant, and when he does come close, it is always on his terms. Only then may sinful creatures approach him without disaster.

In Christ, God came close to sinners. Yet that bridging of the physical distance did not mean that everyone would attain intimacy with God. Even in Jesus' close proximity, God was still terrible in judgment: "I told you that you would die in your sins; if you do not believe that I am the one I claim to be, you will indeed die in your sins" (John 8:24). Even the familiar comfort of John 3:16 is followed by verse 18: "Whoever believes in him is not condemned, but whoever does not believe stands condemned already because he has not believed in the name of God's one and only Son." If we do not accept Christ's substitutionary sacrifice admitting us into the Holy of Holies, we will be judged, regardless of how "spiritual" or sensitive in our devotion to God.

Those who suggest that it is not in God's character to be wrathful or judgmental, as if love were his only attribute, have not sufficiently weighed the biblical evidence. Throughout Scripture we learn that our sins were "laid upon" Christ, our scapegoat, as he carried our guilt upon his own body (Isa. 53:6, 12; John 1:29; 2 Cor. 5:21; Gal. 3:13; Heb. 9:28; 1 Pet. 2:24). In this way, God can be both just and the justifier of the ungodly (Rom. 3:26). How else could God acquit us? If he were too loving to judge us, he would cease to be God, for he himself would violate his own character and become a law-breaker. This is not because the law is somehow above God, but because it is a true expression of his very essence. To violate his law is to violate his character.

God did not have to plant a cross in history. He did not have to send his own Son to redeem sinners. None of this was necessitated by God's own character. To be sure, he is loving, but he clearly warned the human race of the consequence of sin: eternal death. He would still have been true to his loving character if he had refused to rescue those who refused to return his love. Instead, God found a way of saving sinners, reconciling enemies, and acquitting law-breakers that would not violate his justice: He sent his Son as the substitute for sinners.

Because he was God, Jesus could atone for the sins of others. After all, he was not paying for his own sins, and a substitute who is infinite in righteousness can satisfy a debt that is infinite in unrighteousness. God accepted Jesus' sacrifice not as if it were sufficient as a literal payment for sin, but because it was the suffering, death, and blood-shedding of One who was infinitely superior to lambs and goats. Because he was God, Christ could save us from our sins. Because he was also human, it was humanity and not God who bore the responsibility and guilt. Therefore, Christ was not only God but Man. He suffered as God because only God had the power to save; he suffered as Man because only man owed the debt.

This is why the Bible so frequently uses the Greek prepositions *peri, huper,* and *anti,* all of which mean "in place of." This substitutionary language is found in Matthew 20:28, John 11:50, Romans 5:5–8, 8:32, Galatians 2:20, 3:13, 1 Timothy 2:6, and Hebrews 2:9. By his perfect life of constant, uninterrupted obedience to the will of the Father, Christ merited for all believers the right to eat from the tree of life, a right which Adam forfeited on our behalf. By Christ's sacrificial death, our debts were canceled. And by his glorious resurrection, Christ secured a new and living way for us to enjoy the presence of God without consuming fire. Thus, the writer to the Hebrews declares, in view of the frightening scene at Mount Sinai,

> You have not come to a mountain that can be touched and that is burning with fire; to darkness, gloom and storm; to a trumpet blast or to such a voice speaking that those who heard it begged that no further word be spoken to them, because they could not bear what was commanded. . . . But you have come to Mount Zion, to the heavenly Jerusalem, the city of the living God . . . , to Jesus the mediator of a new covenant, and to the sprinkled blood that speaks a better word than Abel.
>
> —Hebrews 12:18–24

Understanding the Gospel

Clearly, the drift from a legal, forensic, objective view of Christ's cross to a subjective, moral, mystical, and relational perspective reflects something larger that is going on in the culture. Modernity, we have seen, has been characterized by Christian and non-Christian historians as a revival of Gnosticism.

And yet, many of those who advocate a rejection of classical Christian orthodoxy in favor of modernity are still considered evangelicals. In fact, Clark Pinnock is quite honest about his project, cheerfully confessing, " . . . we are finally making peace with the culture of modernity."[6]

It is not my intention to suggest that those who depart from such classical doctrinal positions are necessarily gnostics, for there are many other influences. However, one cannot help but notice the contrast between the objective focus of orthodox Christianity and the subjective emphasis of Gnostic mysticism and romanticism.

Once we are taken into ourselves, into our own feelings and the impression of Christ's life and death on our own hearts, we are open to gnostic influences. To the extent that the "culture of modernity" we have been describing is gnostic, it is to that extent that peace-making with such a culture will always entail the acceptance of doctrinal tendencies which threatened to destroy the early church.

Beyond the historical ramifications, we will fail to enjoy the peace that passes all understanding. How can we obtain rest if our intimacy with God is in any way dependent on the condition of our hearts or the inner workings of our spirits? "The heart is deceitful above all things, and desperately wicked," we read in Scripture (Jer. 17:9).

Biblical Christianity is concerned with what happened outside us, two thousand years ago, outside the city of Jerusalem. It is an "over there" religion, not an "in here" religion. It is centered on what happened externally, not on what happens internally. The gnostics replaced the church's teaching on the historical Incarnation, Crucifixion, and Resurrection of Christ with the centrality of the new birth and the activity of God's Spirit within their own spirits.

Christianity does not announce to the world, "If you have a conversion experience, you will be saved, so make sure you have a conversion experience." Anything that has to do with me and my works or my experience securing victory and intimacy with God is sure to lead to despair. It is bad news, not good. And, by the way, this is not to in any way detract from the importance of the new birth or the subjective dimension of Christian experience. It is simply to say that nothing that happens within me is the gospel.

Luther's sidekick, Melanchthon, constantly fell into despair over his spiritual failures and came to Luther for absolution. The German Reformer finally shouted to his introspective friend, "Melanchthon, the gospel is completely outside of you!" Repeatedly, the apostles announce the gospel in the familiar form, "For what I received I passed on to you as of first importance: that Christ died for our sins according to the Scriptures, that he was buried, that he was raised on the third day according to the Scriptures, and that he appeared to Peter, and then to the twelve" (1 Cor. 15:3–4).

"The gospel" does not mean my being born again or experiencing conversion, making a decision or being transformed within. Rather, the gospel is that "He was delivered over to death for our sins and was raised to life for our justification" (Rom. 4:25). The good news is about what happened to Christ because of my failures to believe enough, to obey enough, to serve enough, and to love enough.

The new birth is a marvelous reality, but it is the effect of the preaching of the gospel, not the "Good News" itself. When instructions on how to be born again are preached as the Good News, such a message actually becomes a new law: "Be born again," or "Convert yourself." John 3:5 is often used in this very manner.

Our Lord said, "I tell you the truth, no one can see the kingdom of God unless he is born again." This statement is not in the imperative mood—that is, in the form of a command. He does not tell Nicodemus to make himself "born again." He simply states the reality of the situation: men and women are helpless to save themselves—so helpless, he says, that they cannot even see the kingdom of God and understand the realities of eternal life unless they are first made alive by God. It is the apostolic preaching of the cross, not the motions of one's heart or will, that creates this new birth, as the Holy Spirit awakens sinners to their need through the preaching of the gospel.

Each characteristic of ancient Gnosticism that seeps into our modern world-view, including our religious outlook, is confronted head-on by the cross of Christ. It is corporate rather than purely individualistic; public as well as private; external, historical, objective, and completed, as well as subjectively applied by the Holy Spirit as he acts upon and lives within the human heart.

We can stop focusing on whatever is happening inside us. We can, for the moment, set aside our response to the work of Christ, and turn our full gaze on him who was set forth publicly as the propitiation for our sins. My heart may still be corrupt, my conscience may still condemn me, my soul may still hold on to Christ weakly and clumsily, but Christ was crucified for me. No one can change that. No experience can obstruct that reality. It is finished, once and for all.

Where do we see the glory of God? Is it in those ecstatic moments of reaching emotional heights through praise, singing, prayer, speaking in unknown tongues? Is it through participating in signs and wonders, or having a vision of God in all of his power and might? No, this is the theology of glory. It is strictly condemned by Scripture.

Jesus himself points us toward the glory of God by appealing to Numbers 21:4–9. God's people, as usual, were grumbling. In judgment, God sent venomous snakes and many died in the wilderness. Moses interceded for the people and the Lord said to Moses, "Make a snake and put it up on a pole; anyone who is bitten can look at it and live." Moses did as he was commanded and all those who looked to the brass serpent were instantly healed. Many centuries later, Jesus declared of himself, "Just as Moses lifted up the snake in the desert, so the Son of Man must be lifted up, that everyone who believes in him may have eternal life" (John 3:14-15).

Just as the snake had been the source of disaster, God commanded the emblem of a snake—head crushed and pierced with a stake—to be the remedy. "What the law was powerless to do in that it was weakened by the sinful nature, God did by sending his own Son in the likeness of sinful man to be a sin offering" (Rom. 8:3).

One man had been the source of our guilt and corruption. Another man was lifted up on a cross so that everyone who looked to him might be saved. Our whole church life must be devoted to this task: lifting up "Christ crucified" to a world of sinners like ourselves; pointing and announcing, with John the Baptist, "Behold, the Lamb of God, who takes away the sin of the world."

William Cowper, who suffered from chronic depression, found this message to be the only salve to soothe his accusative conscience:

> Let us love, and sing, and wonder,
> Let us praise the Saviour's Name!
> He has hushed the Law's loud thunder.
> He has quenched Mount Sinai's flame:
> He has washed us in his blood.
> He has brought us nigh to God.
>
> Let us love the Lord who bought us.
> Pitied us when enemies,
> Called us by His grace, and taught us,

Gave us ears and gave us eyes:
He has washed us with His blood,
He presents our souls to God.

Let us wonder; grace and justice
join, and point to mercy's store;
When through grace in Christ our trust is,
justice smiles and asks no more.
He who washed us with His blood
has secured our way to God.

Do you want to see God in all of his glory? Do you long to see Christ in his exalted splendor? Look to the blood-stained cross, with flies and splinters, with angry mockers, with the Father forsaking the Son. True, it is hardly what we would regard as a display of divine power and glory; it appears rather to demonstrate divine weakness and shame. Yet everyone who looks to this Son of Man is saved from sin's guilt and tyranny.

Our sinful nature will continue to draw us back into ourselves, to seek remedies within our own constitutions, through our own powers, piety, and clever techniques. Our eyes are too easily pleased. Our hearts, slow as they are to believe, will often lead us to more dazzling paths. But true spirituality will look outside, not inside. It will seek Christ, who was lifted up on the cross, promising that everyone who looks out to him will be reconciled to God for all eternity. No wonder the apostle Paul said that even though "the message of the cross is foolishness to those who are perishing, . . . to those who are being saved it is the power of God" (1 Cor. 1:18).

Let us, like St. Paul, become "resolved to know nothing . . . but Christ and him crucified" (2:2).

8

❖

RECEIVING CHRIST

*"He has come down to us—all the way down—and has not
left a single step for us to climb."*

God not only takes it upon himself to save us from our guilt; he takes it upon himself to restore us to life and to bring us to faith. In doing so, the riches of Christ, secured at the cross, become ours.

> We must understand that as long as Christ remains outside of us, and we are separated from him, all that he has suffered and done for the salvation of the human race remains useless and of no value for us. . . . All that Christ possesses is nothing to us until we grow into one body with him.[1]

In other words, if there were no subjective work of the Spirit in our hearts, all that we have considered up to this point would remain beyond our reach. Christ's redemptive work in history, objectively won for us, would nevertheless be of no use apart from the work of the Holy Spirit.

When we are united to Christ, we are immediately made heirs of his righteous life. His thirty-three years of complete consecration and total surrender to the divine will become our identity before God. By his circumcision, we are set aside from the domination of sin and made children of God. By his godly life and victory over temptation, we who constantly fail and falter are regarded as holy and acceptable. This is what it means to be identified with Christ's life.

But there is a subjective aspect as well. In this union, Christ's life is not only his active obedience imputed, but his holy life imparted. "I am the true vine, and my Father is the gardener," said Jesus (John 15:1). "Neither can you bear fruit unless you remain in me. I am the vine; you are the branches. If a man remains in me and I in him, he will bear much fruit; apart from me you can do nothing" (John 15:5).

Just as we are declared righteous in justification, we are steadily made righteous in sanctification. We do not look for the one in Christ and the other in something or someone else, even if that someone is the Holy Spirit. For all of our gifts are found in Christ. They are given by the Father, in the Son, through the agency of the Holy Spirit.

We are not baptized into the Spirit, but into Christ by the Spirit. We do not participate in the life of the Spirit, but in the life of Christ by the life-giving power of the Spirit. All of the Spirit's activity has Christ as the reference point, and where the Spirit himself is given center-stage, we can be certain that it is not the Holy Spirit who is active in such settings (John 15:26). We bear the "fruit of the Spirit" only as we are in union with the Vine.

Our justification is perfect, complete, and instantaneous. Sanctification, by contrast, is imperfect, incomplete, and progressive throughout the Christian life. No believer can ever say that he or she has achieved victory over sin, although Christ has accomplished this on the believer's behalf. His victory is imputed perfectly and instantly, while it is experienced in the believer's life only in perpetual conflict with our still-sinful hearts. Thus, our union with Christ in the likeness of his life means that we who once were at peace with our sins are at war with our sins. We who were once satisfied with ourselves are now locked in perpetual battle with our own wickedness and rebellion.

The objective work of Christ would profit us nothing unless it were subjectively received. The historic events of our Lord's passion, death, and resurrection which secured our salvation must be effectually applied by the Holy Spirit working in our hearts. But how is this union secured? If it is not a matter of the soul's direct and immediate access to God's Spirit, how can we possibly cross the infinite chasm between Creator and creature?

HOW WE ARE UNITED TO CHRIST

Sure, God has come in human flesh, but that was two thousand years ago. How does he come to me, today? That is the same as asking, with the Philippian jailer, "Sirs, what must I do to be saved?" And what did Paul and Silas reply?

> 'Believe in the Lord Jesus, and you will be saved—you and your household.' Then they spoke the word of the Lord to him and to all the others in his house. At the hour of the night the jailer took them and washed their wounds; then immediately he and his family were baptized."
>
> —ACTS 16:30–33

In this response there were two "means of grace" which the apostles employed for the salvation of the jailer. The first was the Word.

As we have seen in previous chapters, the Word is divided into two parts—law and gospel. Everything in the Bible that tells us how to live and issues threats for failing to conform to those commands is "law." Everything in Scripture that promises us eternal life on no other basis than the free gift in Christ is "gospel."

We can also express this in the biblical language of "covenant." In the beginning, God promised Adam and his posterity eternal life on the condition of perfect obedience, of which Adam was then capable. Having violated that covenant of works, however, Adam lost his power of free will. Since then, every human descendant has been born spiritually dead, guilty, and incapable of fulfilling God's law or covenant of works (1 Cor. 1:20–21).

After Adam's disobedience, God established a covenant of grace, promising Adam and all of his posterity who would trust in His promise that a Mediator would cover their shame, just as the animal's skins had covered Adam's nakedness. The covenant of works promises, "Do this and you shall live," while the covenant of grace promises, "Live and you shall do this." In the covenant of works, God demands perfect obedience. Christ fulfilled the covenant of works as the Second Adam (Rom. 5:1–21) so that sinners could be received into God's family through a covenant of grace.

It is this covenant of grace, or "gospel," that the apostles presented to the Philippian jailer. This gospel is "the power of God unto salvation for

131

everyone who believes" (Rom. 1:12). It is God's primary means of grace, linking the believer here and now with the historical events of Christ's saving work.

The apostles did not provide steps. They did not explain how to appropriate God's grace. They did not describe how to "make Jesus Savior and Lord." This all would amount to "law"—something for them to do toward the attainment of their salvation, something for which they could claim at least partial credit. The apostles' message is simply, "Believe in the Lord Jesus, and you will be saved—you and your household." The household was even included because, as in the Old Testament administration of this covenant of grace, God still saves families and not merely individuals.

But there is a second means of grace that the apostles appealed to in the conversion of the jailer. Not only did the jailer need the Word to link him here and now to the saving events of history; he also required the sacrament of baptism: "Then immediately he and all his family were baptized" (v. 33). Throughout our discussion of union with Christ above, the repeated references to baptism cannot be lightly dismissed. Gnostics of all ages have insisted that this is not a literal baptism with water, but a spiritual baptism. After all, if the Spirit works directly, why confine his work to such base, earthly elements as water? Don't rituals just get in the way?

The gnostics preferred the "word" directly spoken to the heart or spirit to the "dead letter," and they twisted Paul's words to imply that the Bible was the "dead letter." And as for the sacraments? Those were rituals of a carnal institution, standing in the way of the Spirit's direct communion with God.

The Spirit and the Word

A theology of glory rejects the weakness of preaching and the foolishness of the gospel. Recently, a number of Christian campuses have reported revival. As I have read case after case, one theme running throughout is the "testimony" that the Spirit was working directly in these meetings. Students and faculty alike appeared to applaud the fact that there was no preaching involved. "There wasn't even a preacher," one student exults. "The Holy Spirit was doing it, not some preacher."

What is the assumption in such a comment? It is that the Holy Spirit working directly and immediately (i.e., without means) was superior to the Holy Spirit working through means. By circumventing the Word—and especially the preached Word—the Holy Spirit was perceived as being more intimately and powerfully involved.

Historic Protestantism has always emphasized the preaching of God's Word as sacramental. That is, it is not merely the communication of information, but the effectual means of producing conversion. God alone is the cause of the New Birth, but he calls women and men to himself through the weakness of preaching.

Nowhere in Scripture do we find a pattern of evangelism or revival in which individuals respond to the gospel by simply being "zapped" by the Spirit. They are always responding to the preached Word. It may be one-on-one, or in an assembly, but it is the Word proclaimed that gives life to those spiritually dead. Furthermore, even after they are converted, believers do not grow in their walk, deepen in their Christian experience, or learn new truths by the direct activity of the Spirit apart from God's ordained means.

Apart from the Word, there is no salvation and no activity of the Holy Spirit in the lives of God's people. Where the Word is rightly preached, the Spirit is active in power. Where the Word is not rightly preached, the Spirit is not active in power. It is impossible to have a place in which the Word is preached clearly (as the proclamation of Christ), where the Spirit is absent in his power and saving strength. It is equally impossible for the Spirit to be actively present if the preaching of Christ is not the central focus.

The Reformers faced "the enthusiasts," who were heirs to many of the tendencies of the ancient gnostics. They believed that they knew a better way, a higher path, a secret tunnel of the Spirit that was a short-cut. Luther, for instance, in a sermon on Luke 2:22, warned of "those noxious spirits who say: a man acquires the Holy Spirit by sitting in a corner, etc. A hundred thousand devils you will acquire, and you will not come to God. God has always worked with something physical."

True Christianity is not gained by sitting in a corner, watching and waiting to be filled with heavenly revelation. Rather, as we sit with other sinners in a church, hearing and believing the Word of God, God comes to his people in intimate communion, self-disclosure, and redemption. John Calvin declared, in his commentary on 1 Thessalonians 5:20,

It is an illusory belief of the enthusiasts that those who keep reading Scripture or hearing the Word are children, as if no one were spiritual unless he scorned doctrine. In their pride, therefore, they despise the ministry of men and even Scripture itself, in order to attain the Spirit. They then proudly try to peddle all the delusions that Satan suggests to them as secret revelations of the Spirit.

Our own day is filled with examples of contemporary enthusiasm, or what we would today call mysticism. Defending the Keswick "Higher Life" vision of spirituality, a popular minister and writer asserts, "Sermons are not God's primary method for reaching people. *People* are his method for reaching people." However, it is not any kind of person the writer has in mind, but "people who have discovered the wonderful Spirit-filled life."[2]

Although the author defends the importance of the Bible toward the end of the book, he urges, "God's method for reaching this generation, and in every generation is not preachers and sermons. It is Christians whose lifestyles are empowered and directed by the Holy Spirit."[3]

GOD'S PURPOSE FOR PREACHING

Scripture declares that "faith comes by hearing the message" (Rom. 10:17), since "it [the gospel] is the power of God unto salvation" (Rom. 1:12). But those in our day who emphasize the "higher life" in the Spirit often look for more immanent, direct encounters. This is not a question of the inerrancy or importance of Scripture. At the end of the day, one can hold a high view of Scripture in principle, and still replace its sacramental power with other means of grace.

The underlying premise of such remarks is the notion that relationships are more important than preaching the apostolic truth. But to whom are we introducing people? To Christ or to ourselves? Is the "Good News" no longer Christ's doing and dying, but one's own "Spirit-filled" life? More sobering still, this implies that instead of the Word as a means of grace, "victorious Christians" are themselves mediating divine grace through the example of their own holiness. That makes us sacramental, rather than the Word. This is not Good News, but this is what we get whenever we stray from the preached Word as God's means of grace.

Must we come to Christ and be united to him through the earthly elements of ink and paper? It is not as if the Bible were made of magical material. It is not its ink, paper, binding, and gilded edges that distinguish it from any other literary classic. It is the message that is miraculous. By the working of the Holy Spirit, the law actually brings people to psychological, spiritual, and sometimes even emotional exhaustion. It instills fear of God's righteousness, holiness, and wrath, and it strips us of all confidence in ourselves and in our own performance. The law slays us so that we can be made alive in Christ.

Having left us stripped of our own fig leaves, the law is followed by the gospel, "the power of God unto salvation," that Word of the cross that banishes our fear of death and wrath. When this Word is preached, the Holy Spirit effects the new birth through it. Furthermore, when the minister is faithfully proclaiming the text, drawing on his careful study of the original languages, possible alternative interpretations, and other tools of pastoral scholarship, he is addressing Christ's people in the voice of God himself. The preached Word is the very address of our Judge, Redeemer, King, and Friend.

Far from denigrating the preached Word over the Spirit's direct "whisper" to the heart, the biblical accounts of conversions link the Spirit to the Word in every case. For instance, in the gospel accounts, people respond either in outrage or faith to Jesus' teaching. This preaching of the Word is the Spirit's means of bringing whole crowds to Christ. In fact, this is why Luther said it is difficult to preach the gospel to ourselves.

Scripture is an announcement from God, and therefore requires a messenger outside of us. Our tendency is to twist what we read and deny its impact on our lives. But when we hear it preached by someone else who stands outside our experience and the doubts or fears of our heart, it has a far greater impact. Calvin agreed with this argument. He surmised from Scripture that it is more important to hear the Word preached in church than to read it by oneself, although both are essential. After all, it was not for nothing that Paul said, "Faith comes by hearing the Word of God."

In Acts 2, it is in response to Peter's sermon that "those who accepted his message were baptized, and about three thousand were added to their number that day" (v. 41). In fact, the whole purpose of Pentecost was for the Spirit to empower his disciples to be Christ's witnesses. It is that same Word that brings individuals to Christ one-on-one. Lydia, a businesswoman from Thyatira, was converted in the same manner as Peter's crowds: "The Lord opened her heart to respond to Paul's message. When she and the members of her household were baptized, she invited us to her home" (Acts 16:14–16).

Isaiah's vision changed his life forever when he realized that he was a sinner amidst a nation of lost sinners. After he was forgiven, he cried out, "Lord, here I am, send me!" Later he would write, "How beautiful on the mountains are the feet of those who bring good news, who proclaim peace, who bring good tidings, who proclaim salvation, who say to Zion, 'Your God reigns!'" (Isa. 52:7).

Paul picks up on this language in Romans 10, making the preached Word essential for the Spirit's work of regeneration: "How, then, can they call on the one in whom they have not believed? And how can they believe in the one of whom they have not heard? And how can they hear without someone preaching to them? And how can they preach unless they are sent? As it is written, 'How beautiful are the feet of those who bring good news!'" (Rom. 10:14–15).

The Word, Restoring Life

God has determined to bring that Good News through specific means, and to involve us in this drama. God the Creator of matter is not the enemy of God the Redeemer of spirit. They are one and the same God, who uses the material things in his creation—human language, water, bread and wine, ink and paper—to effect miraculous spiritual transformation. He encounters us in words, and it is by the telling and retelling of these stories of divine redemption that people are reconciled to God and to each other.

The saving efficacy of this preached Word is illustrated in Ezekiel's vision of the valley of dry bones. The Holy Spirit brought the prophet to a valley filled with skeletons. God asked Ezekiel, "Can these bones live?"

> I said, 'O Sovereign LORD, you alone know.' Then he said to me, 'Prophesy to these bones and say to them, "Dry bones, hear the word of the LORD! This is what the Sovereign LORD says to these bones: I will make breath enter you, and you will come to life. I will attach tendons to you and make flesh come upon you and cover you with skin; I will put breath in you and you will come to life. Then you will know that I am the LORD."'

—EZEKIEL 37:4–6

Ezekiel did as God had told him, prophesying (i.e., preaching) to the valley of skeletons. Imagine how silly he must have felt, standing on the edge of a cliff, preaching down to a cemetery. Even if it was merely a vision, what a foolish vision! Yet, Ezekiel did as he was commanded. "And as I was prophesying, there was a noise, a rattling sound, and the bones came together, bone to bone. I looked, and tendons and flesh appeared on them and skin covered them, but there was no breath in them." Another sermon was required:

> Then he said to me, 'Prophesy to the breath; prophesy, son of man, and say to it, "This is what the Sovereign LORD says: Come from the four winds, O breath, and breathe into these slain, that they may live."' So I prophesied as he commanded me, and breath entered them; they came to life and stood up on their feet—a vast army. Then he said to me, 'Son of man, these bones are the whole house of Israel. They say, 'Our bones are dried up and our hope is gone; we are cut off.' Therefore prophesy and say to them: 'This is what the Sovereign LORD says: O my people, I am going to open your graves and bring you up from them; I will bring you back to the land of Israel. Then you, my people, will know that I am the LORD, when I open your graves and bring you up from them. I will put my Spirit in you and you will live, and I will settle you in your own land. Then you will know that I the LORD have spoken, and I have done it, declares the LORD.'
>
> —EZEKIEL 37:9–14

This is precisely what we are called to do. While ministers are appointed by God to prophesy to the dry bones in an official capacity, the priesthood of all believers requires us to prophesy, or preach, to each other. After all, we cannot preach to ourselves. Even the strongest believers find themselves looking away from the cross to themselves, leaving their first love, forgetting the depth of their depravity and the riches of God's grace in Christ.

This is why we need someone outside of us, external to our hearts, to our experience, to our inner lives, calling us to look outside of ourselves to Christ. Even as Christians, we are tempted to begin trusting in ourselves again, thinking that we can save ourselves with God's help. Either that, or we sink beneath the despair of ever finding peace with God because of our ongoing sinfulness. Through a preacher, we find God himself declaring his faithfulness to the covenant of grace.

Education—though it is despised by gnostics who feel that they have access to direct revelations—is indispensable. We believe that the Holy Spirit will link us to Christ through the preached Word, so we come with expectations of divine activity. Israel had the Word of God, but it was the Holy Spirit who, through Ezekiel's preaching, made that Word the active, energetic power behind the spiritual resurrection.

Too often, the preaching in many churches that emphasizes the Word but ignores the Holy Spirit as the divine agent is dry and dull. More like a lecture or a glorified Sunday school class, it lacks the power and authority that comes when truth is not merely explained but proclaimed. It is no wonder that many associated with the lecture-style rather than proclamatory approach become so parched that they begin to look for water in the mirages of popular spiritual fads.

And yet, as Jeremiah points out, there are also opposite dangers when separating the Word and Spirit. The "lying prophets" claim to receive special revelation.

> Do not listen to what the prophets are prophesying to you; they fill you with false hopes. They speak visions from their own minds, not from the mouth of the LORD. . . . But which of them has stood in the council of the LORD to see or to hear his word? Who has listened and heard his word? . . . I did not send these prophets, yet they have run with their message; I did not speak to them, yet they have prophesied.
>
> —JEREMIAH 23:16–21

What Has the Lord Spoken?

Like prophet, like people: "This is what each of you keeps on saying to his friend or relative: 'What is the LORD's answer?' or 'What has the LORD spoken?' But you must not mention 'the oracle of the LORD' again, because every man's own word becomes his oracle and so you distort the words of the living God, the LORD Almighty, our God" (vv. 35–36). The prophet warns of divine judgment for those, whether prophet or people, who claim to hear from the Lord outside of his revealed Word.

This warning was given during a period of active revelation to prophets, when Scripture was still being written. How much more does it apply to us today, after God has spoken fully and finally in his Son (Heb. 1:1)? If we are to see genuine awakening in our day, we must refuse to separate what God has joined together. The Word without the Spirit would be ineffective, and the Spirit without the Word is not the Spirit at all—but the lying delusions of our own imaginative and fallible minds.

It's time we recovered our confidence in the Word and Spirit once again. We must refuse to accept any version of spirituality that seeks the Word without the life-giving Spirit or the Spirit without the actual proclamation, teaching and doctrinal clarity of the actual text of Holy Scripture. Apart from sound doctrine and lively preaching of biblical truth, the Holy Spirit is silent; when that Word is faithfully proclaimed, the Holy Spirit is at work. Then there comes a rattling sound, as the bones come together one by one, forming an army of the Lord in the valley of death.

THE SACRAMENTS—MEANS OF GRACE

It is one thing for an evangelical to believe that the Word is a means of grace. It is quite another to add that the sacraments are a further means of grace. Even the word "sacrament" sounds "Catholic" to many evangelical ears. In fact, it is a biblical concept and enjoys a remarkably high place, next to the Word itself, in Protestant confessions and catechisms. Observe the following classical evangelical definitions. From the Lutheran tradition we discover the following:

> Our churches teach that the sacraments were instituted not merely to be marks of profession among men but especially to be signs and testimonies of the will of God toward us, intended to awaken and confirm faith in those who use them.
>
> —*THE AUGSBURG CONFESSION*,
> ARTICLE XIII (1530)

The Reformed churches concur with this view of the sacraments. *The Scots Confession* of 1560 declares,

> And so we utterly condemn the vanity of those who affirm the sacraments to be nothing else than naked and bare signs. No, we assuredly believe that by baptism we are engrafted into Christ Jesus, to be made partakers of his righteousness, by which our sins are covered

and remitted, and also that in the supper rightly used, Christ Jesus is so joined with us that he becomes the very nourishment and food of our souls." By this supper the Holy Spirit "makes us feed upon the body and blood of Christ once broken and shed for us but now in heaven, and appearing for us in the presence of his Father. Notwithstanding the distance between his glorified body in heaven and mortal men on earth, yet we must assuredly believe that the bread which we break is a communion of Christ's body and the cup which we bless is the communion of his blood

—CHAPTER 21

The Heidelberg Catechism agrees with these definitions, and the *Westminster Confession* adds that

"Sacraments are holy signs and seals of the covenant of grace"
—CHAPTER 27

In every sacrament, two things are involved: the sign and the thing signified. The sign in baptism, for instance, is water; in the Lord's Supper, bread and wine. The thing signified in baptism is regeneration; in the Lord's Supper it is the body and blood of Christ. As the *Westminster Confession* puts it, "There is in every sacrament a spiritual relation, or sacramental union, between the sign and the thing signified; whence it comes to pass that the names and effects of the one are attributed to the other" (ibid.).

In other words, the union between water and regeneration is so close in baptism that Scripture will often speak of both interchangeably, as if the water cleansed in baptism or as if the bread and wine in communion were truly the body and blood of Christ. Thus, Paul speaks of baptism as "the washing of regeneration" (Tit. 3:5–8), and says that communion with bread and wine is actually a participation in the body and blood of Christ (1 Cor. 10:16–17).

When we are bound by this union of the Spirit with his means of grace (word and sacrament), we are truly engaged in a "signs and wonders" ministry. The signs are the written and preached Word, the water, the bread and the wine. The wonders are the supernatural activities of the Spirit that are attached to these signs.

The power or efficacy of sacraments does not lie in their own nature. The efficacy lies in the Holy Spirit who marries them to the spiritual treasures they signify. The same water that is used in baptism could also be used to wash one's hands and there would be no difference in the substance of the water itself. Similarly, there is no change in bread and wine—bread remains bread and wine remains wine. But when the Word and Spirit join these common elements, God promises to be supernaturally present in order to bestow his gifts. Sacraments, therefore, are not chiefly pledges of the believer's loyalty, but of God's. This is why Calvin wrote, "In a sacrament, we bring nothing of ourselves, but only receive." They do not testify to the earnestness of the convert, but to the earnestness of God in saving and keeping his people by his grace.

This was a difficult concept for me, since I was raised in circles where we believed that the significance of baptism and the Lord's supper (indeed, the sermon itself) was to stir us into response. In other words, it was the emotion or piety these actions elicited, not the heavenly gifts that God was giving to me through these means, that defined the moment.

Baptism meant, "I have decided to follow Jesus." The Lord's supper meant, "I remember how much Jesus went through and how much I should therefore do for him." Both the preaching and these ceremonies focused on my intense subjective experience and resolve to do better, rather than on God and his objective grace in Christ. These activities were little more than object lessons for my personal piety.

Although there certainly are emotional effects of receiving the assurance of forgiveness and adoption, the biblical texts make God's grace, not my response, the big news. As the *Heidelberg Catechism* expressed it, the Holy Spirit creates faith in our hearts by the preached Word, and confirms it through the sacraments.

It was for this reason that the Protestant Reformers followed such great church fathers as St. Augustine in calling the sacraments "God's visible Word." The sacraments serve the same purpose as the Word itself, not only offering or exhibiting God's promise, but actually conferring his saving grace by linking us, through faith, to Christ and his benefits.

Someone will doubtless ask, "But if we're justified once and for all, why do we need to continue receiving forgiveness and grace through the sacraments?" It is interesting that we do not ask this question in relation to the Word. We know that we need to hear the gospel preached more than once in our lives, that we need to continually hear God's assurance of forgiveness and pardon extended to us in our weakness and doubt. The sacraments serve precisely the same purpose.

When we receive Holy Communion, we are experiencing the joy of our intimate union with Christ just as surely as his disciples enjoyed Christ's presence in the upper room. Here, in Word and sacrament, our ascended Lord is not far from us, but is himself offering us personal fellowship and all of the gifts he won for us by his ministry. We are so removed from the shores of ancient Galilee, so distant from that first supper. Yet we are instantly joined with the disciples in the upper room and all of the saints of all ages, as together we are united to Christ, sharing in his all-sufficient sacrifice.

Holy communion is not private, but corporate; not merely spiritual, but physical as well; not just representational, but real. When eternity met time, God visited sinful flesh in the physical person and work of Christ. Now, whenever we eat the bread and drink the cup, we meet this incarnate Word and receive the benefits of his passion and resurrection.

We do not meet him by "walking with him and talking with him" in a garden of private devotion that we have imagined or conjured in our own hearts. We encounter Jesus by receiving him in Word and sacrament. In doing so, we are truly taken to heaven by the Holy Spirit, where he places us gently into Christ's arms.

IS ALL OF LIFE SACRED?

Of course, if there is a danger in saying that nothing is sacramental, there is an equal danger in saying that everything is sacramental. We often hear this, even in some evangelical circles which have been influenced by highly aesthetic forms of expression: "All of life is sacred," or "All of life is sacramental."

The Roman Church undermined the importance of God's ordained sacraments by adding sacraments of their own. The Anabaptist enthusiasts undermined them by reducing the efficacy of the two sacraments Christ instituted. We see both extremes in our own day as well. In fact, many who would not be inclined to see baptism and the Lord's supper as actual "means of grace" would have no difficulty applying that designation to any number of other things that are never described as such in Scripture.

I recall hearing an evangelist associated with a group that does not practice the biblical sacraments referring to a short-term mission as "a means of grace." Many of us raised in evangelicalism remember the altar call and rededication, or summer-camp resolutions in this manner. A particularly sinful week could be atoned for by rededicating ourselves in a public meeting to "start over" with Christ. This amounts to nothing less than a Protestant version of penance.

If we do not accept or sufficiently appreciate God's chosen way of coming near to us, we set up scores of other "means of grace." On this point, Karl Barth echoed the Reformation's emphasis on the preached Word as God's means of grace. "Does not God speak through nature too, through history, through Handel's 'Largo,' and all kinds of good art? And can we say that God does not speak directly to people today?" Barth replies, "No, we cannot, is the obvious answer."[4]

While he was criticizing the temptation of German liberals to raise high culture to a sacramental level, we might just as easily charge evangelicals today with raising popular culture to a means of grace. An evangelical missions professor and popular author writes that organ music poses "a theological problem. God has chosen to come close. It is we who choose to push him away—with music, with pulpits, with stilted translations of Scripture, with preaching styles. Somehow, worship with guitars seems to bring him close again."[5]

Imagine replacing "guitars" with "Word and sacraments," in that sentence: "Somehow, worship with Word and sacraments seems to bring Him close again." Many evangelicals would consider this a practically Roman Catholic view, but they have no difficulty embracing other activities that have no command in Scripture as "means of grace."

THE IMPORTANCE OF MUSIC

It is interesting the extent to which many contemporary churches regard music as a means of grace, and not only one sacramental ordinance, but the chief one. In fact, one leader of the church growth movement states, "Music is how to convert a collection of people into a community. It is the most powerful thing we do. That is one of the reasons the new wave of contemporary Christian music and new forms of worship have tended to be highly conspicuous." This writer, in fact, hails the contemporary style that is "spontaneous" and "visual," "freeing the preacher from the pulpit," and "replacing the word 'worship' with the word 'celebration.'"[6]

Where in Acts 2 do we read that "music is how to convert a collection of people into a community"? We see Word and sacrament, but where is the sacramental efficacy of music? Yet the contemporary worship style, in which music plays an important part, is now viewed by many as the only means of grace. It is seen as the only way of reaching the lost and creating community. In other words, we create this community by our style, rather than by seeing God create it by his grace, working through his ordained means.

The very suggestion that matters of musical style or church furniture and architecture do not matter is gnostic, ignoring the physical embodiment of the message. But Karl Barth was one theologian who recognized this danger in liberalism as we see it now in evangelicalism:

> It has now become a most unusual consideration, common only in the language of edification, to say that people go to church to hear God's Word—no, they go to hear Pastor So-and-So—or to say of the pastor that his task is to proclaim God's Word—no, it is to offer his expositions, meditations, applications, and demands! I need hardly say that the devastating lack of tension and dynamic, the lukewarm tediousness and irrelevance of Protestant worship, is closely connected with this consideration.[7]

Preaching, Barth said, used to be God's Word to his Church, but now it has become the preacher's wit and inspiration for the customers. He explains why Reformed churches have high pulpits and related expressions of God's "aboveness" and "otherness":

> Preaching takes place from the pulpit (a place which by its awesome but obviously intentional height differs from a podium), and on the pulpit, as a final warning to those who ascend it, there is a big Bible. Preachers also wear a robe—I am not embarrassed even to say this—and they should do so, for it is a salutary reminder that from those who wear this special garment the people expect a special word. A formidable and even demonic instrument, the organ, is also active, and in order that the town and country alike should be aware of the preaching, bells are rung. And if none of these things help, will not the crosses in the churchyard which quietly look in through the windows tell you unambiguously what is relevant here and what is not?[8]

How morbid is this Barth, not only binding preachers to high and distant pulpits with big Bibles and robes, but praising cemetery crosses which can be easily observed through the windows. Contemporary worship cannot even deal with death, so deeply entrenched is its Gnosticism. For instance, in the article cited above, Lyle Schaller approvingly explains,

> The best illustration of this [shift from 'worship' to 'celebrations'] is that we used to have 'funerals.' Then we went to 'memorial service.' Now we have a 'celebration' of the life and ministry of the departed person. That's a shift in the whole atmosphere of what happens during that period of time. It's gone from pain, sorrow, grief, and crying to celebration.[9]

Even in the face of death, which Barth pointed up as a reminder of our weakness and humanness, contemporary worship refuses to sober up and adopt a serious posture. If death is an occasion for informal "celebration" and cheerful smiles, is there anything that will cause us to take the realities of this earthly existence seriously? Can nothing remind us that we are but dust—creatures—and sinful creatures at that? If there is no confession of sin anymore in the service, no declaration of pardon, no high and exalted Word, and no sacrament to visually confirm the Word, is it any wonder that so many either stop attending church altogether or seek other so-called means of grace?

So how do we bridge the gap then? If the service is to stress God's distance, how will people be encouraged to get close to God? That is the point: We don't bridge that gap, not by music, not by "celebration," not by signs and wonders, not by all-night prayer meetings. It is God who bridges the gap; it is he who comes close to us, and he does this as he reveals himself to us and dispenses his forgiveness through Word and sacrament. These are God's activities, not ours. As such, the focus of our services ought to be on God and not on the celebrants.

God is free to be or to do whatever he chooses, whenever he chooses, however he chooses, for whomever he chooses. This is the very essence of God's character, which he revealed to Moses and to all generations through him. His mercy and his presence can never be presumed upon or "conjured" by techniques on our end, whether inspiring music or testimonies, moving altar calls or mass meetings of prayer, praise, fasting, and confession. He answers the call neither of the organ nor of the guitar, but promises to be present in the weakness of preaching. Still less is he awakened and summoned to our meetings by odd phenomena of barking, laughing, and roaring that somehow come to be identified with "revival." God comes to us on his terms.

FURTHER UP, FURTHER IN

In a recent issue of *Christianity Today,* Quaker writer Richard Foster wrote an article on "the means of grace."[10] Beginning with the title, "Becoming Like Christ: Further Up, Further In," the author sees the means of grace as having to do exclusively with our spiritual and moral transformation. Thus, it is a subjective rather than objective ministry that these means perform.

"Further Up, Further In," underscores the direction we have been arguing against throughout this book. That is not to say that we are not to set our minds on things in heaven, for we have already seen how this is where we are seated in Christ. Nevertheless, it is not the purpose of sacraments to lead us ever-higher until we finally experience something akin to the "Beatific Vision" known to mystics and monks in the Middle Ages. The whole purpose of sacraments is to drive us further *out* of ourselves, not *into* ourselves! They take our focus off of our own experience, performance and imagination, guiding us to Christ's cross.

In this article the author offers an abundance of "means of grace," leading off with work. Although our work in the world is a gift of common grace and is shared by Christians and non-Christians alike by virtue of creation rather than redemption, Foster sees it as a channel of grace. Trials can be a means of grace, as are "movings of the Spirit." Still other means of grace include the spiritual disciplines: "prayer, study, fasting, solitude, simplicity, confession, celebration, and the like."

The reality is, all of life is not sacred or sacramental. Still, that does not denigrate the common. God is as much the Lord and sustainer in our common daily activities as he is in the supernatural activities of Word and sacrament. We need not "spiritualize" that which God has already himself created, whether music, art, science, or any other cultural pursuit, for the common is as truly created and ruled by God as is the holy.

However, God is active in a different way when he meets us where he has promised. God is involved with our lives whether we are in church or at work, but his involvement is different in each case. We are to do all that we do—whether we eat or drink—to the glory of God. Yet such a common meal, graced with God's pleasure and provision, is not sacred. It is common time, not holy time. It is a common place and a common activity, but supported by God and a meal in which he takes great delight.

We do not have to say that something is "sacramental" or "sacred" for it to be honoring to God. That is Paul's point when he directs us to do all things to the glory of God. But in the sacraments, God promises to meet with us in a different way, separate from all normal, common activities of daily life, in saving grace rather than common grace. We must not doubt that his promise is true.

Can we really say that every time we have a meal we are receiving Christ's body and blood? Surely not, for we have no promise from God that he will provide these gifts except as he has ordained. We do not receive God's gifts whenever and however we choose, but must find them in the time, place, and manner that he has chosen. The Good News is that God has bridged the gap—not only in providing Christ for our salvation, but in giving him to us and applying his benefits in our lives here and now. He has come down to us—all the way down—and has not left a single step for us to climb.

9

◦❈◦

LIFE IN THE SPIRIT

"I believe in the Holy Spirit, . . . who with the Father
and the Son is worshipped and glorified."
—NICENE CREED

The Pentecostal evangelist was engaging in "power evangelism," and according to all reports, even non-Christians passing the stadium apparently were falling under the power of the Spirit. "With a high-volume, high-energy, prolonged challenge, he taunts the spirits until they manifest in one way or another," reported C. Peter Wagner. "It may appear to the inexperienced to be utter chaos," Wagner continued, "but for the evangelist and his veteran team, it is just another evening of power encounters."[1]

It's difficult to imagine the apostle Paul referring to his gospel as "high-volume, high-energy . . . power encounters." Nor can I envision Peter saying, "At the same time I'm gathering information with my five senses I'm sending up my antenna into the cosmic reality" (John Wimber's words).[2] This search for something beyond natural knowledge gained through the five senses and "plugging in" to a higher *gnosis* is part of modern evangelicalism's approach to spirituality. It is also, as we have seen, nothing short of Gnosticism.

In what sometimes appears to be more science fiction than biblical or theological reflection, leaders of the so-called Third Wave of revival reflect the gnostic tendency to blend magic and technique. This is not to say that those who endorse this approach are explicit gnostics, for they would, no doubt, affirm the essentials of classical Christianity. Nonetheless, the impact of Gnosticism on the broader culture and, especially, upon evangelical attitudes and practices, is unmistakable.

The longing for a new Pentecost is certainly understandable. We have seen one fad after another raise our hopes, only to leave us tired and depressed again the morning after. Desiring more intimate fellowship with God, we turn to the One who was sent from the Father as our comforter, the Holy Spirit. Yet we still fail to find this sweet communion as an abiding, perpetual source of strength and spiritual fulfillment.

THE SPIRIT AND THE WORD

What is wrong here? I believe the problem lies in the fact that we have divorced the Spirit from his Word, much like divorcing a king from his army or a soldier from his weapons. If the Spirit worked apart from ordinary means, we could expect him to sustain us by "power encounters," mass meetings of prayer, confession, and revival. We could reach him by abandoning ourselves to strange phenomena, such as laughing, barking, and so on.

Just think of the Pentecost that did occur in real human history—the one that was recorded in Acts 2. Dick Lucas, a Church of England rector, reminded me of this point. The power of the Spirit fell on the people who had been gathered there from around the world and Peter preached a very long sermon. In fact, throughout Acts, we learn that the great advances of the church in terms of missions, evangelism, and outreach did not involve miracles, but were in response to the preached Word.

It is essential for us to remember that, in Scripture, we do not find the Spirit calling attention to himself. Jesus said, "When the Helper comes, whom I will send to you from the Father, that is the Spirit of truth, who proceeds from the Father, he will bear witness of me, and you will bear witness also, because you have been with me from the beginning" (John 15:26–27). Jesus says that the Spirit will not speak about himself, but about Christ.

Nearly every religion has a place for a Great Spirit. However, none claims that its whole existence turns on the historical life, death, and resurrection of the Son of God incarnate. To whatever extent any group of professing Christians replaces the focus on Christ with a focus on "power encounters," to that extent such a group is removed from the original power of Pentecost. Peter did not consider his sermon a necessary prelude to the "real excitement," as many power evangelists seem to view the brief message before the "ministry time" of signs and wonders. Peter's preached gospel was "the power of God unto salvation for everyone who believes," as Paul declared (Rom. 1:13), and many responded to that preached Word whenever it was proclaimed.

This, of course, coincides with the purpose for which the Holy Spirit was sent. Jesus commanded his disciples to gather themselves in Jerusalem, to wait for the coming of the promised Holy Spirit. In case they were wondering if this meant the end of the world or the consummation of the kingdom, Jesus gave the reason for this Paraclete's entrance: "But you shall receive power when the Holy Spirit has come upon you. . . ." Now there is some excitement—power!

But Jesus was not finished: " . . . power to be my witnesses both in Jerusalem, and in all Judea and Samaria, and even to the remotest part of the earth" (Acts 1:7–8). That is why the centerpiece of Pentecost was a sermon. If the church is still extending the kingdom through the gospel "even to the remotest part of the earth," there is no need for another Pentecost.

This power, which was promised by our Lord, is still enjoyed by all who faithfully hear and proclaim the Word of truth. Yet at times we seem ashamed of the foolishness of preaching, missing God's real presence because he is clothed in simplicity. In our Christian culture, the preaching of the cross is not as exciting as Pentecostal power-encounters.

From that perspective, we might conclude that there is little place for the Holy Spirit. That is because we tend to associate the work of the Spirit with our own personal experience rather than with his proper role as the giver of life and illuminator of Holy Scripture. If we are looking for the powerful presence of the Holy Spirit apart from Word and sacrament, we will indeed be disappointed with the churches that are anchored in biblical orthodoxy. But for those who believe that these divinely-ordained activities provide genuine encounters with the living God, the Spirit-led life will be rich indeed. Life in the Spirit is the privileged possession of every believer, and no Christian is excluded from his saving benefits.

A Personal Encounter

When I was a teenager, my brother, then an assistant football coach at Arizona State, introduced me to Danny White, who was at the time the star quarterback for the Sun Devils. I was only twelve years old and in awe of White. Meeting him was one of those times when I was aware of every movement I made, of every nervous gesture. As we walked toward him on the football field, I could feel my feet become lead. Fear gripped me. I almost wanted to retreat, but there was no turning back now. With a dry throat and clumsy handshake I met White, and my brother abruptly excused himself.

There we were, Danny White and this awkward teenager who was unusually short on words. But Danny immediately broke the tension when he said, "Hey, Horts, how about a few passes?"

"What's he talking about?" I wondered. I would have understood his straightforward invitation, had I not been so nervous.

"You mean passes to a game?"

"No," he replied, "I mean throwing some passes here on the field for a while."

For the next twenty minutes or so there we were, Danny White and Mike Horton, throwing the ball around and getting to know each other—not just as a fan gets to know a hero by following his career, but as friends. My brother was the "mediator" who had created this opportunity for friendship.

Since then, I have had the opportunity to meet some other people who made me feel rather nervous. But no meeting presents a greater challenge than when we meet God in the person of the Holy Spirit. It is a wonderful opportunity, to be sure, but it is also a challenge. We do just fine in the stands, shaking our heads at the unbelievable skill and energy of the Holy Spirit. We follow his work closely through the years. But to actually *meet him?* To get to know him, not just as an awestruck fan meets a celebrity, but as two friends out on the field together? Those of us who are especially worried about charismatic excesses often find such intimacy beyond what we can (or should even attempt to) reach. But it is at God's invitation that we leave the stands, walk out to the field, and befriend God through the person of the Holy Spirit.

God the Father longs to have a relationship with us. He "loved the world so much that he sent his only begotten Son" to save us so long ago.

When God the Son took on flesh, suffered, died, and rose again, he brought us everlasting peace with God. However, if it were not for the Holy Spirit, we would still be up in the stands, unrelated to God as anything other than admiring fans. It is through God the Holy Spirit that the Father's initiative in Christ—adoption and reconciliation—is finally fulfilled.

GETTING TO KNOW THE HOLY SPIRIT

When we gather for worship, many of us affirm that we "believe in the Holy Spirit, the Lord and Giver of Life, who proceeds from the Father and the Son, who with the Father and the Son is worshiped and glorified." This ancient declaration, first officially affirmed in this form in 325 A.D., arose in response to the heresies that tended to deny the Trinity, including the deity of the Holy Spirit and his distinct personality within the Godhead. At the other end of the spectrum there have always been those, like the Montanists, who placed the spotlight on the Holy Spirit. They did not recognize that the "shy member of the Trinity" was sent to spotlight the person and work of Christ. The symbolism in many charismatic congregations reflects this distortion. A visitor often finds a large outline of a dove in the front of the auditorium, while there is no cross to be found in the sanctuary.

Unfortunately, all of this fanaticism with the Holy Spirit can cause a negative reaction of cynicism about his person and work. That cynicism, however, will not only turn us away from the source of Christ's life in us; it will actually deny something essential to our faith and endanger our very souls. I even understand that there is a T-shirt for anti-charismatics with a bar going through a circle, laid over a dove, much like the "no smoking" logo. In reacting against hyper-spiritualism, many risk blasphemy.

Here is an important question: Do you worship the Holy Spirit? How long did it take you to answer? Did you have to think about it for a second or two? It is time we seriously reconsidered what we mean when we say in the Nicene Creed, "I believe in the Holy Spirit, . . . who with the Father and the Son is worshiped and glorified."

God the Holy Spirit is . . .

- Creator and Preserver (Gen. 1:2; Ps. 104:30)
- Source of the virgin conception of our Lord (Luke 1:35)

+ The One by whom the prophets and apostles spoke the Word of God (2 Tim. 3:16; Eph. 3:5; 2 Pet. 1:21)
+ Author and sustainer of the new birth (John 1:13; 6:63; Acts 1:5; Rom. 8:4, 9; 1 Cor. 2:14; 12:13; 2 Cor. 3:6; 5:5; 2 Thes. 2:13)
+ Person of the Godhead who indwells every believer (1 Cor. 6:19; ; 2 Cor. 1:22; 5:5; Eph.1:13)
+ God, sharing equality, substance, and eternality with the Father and the Son (Ps. 139:7; 2 Cor. 3:17; Eph. 2:22; 4:30)

The Holy Spirit is not only worthy of our worship, but demands it by his very essence and attributes. He is not a force, or a principle of deity. He is a divine Person, just like the Father and the Son.

From the historic definition of the Holy Spirit, we also focus on his activity in saving and revealing. In salvation, he is "the Lord and Giver of Life." Apart from him, the great riches of the Son's work would remain securely held within heaven's vaults. It is he who takes the Son's active and passive obedience and makes sure this is imputed to our charge through the faith he gives us. We do not believe on our own. We do not have the power to regenerate ourselves by believing.

It is intriguing that Wesleyans, Pentecostals, and charismatics are seen as the defenders of the Holy Spirit. Of course, it is understandable from a historical point of view: orthodox evangelicals have been rather nervous about the Third Person since the excesses of revivalism. Nevertheless, both groups are in the wrong on this point. Wesleyans, Pentecostals, and most charismatics are Arminian in their theology. That is, they believe that it is the human will that gives life; God merely offers it. In other words, God cannot unilaterally create new life apart from the activity of the creature.

Doesn't this limit the power and authority of the Holy Spirit in this matter of salvation? It clearly denies texts that suggest otherwise (see John 1:13; 6:37, 44, 63; 10:14, 25–30; Acts 13:48; Rom. 8:30; 9:10–26; 1 Cor. 2:14; Eph. 2:1–10; Phil. 2:13, etc.). To suggest that the Spirit's work depends on human activity, not only in regeneration, but in day-to-day maintenance of this new life, seems to place more emphasis on the power of man than on the power of the Spirit. I cannot see how Arminians can have a high doctrine of the Holy Spirit, even if they speak often of his role in their lives.

The Spirit's Work In Orthodoxy

Finally, the creed affirms the biblical teaching that the Holy Spirit "spoke through the prophets." Again, there is no difficulty affirming the feverish activity of the Holy Spirit in orthodox Christianity, but it has a different focus. As we have been arguing, the Holy Spirit works through means. He spoke "through the prophets." Peter wrote, "Above all, you must understand that no prophecy of Scripture came about by the prophet's own interpretation. For prophecy never had its origin in the will of man, but men spoke from God as they were carried along by the Holy Spirit" (2 Pet. 1:20–21).

Just as the new birth does not have its origin in the will of man, neither does divine revelation. God did not merely inspire the prophets and apostles by influencing their emotions and by placing ideas in their heads. He sovereignly breathed his words into existence through the ministry of human beings who may well have thought at the time that they were simply recording their own thoughts and words.

So here again, the Reformation tradition parts company with its brothers and sisters who would downplay the omnipotence of the Holy Spirit. It refuses to overlook the fact that the Holy Spirit saves and speaks through means: historical acts (the Exodus, the Crucifixion, Resurrection and Ascension, the Second Coming, and Judgment); physical signs and seals (water, bread and wine, paper and ink).

Our charismatic brothers and sisters sometimes assume that we diminish the role of the Holy Spirit simply because we do not talk about the gifts of healing, tongues, and prophecy. Even if we were to say that such gifts have ceased, it is quite erroneous to identify the work of the Holy Spirit exclusively or even chiefly with these spectacular activities—even if these gifts are still in effect.

Regardless of their view concerning the gifts, for Reformation Christians, the most important activity of the Holy Spirit is not raising the dead here and now, but raising to spiritual life those who "were dead in trespasses and sins" (Eph. 2:1). He will complete the work of redemption by raising the bodies of the dead at the end of the age. His business is not healing asthma, but healing the breach between God and human beings; not giving us the power to bind the forces of demons, but giving us the power to be Christ's witnesses.

While we do not discount the miraculous and the spectacular, Reformation Christians see the activity of the Holy Spirit in the common, everyday, and mundane. The new birth is as supernatural as a physical resurrection. An answered prayer is a spiritual gift. If we cannot see the center of the Holy Spirit's activity as being the miracle of regeneration, the gift of faith, union with Christ, sanctification, and the Word and sacraments, then we have missed entirely the person and work of this member of the Godhead. God reveals himself through the Word that his Spirit inspired, and that same Spirit illumines us to understand its meaning.

Two things become apparent at this point. First, in practice, we as "orthodox Protestants" often do not affirm that the Holy Spirit is "worshiped and glorified" with the Father and the Son. Meanwhile, Pentecostal and charismatic believers often do not affirm the power and authority of the Holy Spirit in such a way as to render the Third Person a suitable object of worship and admiration. In both cases, the greatness and glory of the Holy Spirit, which Scripture eagerly ascribes to him, is underplayed and the church is the poorer for it.

The danger in orthodox circles is to react against the subjectivism that exults in the freedom of the Spirit. In doing so, we try to control the Holy Spirit. This is a reactionary tendency we see throughout church history. For instance, the growth of "sacerdotalism" (i.e., the view that the priest, acting on behalf of the church, actually controls the salvation of believers by the sacraments) in the ancient and medieval church was in part a reaction against the unrestricted "enthusiasm" and individualism of the gnostic sects that plagued the church throughout the Middle Ages. Having been faced with disorder and confusion in the name of the Spirit, they were now committed to tradition, powerful ecclesiastical authority, institutional order, creedal consensus, and sacramentalism.

The Holy Spirit could, in a sense, be controlled by the church in this way, as the church decided how and to whom God's grace would be dispensed. The medieval way of referring to the operation of God's grace in the sacraments was, *ex opere operato*— "by doing it, it is done." It is like flipping a switch or pushing a button, and thus the Holy Spirit is given or withheld at the pleasure of the church.

THE CREEDS AND THE SPIRIT

At the time of the Reformation, there was a recovery of biblical balance. The medieval church had so institutionalized the Word and the gospel that its own interpretations were viewed as God's Word along with the text of Scripture. When the gospel message was corrupted by the church's teaching, there was no remedy, because the church was in control of the Word. It could not possibly judge or correct the church.

To make matters worse, the sacramental system led many to live in fear of being barred from paradise for having offended a clergyman or for failing to buy a papal indulgence. The radical Reformers, whom Luther and Calvin referred to as "enthusiasts," wanted not merely to reform, but to abolish. Like the ancient gnostics, some pitted the Spirit against creeds, institutional authority, tradition, sacraments, and even the Word itself.

In his own inimitable style, Martin Luther once quipped, "They think they have swallowed the Holy Spirit, feathers and all!" Just as the Roman Church had given the impression that she "controlled" the Spirit by the infallible teaching office, the enthusiasts thought that they controlled the Spirit through his personal indwelling of every believer. They insisted that they were freeing the Holy Spirit from the gilded cage of medieval authority.

The Reformers avoided both extremes, arguing on one hand (against the medieval church) that the Holy Spirit, and not the priest, the church, or the sacrament itself, is the effective agent in bringing people to Christ. He is not bound to the church or to its authority, but rather leads and guides the church into all truth. This requires constant criticism and reformation.

Against the enthusiastic sects, the Reformers insisted that God has freely and sovereignly willed to give his Spirit whenever and wherever the Word is rightly preached and the sacraments are rightly administered. It is a person—God himself—meeting the worshiper through the mediation of Christ alone. It is not the church's action, but God's. It is not controlled by human technology or spiritual elitism, but freely dispensed from the nail-scarred hands of our risen Lord. It is not an encounter with a system of rituals, but with the living Christ who nevertheless promises to be with us, personally and really, through these ordained means.

Only with this biblical balance, acknowledging the freedom of the Spirit who, like the wind, blows wherever he will in the context of his Word and sacraments, can we avoid institutionalism and enthusiastic individualism. The individual no less than the church has no right to expect that he or she will ever possess the Holy Spirit as much as that he or she will be possessed by the Holy Spirit. We never, individually or collectively, control the Word and Spirit, but are controlled by the Word and Spirit as they conspire together for our salvation.

One of the things we need in our day is a recovery of the biblical doctrine of the Holy Spirit. This will amount to a revolutionary reaquaintance, but it is a necessary one. He will disturb us all: contradicting those whose notions of human freedom place restrictions on the Spirit's sovereignty and freedom; unsettling the rest of us in our practical rejection of his freedom. The Holy Spirit is active in the twentieth century—in fact, more active than we are used to thinking. He is at work through his preached Word and sacraments, and the more faithfully we dispense them, the greater the possibility for genuine spiritual awakening.

WHAT ABOUT GUIDANCE?

Any discussion of life in the Spirit necessarily raises the question of God's personal leading in our lives. On one hand, some believers seem to believe that the Holy Spirit is not active in their daily existence. They are, in fact, suspicious of the activity of God's Spirit in our lives.

On the other hand, there are those who insist that they can discern whom to marry and where to work by direct revelation from the Holy Spirit. Such brothers and sisters are confident that God is still speaking, and that this divine speech is not confined to the limits of Scripture. Sometimes this is even expressed in a manner that disparages the written and preached Word.

In his epistle, James gives us the only command I have been able to find on this subject: "If any of you lacks wisdom, he should ask God, who gives generously to all without finding fault, and it will be given to him" (James 1:5). We can only act on promises. God has "minted" his will into the "coins" of promises and apart from the coinage of the realm, we cannot know God's mind or heart. Here in James we have a promise we can boldly claim in our life decisions: we can ask God for wisdom, and he will not withhold it!

Historically, biblical interpreters have offered a distinction that is quite helpful here. They speak of revelation and illumination. In the case of the former, God utters new sentences that have not yet been recorded in Holy Scripture. Through his appointed prophets and apostles, there is fresh revelation. Furthermore, spectacular signs and miracles cluster around these fresh stages of biblical revelation. We see them cluster, for instance, around Moses and the prophets and then again around Jesus and his apostles. Centuries passed in between the various stages of fresh revelation in which no miracles are recorded. During these times, God's people apparently had to rely on the revelations that had been given to their fathers.

I believe we live in such an era. "In the past God spoke to our forefathers through the prophets at many times and in various ways, but in these last days he has spoken to us by his Son. . . ." (Heb. 1:1). Jesus is the Prophet, Priest, and King to whom all of Israel's prophets, priests, and kings pointed. Imagine suggesting that after Christ there would come other priests who would die for our sins and secure our reconciliation with God, or other kings who might declare supremacy over Christ's realm. Of course, this would be a blasphemous suggestion. And yet, many people seem to have no difficulty in saying that Christ and the inspired testimony of his apostles are not the fulfillment of all Old Testament prophecy. There is still more to be added, they say. If so, can we not conclude that something is lacking in the revelation of Christ?

I believe that this is precisely the impression that is made in many circles today, where it is not enough that Scripture presents Christ and our eternal happiness in him through promise and fulfillment. The Bible has to tell us where we left our keys last; it has to help us raise our kids; it has to guide us to our spouse. If the Bible will not provide this data, we will find another source—another avenue to the mind of God.

This is where contemporary views of revelation concern me, in that they are increasingly open to gnostic directions. Saying that "God told me whom to marry" is tantamount to saying, "I am a prophet and God has just made me an agent of revelation." And yet, even in Scripture, prophetic utterances are not characterized by their personal usefulness to the prophets themselves. Where in all of God's Word do we have the expectation, by example or by promise, that revelation will be given for individual decision-making?

Wisdom, yes. And illumination of God's Word by the Spirit, to be sure. But revelation? We simply must stop going to verses such as Matthew 7:7 ("Ask and it will be given to you; seek and you will find; knock and the door will be opened to you") and concluding that it applies to anything and every-thing. Seen in this context, God cannot be held responsible for promising to provide us with fresh revelation of his secret will for our own personal happi-ness and success in life. Those who treat the Bible as a crystal ball or set the

Bible aside when it does not provide such magical information are seriously misunderstanding the intention of this passage.

After Moses had received the revelation of God's law and promise, he still faced an uncertain future. He wondered what God had in store for his people. In one particular instance Moses was not even looking out for his own personal interests, but was wondering about the future of the elect nation God formed and redeemed. Still, Moses concludes, "The secret things belong to the LORD our God, but those things which are revealed belong to us and to our children forever, that we may do all the words of this law" (Deut. 29:29).

As we saw from Jeremiah's confrontation with the false prophets, God takes the claim to private revelation very seriously. Those who say, "The Lord said," or "I have a word from the Lord," are commanded to stop saying this: "This is what each of you keeps on saying to his friend or relative: 'What is the LORD's answer?' or 'What has the LORD spoken?' But you must not mention 'the oracle of the LORD' again, because every man's own word becomes God's oracle and so you distort the words of the living God, the LORD Almighty, our God" (Jer. 23:35–36). God pronounces an eternal curse on those who claim divine authority for their own dreams and imagined revelations (v. 39).

This distinction, therefore, between revelation and illumination preserves us from transgressing the limits. While we should not expect fresh words from God, we have every reason to expect and pray for fresh illumination from God's Spirit. He who inspired the very words of Scripture is qualified to give us understanding of that Word, and we have his own promise that whoever seeks, knocks, and asks will be satisfied with having heard the very words of God himself.

As for "the secret things" to which Moses referred, those "belong to the LORD." Seeking to know the future—whom we should marry, where we should live or work, whether we should take one course of action or another—intrudes on the secret plan that God has for our lives. God has planned every inch of our lives, so careful and concerned is he about each of us. In fact, says Jesus, "Even the very hairs of your head are all numbered" (Matt. 10:30). However, he did not go on to promise that he would tell us how many hairs we would have on our head by the time we reached mid-life crisis!

God's secret files cannot be accessed by clever technicians, but he has left us with more revelation than we will ever master in our lifetimes. He has told us what we need to know for salvation and godliness, and, in fact, this is the purpose of Scripture. However tempting it may be—and we all feel the temptation—we must not allow our narcissistic preoccupation with self determine the usefulness or the content of divine revelation. God does not speak to us merely as individuals, but as a lost world and as a gathered body of redeemed children, and he reveals everything that we must know for his purposes, not for ours.

SANCTIFICATION: IMMEDIATE OR PROGRESSIVE?

As we have seen in previous chapters, the gnostic revival is more interested in the Spirit than in the Son, for the Spirit is the symbol of freedom, experience, and disembodied existence. The Son is rooted in human history, incarnate in human flesh, and saves us by a bloody death that is applied to us through material means. One well-known evangelical author goes so far as to say, "A Christian is a Christian because he is rightly related to Christ; but 'he that is spiritual' is spiritual because he is rightly related to the Spirit, in addition to his relation to Christ in salvation."[3]

Not only is justification separated from sanctification; Christ is separated from the Holy Spirit. By contrast, the Scriptures teach that the believer receives nothing by union with the Spirit, but that every spiritual blessing is found in union with Christ. Although the Spirit effects this union, it is union with Christ that is in view at every point.

The mystical heritage has always emphasized the "higher life" attained by super-saints who have realized the possibilities for living above defeat and sorrow. A crisis experience leads to a new level of faithfulness and a greater depth of spiritual insight and encounter with God. Through William Law's *Christian Perfection,* English Protestantism received a strong dose of this medieval mysticism, particularly in its perfectionistic strains. But it was John Wesley who made Law's perfectionism part of mainstream teaching.

Wesley believed that "even newborn baby Christians are so far perfect as not to commit sin."[4] So how do we interpret such passages as 1 Kings 8:46, where Solomon declares, "There is no one who does not sin"? Says Wesley, "Doubtless thus it was in the days of Solomon, yes, and from Solomon to Christ there was then no man that did not sin." But things are different now. What do we do with the statement in James 3:2, that "we all stumble in many ways"? Of course, "the apostle could not possibly include himself, or any other true believer. . . . Surely not apostles! Not believers! . . . A Christian is so far perfect as not to commit sin." This is because the Christian receives sanctification all at once, immediately, through one act of faith that is separate from justification. "If, therefore, the heart is no longer evil, then evil thoughts can no longer come out of it."[5]

The classic Protestant teaching is that the moment we trust Christ, justification is instantaneously declared, while sanctification is merely begun. Both justification and sanctification, however, are given through this same union with Christ through faith. No further crisis is required. There is no "second blessing" from the Holy Spirit, for all of our spiritual blessings are given to us in Christ and these are the possessions of every believer (Eph. 1:3–4).

Sanctification, however, is a process. Nowhere in Scripture is it described as an instantaneous perfection of the heart. The heart of the Christian is still deceitful and wicked, although it is alive to God and at war with indwelling sin (Rom. 7:7–25).

Wesley said he knew of no instance "of a person's receiving in one and the same moment remission of sins, the abiding witness of the Spirit, and a new, clean heart."[6] These required two separate crisis events. It is this separation of Christ from the Holy Spirit and justification from sanctification that has created a distinction between "victorious Christians" and "carnal Christians," between Spirit-filled believers and those who lack this precious filling.

Like the medieval mystics, Wesley believed that the Christian could be so thoroughly purged of sinful thoughts and desires that sinful actions would cease. And what happens when people continue to sin? Wesley is compelled to redefine sin in order to suit this scheme. Christians still make "mistakes," Wesley conceded. After all, "these are all deviations from the perfect law, and consequently need an atonement. Yet that they are not really sins, we apprehend may appear from the words of St. Paul, 'He who loves his fellow-man has fulfilled the law. . . . Therefore love is the fulfillment of the law' (Rom. 13:8, 10). Now, mistakes, and whatever infirmities necessarily flow from the corruptible state of the body, are in no way contrary to love; nor therefore, in the scriptural sense, sin."[7]

Those who think that the high purpose of the law—love of God and neighbor—is easy or perfectly attainable in this life do not know the sinfulness of their own hearts. They have to lower their estimation of sin, as Wesley did, by calling such shortcomings "mistakes" instead. This, of course, creates two kinds of Christians, to be sure, but not the sort Wesley intended: deluded Christians who think that they really are living above sin, and despairing Christians who know that they are not.

It is worth noting that the chief division between Rome and the Reformers was the former's insistence that justification was the result of "faith working by love," rather than faith alone. When Wesley declares, "Faith working or animated by love is all that God now requires of man, he has substituted (not sincerity, but) love, in the room of angelic perfection,"[8] he is in the path of the medieval mystics and the official teaching of the medieval system. No wonder he counseled his followers to "beware of believing that faith alone, apart from works, is sufficient to justification. . . ."[9]

Wesley was not always clear in his mystical and, frankly, Roman Catholic orientation. He even declared his confidence in justification by faith alone on other occasions. He was clearly confused on these vital matters and opened the door to a mystical tradition within the mainstream of evangelical Christianity. That tradition persists to our day, especially in the form of the Keswick movement.

THE HOLY SPIRIT: SEVEN EASY STEPS

Gnosticism views God as a force or source of power, "accessed" through various techniques and methods. And faith becomes a technique for "plugging in" to divine energy, rather than its classic definition as knowledge, assent and trust. The industrial revolution gave mystics objects to lend credibility to metaphors of mechanics. An example of this sort of thinking is found in the writings of R. A. Torrey. Scottish theologian Donald Macleod has written a marvelous critique of Torrey's "steps" that is well worth considering. "There is," says Torrey, "a plain path, consisting of seven very easy steps, which any one here can take today, and it is absolutely certain that any one who takes those seven steps will enter into blessing."[10]

Torrey tells us that the first step in this process toward obtaining the Spirit is to accept Jesus as Savior. But this is only the first step, according to Torrey. Donald Macleod is therefore justified in his claim that Torrey denies *sola fide*, or "faith alone."[11]

According to Scripture, we have everything that we need in Christ.

We do not find some spiritual blessings in Christ and others in the Holy Spirit, each according to a different set of criteria and conditions. Rather, in Christ we have all spiritual blessings in heavenly places (Eph. 1:3–4). The Spirit does not give us anything of his own, but gives us what belongs to Christ. Everyone who is in union with Christ is given the Holy Spirit (Eph. 1:13, 14).

But to receive the Holy Spirit, Torrey insists, one must move on to step two: "Renounce all sin."[12] How one can renounce sin apart from the baptism in the Holy Spirit (which one does not have until the final "step") is rather remarkable and looks hauntingly familiar in the light of Galatians 3:2: "I would like to learn just one thing from you: Did you receive the Spirit by observing the law, or by believing what you heard? Are you so foolish? After beginning with the Spirit, are you now trying to attain your goal by human effort?"

R. A. Torrey, it must be pointed out, stood in a line of revivalistic perfectionism, from Charles Finney down through the Keswick "Higher Life" Bible teachers such as Hannah Whitall Smith and others, who continue to exercise an enormous influence through many leading evangelicals today. In this scheme, the believer must "surrender" completely to the Holy Spirit in order to receive the baptism or filling of the Spirit, and this means renunciation of all sins. Of this sort of spirituality Donald Macleod wisely cautions, "That may comfort the deluded. But it will drive the realist to despair."[13]

Step three for Torrey is, "Open confession." After the believer has announced to the world that he or she has renounced sin and accepted Christ, that individual is well on the way to receiving the Holy Spirit. Macleod observes, "In the New Testament, confession is Christ-centered: He is great (Heb. 4:14). The testimony is not that we have renounced sin but that Christ saves us from it."[14]

"Obedience" is the fourth step on Torrey's ladder of glory. Torrey writes, "Obedience is not merely doing one, two, or three things that God commands, but doing everything that he commands."[15] In one sense, this is true: The believer never conforms to any one of the commands perfectly, but begins to imperfectly conform to all of them the moment he is reconciled to God and united to Christ. But Torrey is implying that perfect obedience is a necessary condition of receiving the Holy Spirit: "This is one of the most fundamental things in receiving the baptism with the Holy Spirit, the unconditional surrender of the will to God."[16]

Macleod asks, "Why should such a person need the baptism with the Holy Spirit? Has he not already, by his own strength, done everything for which the Spirit's gift might be desired? . . . Only a seared conscience or a benighted theology could persuade any man that he had made an absolute surrender of his will to God and was obeying all his commands."[17] James wrote that the one who keeps the whole law but offends at even one point is guilty of breaking the whole law (James 2:10).

The fifth step is to "thirst." When Jesus said, "Blessed are those who hunger and thirst for righteousness, for they will be filled" (Matt. 5:6), he was not suggesting that we begin to hunger and thirst. Rather, he was assuming that this is already the case of those in whom the Spirit is working. However, for Torrey and other "victorious life" teachers, it is a command, a condition of receiving the Spirit. Torrey writes, "When a man really thirsts, it seems as if every pore in his body had just one cry, 'Water, water, water.' When a man thirsts spiritually, his whole being has just one cry, 'The Holy Spirit, the Holy Spirit, the Holy Spirit, O God, give me the Holy Spirit.'" But it is not enough to thirst earnestly; one must thirst with pure motives, he says.[18]

Step six is, "Just ask Him." Ralph M. Riggs, another "victorious life" teacher, suggested, "This is God's elimination test to determine whom he considers worthy to receive this priceless gift."[19] Here we see not only the perfectionistic and mystical tendencies of gnostic spirituality, but spiritual elitism as well. Holiness spirituality will always create two classes of Christians: the "haves" and the "have-nots," and it is in full view here.

Those who have made it to the sixth level are worthy of asking God for this gift, but it is not really a gift, since so many believers have already been disqualified by this "elimination test to determine whom he considers worthy. . . ." And, as Macleod points out, for Torrey, this "just asking" is not as simple as it sounds. Not any old prayer will do. It must be a direct, mystical encounter. Torrey tells us how he reached this state: "About midnight God gave us complete victory. And oh! what praying there was from that time on up to a little after two in the morning. I think I had never heard such praying before and have seldom heard such praying since."[20]

Finally, the successful seeker has reached the seventh step to the Spirit: "Faith." Faith? At the end? At least in the medieval scheme the monk would begin with faith as he climbed up the stairway of glory. But Torrey holds it out as the conqueror's crown. Until now, everything that the believer has done presumably has been accomplished without faith, despite the biblical warning that "without faith it is impossible to please God" (Heb. 11:6).

THE KESWICK MOVEMENT

This process matches the medieval "ladder of glory" rather closely, with the steps of confession, penance, purgation, illumination, and union leading to the "beatific vision." This Wesleyan-Holiness theology not only underlies much of Pentecostal and charismatic understanding, it has deeply influenced mainstream evangelicalism through the Keswick movement.

This "Higher Life" scheme, employing phrases like "the victorious Christian life," and "the wonderful Spirit-filled life," adopts this Wesleyan and Pentecostal distinction between *justifying* faith and *sanctifying* faith, each separate acts. Victory over sin's tyranny is accomplished not by Christ and our union with him through faith, but by a separate crisis in which we receive the Holy Spirit and victory over known sin.

What is remarkable as one scans the list of participants is that the majority of the most identifiable names on the roster, from a variety of denominations, are held together by a common heritage in the theology and practice of Charles Finney. "Finney bristled with eccentricities. Fads were exaggerated into fanaticisms, foibles into gospels." So charged B. B. Warfield in 1921, at the beginning of a massive study of perfectionism from Finney to 1920.[21]

Much of Warfield's work describes and critiques the merging of Wesleyan and Finneyite perfectionism in the Keswick Movement that came to be identified by the terms "Deeper Life," "Higher Life," and "the Victorious Christian Life." This movement, burgeoning in the second half of the last century, turned many classical Protestants into evangelical mystics overnight.

In classical Reformation Christianity, there are two categories, law and gospel. "Law" demands perfect conformity to God's righteous will and allows no shortcomings in holiness; "gospel" promises full remission of sins and imputation of Christ's "alien righteousness" apart from human merit. Luther confronted the "ladders of ascent" through which a devoted Christian could seek God's face through confession, purgation, and eventually union, leading to the ecstatic experience of a direct encounter with God. Protestants have proved themselves to be just as clever in the assembly of such ladders.

Keswick leaders themselves cited in their list of predecessors such mystics as William Law, Thomas a Kempis, and Madam Guyon.[22] J. I. Packer notes that, according to J. B. Figgis, the list of "Wesleyan Perfectionists and mystical Quietists" also includes Francis de Sales and Molinos (a Counter-Reformation theologian).[23] Like the mystics of old, these "victorious Christian life" proponents lowered the expectations of the law. No longer did God require absolute perfection, but "absolute surrender."

It was not external works of obedience that God required, but "complete consecration" and "yieldedness." Those, however, who attempt to "yield," "surrender," and "love" as God commands soon realize that this is even more difficult than conforming outwardly to divine commandments. This is why Jesus summarized the moral Law as loving God and one's neighbor perfectly.

But many of those in the later Wesleyan line, including the advocates of Keswick teaching, set aside God's moral Law as the guide for the believer's life and replaced it with a law of love and surrender. By doing this, they were able to say, with Wesley, that Christians are capable of attaining such a degree of perfection that they are able to live above all deliberate acts of sin.[24] With the advent and rapid growth of Dispensationalism, leaders of the movement declared, "The grace teachings are not laws; they are suggestions. They are not demands; they are beseechings."

So God's law is replaced with "suggestions," short-circuiting the conviction of sin, while God's gospel is basically merged together with this single category of "suggestions" and "beseechings."[25] It is neither law nor gospel, but a confusion of both. In the place of God's moral law, one dispensationalist substituted "three laws or principles, which characterize the teachings of grace concerning the manner of the daily life of the believer." These "laws" are "the law of perfect liberty," "the law of expediency" and "the law of love." Their perfections are achieved not by rigorous human achievement, but by "full surrender" to the Christ who is at work within the believer.[26] "The code of rules contained in the law has been superseded by the injunctions and beseechings of grace."[27]

Warfield challenged such teaching concerning the Christian life in a *Princeton Theological Review* piece reviewing the Bible teacher's *He That Is Spiritual.* However, these views gained prominence in countless Bible and prophecy conferences throughout this century. Today's spiritual advisers are also ready with techniques, principles, and fail-proof steps to victory—for those who have enough faith to employ them.

Additional examples demonstrate the abiding popularity of the Keswick teaching. Henry T. Blackaby and Claude V. King have co-authored *Experiencing God* and *Fresh Encounter*, and although these are celebrated as fresh treatments of the subject, they are simply repetitions of the Keswick "Higher Life" teaching. In fact, in an article for *Charisma* magazine, the authors offer seven steps or principles for experiencing God. "In our day, God speaks through the Holy Spirit, using the Bible, prayer, circumstances, and other believers."[28] In addition to the Word, then, prayer, circumstances, and other believers become channels of divine grace, but the sacraments are absent. Upon reaching the seventh point, the authors state,

> You come to know God by experience as you obey Him, and He accomplishes His work through you. After you have determined to follow God by faith and you have made the required adjustments, you must obey Him. When you do what He tells you to do, no matter how insensible it may seem, God accomplishes what He purposed through you. You experience God's power and presence and so do those who observe what you are doing. . . . The Holy Spirit is the one who will guide you as you apply these seven principles according to God's will.[29]

In a defense of Keswick teaching, one leading advocate agrees that there are "means of grace," but he calls them "conduits of divine energy," in keeping with the mystical analogies of the system. Furthermore, the "means of grace" he mentions are prayer, Scripture, church, and suffering, while baptism and the Lord's Supper are not even mentioned.[30]

Even Southern Baptist piety has been influenced by the Wesleyan and Pentecostal "second blessing" theology through the Keswick movement. "I believe," one Southern Baptist pastor writes, "there is a definite distinction between being baptized by the Spirit and filled with the Spirit. . . . The filling of the Spirit is something that takes place in accordance with our willingness to surrender to the influence of the Spirit."[31]

While noting this laudable concern not to divide Christians into "haves" and "have-nots," Eric Casteel observes, "He simply replaces the haves and have-nots with the willings and the willing-nots, or surrenderers and surrenderer-nots."[32] Willing our way into God's presence is no less legalistic and human-centered than working our way into his presence, but Paul gives us the Good News: "It does not therefore depend on man's will or effort, but on God's mercy" (Rom. 9:16).

Once we understand that we are already "in Christ" and are therefore enjoying the full benefits of life in the Spirit, regardless of how deeply we struggle, the commands are no longer threatening. The believer knows that he or she is already justified and that this status cannot be improved or lost by the degree to which one conforms to the imperatives, whether the Ten Commandments or the fruit of the Spirit. This frees us to pursue godliness with vigor and excitement, knowing that it is not establishing our relationship with God, but responding gratefully to the fact that we already possess in Christ all spiritual riches. The fear of punishment and the hope of rewards now become obsolete motivations for the Christian life, as the believer serves God as a full heir rather than a slave.

This was one of the reasons why the Reformation freed men and women to pursue their worldly vocations with excellence. Calvin, in fact, complained to Cardinal Sadoleto that the mysticism and merit-claiming system of medieval religion led the average Christian to "merely seek and secure the salvation of his own soul. I am pursuaded, therefore, that there is no man imbued with true piety, who will not consider as insipid that long and labored exhortation to zeal for heavenly life, a zeal which keeps a man entirely devoted to himself, and does not, even by one expression, arouse him to sanctify the name of God."[33]

So too, so much of contemporary spirituality and piety is focused on self. "How am I doing spiritually?" "How is my walk?" "Am I living in victory?" Reformation spirituality lifted people out of a purely introspective, inward-looking piety and directed them outside of themselves to Christ and the cross, from which vista they could now look out across the needy world. Abraham Kuyper wisely warned,

> Many well-meant efforts at so-called sanctification become sinful. For the man who applies himself earnestly and diligently to good works, solely to attain a holier status and thus become a holier person, has lost his reward. His end in view is not God, but himself; and . . . this wrongly planned sanctification causes self-exaltation and spiritual pride.[34]

Since redemption is a completed work, the believer was liberated to serve God and neighbor without thought of rewards or punishment. If we recover this objective, external, outward-looking theology, piety will follow. And this is becoming increasingly necessary in a world in which so many of us spend so much time contemplating our navel that there is such little long-term influence in the world as salt and light.

Receiving the Holy Spirit, then, is not distinct from receiving Christ. When we are brought by the Holy Spirit into a saving union with the Son of God, we are given all of the blessings that belong properly to Jesus Christ himself. The "fruit of the Spirit" (Gal. 5:22–24) is in reality the produce of Jesus Christ, because it is the Holy Spirit who grafts us onto the Vine, to make us living, fruit-bearing branches.

The theology of the cross stands opposed to all schemes of perfectionism, mysticism, spiritual elitism, and works-righteousness that can only lead to despair. We must therefore recover the Reformation's warm devotion to the Holy Spirit who points only to Christ. He gives everything that is Christ's to everyone who is in union with the Redeemer—by faith and faith alone.

10

⋖⋗⧬⋖⋗

THE WAY OF THE CROSS

"Oh Christ, Where is truth? Where is any consolation?
—KARL GORDELER

Mind you, I'm not one of those writers who is searching for evidence of the New Age movement behind every tree. Nevertheless, I cannot help but notice the increasingly blurred lines between popular mysticism (perhaps even superstition) in the wider culture. Meanwhile, there is a trendy obsession with "spirituality," even among so-called evangelicals.

Twenty percent of Americans say they have had a revelation from God in the last year and 33 percent report a mystical experience.[1] Angels suddenly became a hot item in secular bookstores a few years ago and now books on these divine messengers, fiction as well as non-fiction, roll off the evangelical presses, accompanied by collectable figurines and related paraphernalia. Books about life-after-death experiences continue to outsell the best of bestsellers. The most outlandish movements, dying as quickly as they rise, are declared "revivals" and, therefore, off-limits to criticism.

There is an ongoing search for meaning in the sacred, but it is not new. Fascination with the spiritual, and indeed even with the occult, reaches back to the transcendentalists of the last century. And several of these individuals were the founders of sects that are now regarded within the culture as fairly mainstream, such as Christian Science and Mormonism.

Newsweek's Kenneth Woodward writes, "Americans love the search so much that the idea of a destination is lost."[2] Liberal churches are exploring ancient gnostic texts, such as the Quest program at San Francisco's Grace Episcopal Church. There, students experiment with "artistic creativity, mystical experience, reclaiming the feminine as divine, and the integration of Eastern and Western spiritual disciplines." Woodward adds,

> Disguised in the secular language of psychotherapy, the search for the sacred has turned sharply inward—a private quest. The goal, over the last forty years, has been variously described as 'peace of mind,' 'higher consciousness,' 'personal transformation' or—in its most banal incarnation— 'self-esteem.'. . . . In this environment, many searching Americans flit from one tradition to the next, tasting now the nectar of this traditional wisdom, now of that. But, like butterflies, they remain mostly up in the air.[3]

At the same time, evangelical megachurches appeal to the same market of "seekers" by offering classes in self-esteem, transformation, spiritual disciplines, and journeys. Sometimes they even incorporate the works of Thomas a Kempis, Theresa of Avila, and others in the mystical tradition, writers who are enjoying a revival thanks to evangelical as well as secular publishers.

The inward tendencies of pietism in the evangelical tradition seem to be creating a greater openness to medieval spirituality, and the marketplace dictates the current obsessions. This means that without a clear theological rudder, evangelicalism will be increasingly drawn by the siren's song of popular trends. The lines between Christian truth and popular spiritual fads are increasingly blurred.

UNITED WITH CHRIST

We are supposed to relate the cross as a historical, saving event, and to the way of the cross as the pattern for our own lives. We know we were baptized into Christ, and our identity as self-oriented creatures has been not merely revised or amended, but buried. Christ's cross was more than God's method of saving us; it is our own cross, our own death, burial, and resurrection. We are united with Christ.

Yet today's Christian culture seems intoxicated with power and glory. We see this in the church growth movement, in the fascination with celebrities who become Christians, in marches on Washington, and the pride of influence in the halls of government. We see it in the over-done religious musicals that often pass for church services, and in the mass crusades during which hundreds come forward but few become disciples.

We "celebrate" our way into God's presence, climbing a sentimental ladder, singing songs that replace Christ and his cross with me and my desire to see God's face, to experience his power, to see his glory, to feel his touch. Meanwhile, despite all the pomp and show, secularism continues its steady march uninterrupted as the noise from the theology of glory drowns out any dissent that might be heard coming from the ranks of the faithful.

Being united to Christ sounds like wonderful news at first. We hear inspiring testimonies about how much happier and more fulfilled people were after they "found Christ." But we seldom hear, and often forget the far-reaching ramifications of this identification. Not only are we identified with his victory, but are also destined to share in "the fellowship of his suffering."

SUFFERING IN CHRIST

There have been other periods of relative ease for the church when it enjoyed popularity, success, power, and glory. But in no other era has a theology emerged that was so completely pagan in its view of suffering. During earlier epochs, suffering was perhaps avoided (as indeed it should be, if at all possible), but worldly ease lacked the sublime benefits promoted by today's prosperity evangelists. According the them, suffering, sickness, pain, poverty: all of these things are the results of failing to properly "plug in" to the spiritual realm, to appeal to the appropriate incantation, to know the secret principles and formulae. Norman Vincent Peale or Robert Schuller might locate these principles in popular psychology and various mental-health fads, while others tap into the spiritual "other side" in more esoteric ways.

According to Scripture, faith is trust in the finished work of Christ for salvation from divine judgment. But according to one faith movement preacher, faith has a much different definition: "Faith is a power force. The force of faith is released through faith-filled words. Faith-filled words put the law of the Spirit of life into operation."[4] Even more mainstream evangelicals have confused faith with "positive thinking."[5] This is the sort of gnostic (and in its modern expression, New Age) spiritual technology that one can only describe as magic. It is the theology of glory taken to the ultimate extreme.

Meanwhile, to suggest in many Western Christian circles that God sends us suffering, or that he reveals himself in and through suffering, sounds almost as blasphemous as the prosperity gospel would have sounded to past generations of Christians. Even in mainstream evangelical circles, there does not seem to be a clear theology of suffering. And when people actually encounter a crisis, they discover that the shallow platitudes and clichés they have heard do not suffice. They begin to question God and his ways. They have nothing beyond their agonized questions to hold them fast.

We cannot know the divine purpose for specific encounters with pain. However, the message of the cross provides us with some profoundly helpful ways of understanding and coping with the whole notion of suffering. The apostle Paul, of course, experienced more than his share of suffering. He was beaten, imprisoned, stoned, and as a result lost much of his eyesight. He also suffered great emotional and spiritual pain as he received rather regular news that one of his church plants ended up playing around with other gospels. "I have often been cold and naked. Besides everything else, I face daily the pressure of my concern for all the churches. Who is weak, and I do not feel weak? Who is led into sin, and I do not inwardly burn?" (2 Cor. 11:27–28).

Is this the sort of reporting one should expect from an apostle? Should he not be triumphant, hiding his own problems in order to magnify the power, joy, happiness, and success that God gives to faithful servants? How will Paul's readers find sufficient motivation and inspirational example for their own lives amid such "negative confessions"?

Instead, he says, "If I must boast, I will boast of the things that show my weakness" (v. 30). When Satan tormented Paul with a mysterious "thorn in the flesh," the apostle repeatedly asked God to remove it, but the only word he heard from God was, "My grace is sufficient for you, for my power is made perfect in weakness" (12:9). "That," said Paul, "is why, for Christ's sake, I delight in weaknesses, in insults, in hardships, in persecutions, in difficulties. For when I am weak, then I am strong" (v. 10).

What kind of theology is this that recommends suffering? Yet that is actually what Paul is suggesting—that believers look assiduously for opportunities to be weak. This is no superficial masochism that the apostle is outlining, no Stoic "stiff-upper-lip" theology. Rather, it springs from his theology of the cross, which he has argued so insistently in other places.

THE HIDDENNESS OF GOD

In Romans 5, Paul writes, "And we rejoice in the hope of the glory of God." This glory is not something we see or experience right now, except under the form of its opposite: shame. This is what Luther also meant by the "hiddenness of God," and, like Paul's, Luther's life became the crucible in which this teaching began to make sense. Not only was Luther constantly under attack; there was a question about God's presence in a church that was so corrupt and in a world that was so full of darkness, disease, and superstition. This question became even more acute in Nazi Germany over four centuries later. Alister McGrath writes,

> Luther's theology of the cross assumed its new significance because it was the theology which addressed the question which could not be ignored: is God really there, amid the devastation and dereliction of civilization? Luther's proclamation of the hidden presence of God in the dereliction of Calvary, and of the Christ who was forsaken on the cross, struck a deep chord of sympathy in those who felt themselves abandoned by God, and unable to discern his presence anywhere. One such individual was Karl Gordeler, executed as a conspirator against Hitler in the darkest days of the war.[6]

As McGrath explains, Goerdeler's experience of God's absence was even more worrying than his physical torment. Goerdeler wrote,

> In sleepless nights I have often asked myself whether a God exists who shares in the personal fate of men. It is becoming hard to believe this. For this God must for years have allowed rivers of blood and suffering, and mountains of horror and despair for mankind to take place.... Is this meant to be a judgment? ... Like the psalmist, I am angry with God, because I cannot understand him.... And yet through Christ I am still looking for the merciful God. I have not yet found him. O Christ, where is truth? Where is any consolation?[7]

If we look only for the God of glory, we will find no consolation, for we are but dust. Furthermore, we are sinful creatures, and God's power and majesty, holiness and grandeur, will drive us—like Adam and Eve—deep into the forest where we hope to escape his heavy presence. What we must look for is not God as he is in himself, but as he has hidden himself in Christ.

This means that the entire revelation of God will be found in the very opposite of where we would normally look: in a stable rather than a palace, among the poor, weak, sick and immoral rather than among the wealthy, powerful, healthy, and self-righteous. We can only look upon God and live as we see him hanging on a cross for our sins, not in the blinding light that hides him from our unholy eyes.

During the Third Reich, evangelical pietism blended with German nationalism to produce a theology of glory that enabled the churches to embrace the power and prestige of the Nazi regime. And it was Paul's theology of weakness that upheld the Lutheran and Reformed clergymen and laypeople who opposed Hitler by forming the Confessing Church. Martin Niemoeller, Herman Sasse, Dietrich Bonhoeffer, and Karl Barth were among those who opposed the Nazis, finding great strength in Paul's message of weakness. Formed from the Young Reformation League, the Confessing Church insisted on recovering this message for another generation.

Whenever God comes to us, hidden in what appear to be moments of darkness, suffering, doubt, and despair, it is in that very "hiddenness" that he reveals himself. In the Incarnation, God revealed himself by concealing his glory in human flesh, and in our own experience God often makes himself most powerfully known to us in the moments of our greatest weakness and need. Of course, human reason abhors this paradox, despising its realism as unnecessarily pessimistic.

Like Paul, Luther took a similar view. McGrath notes, "Far from regarding suffering or evil as a nonsensical intrusion into the world (which Luther regards as the opinion of a 'theology of glory'), the 'theologian of the cross' regards such suffering as his most precious treasure, for revealed and yet hidden in precisely such sufferings is none other than the living God, working out the salvation of those whom he loves."[8]

Just as the Law's terrible judgments and threatenings are necessary in order to drive us to Christ, so suffering serves a similar purpose. It strips us of our pride, self-sufficiency, complacency, and our oblivion to the things to come. Eternity is more deeply engraved on the rough palms of God's suffering children.

In the face of suffering, the believer is not to look for the "hidden God"—that is, God in his secret majesty. We cannot even attempt to figure out by speculation why we are suffering. We can only, with Moses, look upon God's "back-side," his compassion and mercy as revealed in Christ and his cross. While God's hidden will in suffering cannot be found, and searching for it can only drive one to depression or delusion, his revealed will is displayed in the suffering of Christ, in which his people are called to share.

Suddenly, in light of this, the dark, mysterious, fearful spectre of suffering is removed even though the pain, even though the physical and emotional realities continue unabated. Still bewildered by the problem of pain, the soul at least is at rest, confident in God's mercies in Christ. Again, God chooses what is foolish, despised, weak, ridiculous, and offensive to us and makes this the very way in which he will come to us in wisdom, power, and salvation. Just when our own reasoning judges God the furthest away, he is closest. When the heart seems to be apprehending God's judgment and wrath, the Father is most deeply revealing his love and grace.

So, Paul says, "And we rejoice in the hope of the glory of God. Not only so, but we also rejoice in our sufferings, because we know that suffering produces perseverance; perseverance, character; and character, hope. And hope does not disappoint us, because God has poured out his love into our hearts by the Holy Spirit, whom he has given us" (Rom. 5:2–5).

While "life in the Spirit" for many might mean constant victory over temptation, doubt, suffering, and pain, Paul tells us, "Now if we are children, then we are heirs—heirs of God and co-heirs with Christ, if indeed we share in his sufferings in order that we may also share in his glory" (Rom. 8:17). Like the wind and waves against the rocky coastline, suffering becomes one of God's ways of shaping our spiritual topography, reshaping our character, disciplining our constitutions, and conforming us to the image or likeness of Christ.

It must be said at this point, however, that although "God works all things together for good" on behalf of his people, not all things *are* good. Sometimes people so emphasize God's sovereignty in suffering and his good purposes that they give the impression that suffering itself is good. That is not what the "way of the cross" intends to convey.

If there had been no fall in the first place, there would have been no suffering. Suffering, like death, therefore, is an effect of original sin, Adam's rebellion in the garden. We must not call good that which is inherently bad and expect people who are enduring great pain to take much courage in the misguided notion that they are to thank God for the suffering. We have no more of an obligation to thank God for suffering than we thank him for sin.

Just because God is so much greater than our sin and pain that he can reveal himself in the midst of it does not mean that sin and pain are less evil. This is why the psalmist can become angry at God without calling into question his providence. Intellectually, we can know that God works all things together for good and still wonder in our own experience why he allowed the bad in the first place. From our vantage point, suffering is still as nasty as it ever was. But God always has the last word and even the devil, as Luther put it, "is God's devil."

World-Affirming Piety

One of the differences between Reformation Christianity and many other approaches is its distinctively world-affirming character. Although suffering has a place, so too does vigor. While others might focus on the inner life, spiritual progress, and private well-being, the approach set forth by the biblical writers is one of looking beyond ourselves to serve a world in need. It begins with one's family, reaching out to one's church and vocation, and on into the related spheres of public and private life. If I am preoccupied not only with my personal salvation and keeping my relationship with Christ intact, along with figuring out God's secret will for my life, how can I have any time or energy for others? The way of the cross—the spirituality proposed here—provides our best way of understanding our relationship to the world.

Scripture refers to "world" in two senses: first, as that which God created and redeemed (Rom. 8:20–23). The creation is not somehow evil in and of itself, but is corrupted because humanity is in rebellion against God. That is why the world is called an enemy of the believer. This is the second sense: "world" as the system of opposition to God's reign. This speaks of the creation in its hostility to God, not in its essence as created by God. Therefore, the world is not an evil realm (as Gnosticism maintains), but an arena in which the war between good and evil, belief and unbelief, truth and error, is being played out in history.

Calvin referred to the world as "the theater of God's glory." This surely stands in opposition to any gnostic tendencies that seek to draw Christians away from this theater and sequester them in spiritual monasteries or ghettos. Believers are called into the world that God created and redeemed, but they are called into the world as new people.

Christians no longer fight on the same side as before, nor do they employ the same weapons. Their world has ceased to revolve around cutthroat business practices, greed, empire-building, and jealousy. Indeed, the theology of the cross not only becomes the way of salvation, but the way in which the crucified are meant to walk. It is Christ's cross and resurrection that define the believer's life, as he or she has been crucified and raised with him. "May I never boast except in the cross of our Lord Jesus Christ," said the apostle Paul, "through which the world has been crucified to me, and I to the world" (Gal. 6:14).

In Alexandre Solzhenitsyn's *Gulag Archipelago,* the hero endured his imprisonment by determining from the outset that he was dead. By watching the guards and their treatment of the prisoners, he came to realize that those who were the first to collapse under the strain of their imprisonment were those who simply could not accept their fate. Those who made it through each day were those who lived as though they were dead to the guards and to their prison existence.

Similarly, Paul argues that when someone is dead, that which once exercised such inexorable tyranny no longer has a claim on the life of the deceased. The government cannot indict a criminal who is dead; the Mafia cannot execute a murder contract on someone who is no longer living. And in our case, the world no longer has a claim on us because we were crucified with Christ. The cross is God's "witness protection program." We are now defined by his world, "the age to come," rather than "this present evil age" (Heb. 6:5).

Many of us live as though we were still "dead in trespasses and sins" (Eph. 2:1), as though Christianity were there merely to provide forgiveness and inspiration to engage in spiritual activities. But in reality, those who are united with Christ in the likeness of his death, burial, and resurrection are actually made new creatures and their relation to the world is changed. Before, the world defined everything: Success, happiness, pleasure, meaning, purpose. Now we no longer have to live under that kind of pressure and tyrannical obsession.

Christ is Lord, not the world. He has gained our freedom and we are now defined by his life, death, and resurrection. And here is one of the ironies in all of this: When our relation to the world changes, the world itself changes in our perspective. It is not just that we are different, but that we view the world differently, through Christ's lens. We "read" the world with a wisdom that values the eternal and the redemptive story as the real meaning behind all of history. We begin to see the struggle between the defeated serpent and his victorious rival as the "story behind the story" of human existence. We recognize this world as the place where the last gasps of Satan's fury are conquered by the return of Christ to his redeemed theater.

Once one has accepted death to sin, the world, and the devil, genuine life is possible. Here again, we see the paradox of this message of the cross. It is this message alone that distinguishes the preaching of Christians from that of, say, Mormons. In such moralistic religions, the purpose is to enhance and improve the unregenerate; in Christianity, the goal is to slay the sinner, only to raise him or her from the dead. It is only by losing our lives, said Jesus, that we will gain them back again (Matt. 10:39).

Those who seek a way of glory as the pattern for their lives, whether "spiritual" glory or personal, national or corporate glory, will be left disillusioned in the end. Those who have accepted their death and their new identity in Christ are prepared for suffering, unpleasantness, disappointment, and frustration both in Christian growth and life in general. They are not surprised when it comes, because they know the story. They have read the script and they know that their plot-line is defined by the central figure in the play. Furthermore, they know how it turns out in the end and are willing to confess, "I consider that our present sufferings are not worth comparing to the glory that will be revealed in us" at the end of the age (Rom. 8:18). Glory comes, not now, but then. For now, it is the cross.

AGAINST THE WORLD, FOR THE WORLD

The way of the cross, then, is a way of death: a once-and-for-all death of the Son of God that defines the rest of our lives, and the daily death that we undergo as we turn from self to Christ, from looking within to looking without, from seeking our own happiness and glory to seeking God's glory and the good of our neighbor. We are not simply imitating Christ's cross; we are baptized into Christ's cross. It is not merely ours by example, but by ownership.

We are crucified to the world so that we may serve the world as participants in Christ's ongoing ministry of reconciliation. This is an important point, because there are those who will take this message of being dead to the world and alive to Christ and respond by hating not only worldliness, but the world itself including its culture, education, and arts. They simply negate the world. We, however, must seek to win the world by resisting the world and by setting up God's confrontation with the world in the public square in the form of law and gospel, judgment and justification, sin and grace. Some have expressed this biblical argument with the slogan, "Against the world, for the world."

Imagine the effects that this could have on our public witness! We have seen it before, when the early church followed the theology of the cross. We saw it during the Reformation, as men and women sacrificed their lives and popularity for the glory of God and the good of the world. Sacrifice is almost entirely lost from our Christian character in many Western, highly industrialized nations. Christianity is perceived as the best way of fulfilling ourselves, not the only way of finding peace with God through Christ's death, which calls for the death to self. Biblical religion does not call us simply to a better way of being preoccupied with self, but judges the entire enterprise.

Those who follow the theology of the cross, then, will find that this death is not an end in itself, but the very portal to new life, a life that transcends narcissism. It is not a negative, morbid, ascetic lifestyle that this path has in view. It is a marvelously liberating outlook that frees us from being constantly shaped and defined by this fading, evil age.

TRYING TO GET WHAT WE WANT

"I Still Haven't Found What I'm Looking For." Whatever their intention, this lyric from the band U2 expresses the sentiment of the biblical writers. The message of the cross is not only foolish to the perishing because of the method of redemption, but also because it runs counter to all of our expectations. We are looking for quick fixes, for a satisfaction-guaranteed scheme that will bring instant gratification. It is no coincidence that the same theology of glory that creates the prosperity gospel's emphasis on "naming and claiming" health, wealth, and happiness also suffers from an impatience with God's timetable. How often have new believers been led into ecstasy, expecting triumph over personal sin and suffering, only to feel disillusioned in the days and weeks that follow when their personal dreams have not come true?

Gnostic escapism is apparent in the demand for instant liberation, not merely freedom from the effects of the Fall, but from Creation itself. One preacher states, "The problem area is not in your spirit; it lies in your mind and body."[9] If we could only transcend our physical existence, instant gratification would ensue. This is the position taken by Christian Science and similar mind-science cults as well. A charismatic leader tells us to "speak to" our sickness and to simply "command the money to come to us."[10]

We are not used to waiting, especially in as technologically sophisticated a culture as ours. Microwave dinners, instant transmission of letters and E-mail, and air and space transportation all conspire against the virtue of patience. So it would stand to reason that modern Gnosticism would find fertile soil in a pragmatic culture that tends to see every problem as something that can be easily conquered by applied technology—in this case, spiritual technology, "mind over matter," positive confession, and positive thinking over the realities of human life.

The problem, of course, is that God does not operate on the same principle as microwave ovens, and there are no "laws" or "principles" of the spiritual world that are roughly equivalent to those of physics. If one is looking for magic, there are many who are more than willing to oblige. Christianity, however, refuses to engage in magic.

We want it all. We want it now. We cannot wait to see God in his majesty, face-to-face, so we create our own encounters. We cannot wait to receive the restoration of our bodies, so we "name and claim" health. We cannot wait to be glorified, free of sin and entirely sanctified in heaven, so we invent schemes of perfectionism here and now for those who want to go "first class."

LORDS AND MASTERS; SERVANTS AND FRIENDS

All of these pursuits—faith healing, secret revelation, spiritual technology, and perfectionism—exemplify gnostic spirituality. And they all find their source, at least partly, in our own impatience. After Jesus had announced to the twelve that he would be crucified and raised on the third day, the mother of James and John asked Jesus to grant that one of her two sons would sit on his right hand and the other on the left in his kingdom.

But Jesus answered and said, 'You do not know what you ask. Are you able to drink the cup that I am about to drink, and be baptized with the baptism that I am baptized with?' They said to Him, 'We are able.' So He said to them, 'You will indeed drink My cup, and be baptized with the baptism that I am baptized with; but to sit on My right hand and on My left is not Mine to give, but it is for those for whom it is prepared by My Father.' When the ten heard it, they were greatly displeased with the two brothers. But Jesus called them to Himself and said, 'You know that the rulers of the Gentiles lord it over them, and those who are great exercise authority over them. Yet it shall not be so among you; but whoever desires to be first among you, let him be your slave—just as the Son of Man did not come to be served, but to serve, and to give His life a ransom for many.'

—MATTHEW 20:20–28

The theology of glory creates lords and masters; the theology of the cross creates servants and friends. Here the two sons come, allowing their mother to mediate in their behalf, in order to secure heavenly rank. This is the pursuit of glory. Jesus left glory behind in order to serve humankind by giving his life as a ransom for many. Meanwhile, James and John wanted to escape a life of service. They wanted to avoid the laborious task of following the flock, keeping any stray or wandering sheep from getting lost.

Jesus asks them a hard question: "You do not know what you ask. Are you able to drink the cup that I am about to drink, and be baptized with the baptism that I am baptized with?"

Well, of course, they were! Isn't every believer? Everyone wants to experience everything Jesus experienced and walk in his footsteps. Were there powerful signs and wonders in his day? There should be in ours. Were the disciples' lives filled with excitement and healings? That is what I want, then, too. Why should they experience all that glory? I want my share!

And yet, there was a high price to be paid for being among the twelve. With the exception of Judas, who had his own problems, martyrdom awaited those who defended the cross and the resurrection. Peter was crucified upside down, refusing to allow men to compare his death to Christ's. Are we as anxious to suffer a similar fate as we are to experience their glorious moments of signs and wonders?

Indeed, James and John did not know what they were asking. To be first in the kingdom of heaven is to be last on earth, to be the servant of all, to be crucified upside down. This is what the Scriptures mean when they declare that we are heirs "if indeed we suffer with him, that we may also be glorified with him" (Rom. 8:17). "For to you it has been granted on behalf of Christ, not only to believe in him, but also to suffer for his sake...." (Phil. 1:29).

In one sense, of course, it is impossible for the believer to drink the cup Jesus drank or to be baptized with the baptism of fire he experienced. Jesus alone fell under the condemnation of God's just sentence for the sins of the world. It was an unrepeatable substitutionary atonement. But in another sense, every believer shares in the death and resurrection of Christ. We are called not to sit on thrones in glory, but to come and die at the foot of Golgotha, and to rise again as servants of the weak, the outcast, the poor, the alien—to be servants to the very people who are considered the servants of society.

LONGING FOR PERFECTION

Perfectionism, as we have seen, is another major characteristic of Gnosticism, and it is alive and well in American revivalistic history, through the influence of pietism, John Wesley and the Holiness tradition, Charles Finney, and the Keswick movement. J. I. Packer reminds us that such teaching is "delusive."

For it offers a greater measure of deliverance from sin than Scripture anywhere promises or the apostles themselves ever attained. This cannot but lead to self-deception, in the case of those who profess to have entered into this blessing, or to disillusionment and despair, in the case of those who seek it but fail to find it.[11]

Christians who are most deeply aware of their weakness are far more mature than those who claim to have attained a level of victory. The experience of the apostle Paul is normative for the Christian life, as he takes in the full scope of sanctification. In Romans 6, we read the triumphant report of what God has already accomplished for us in Christ: freedom from sin's dominion and new life in Christ. But in Romans 7, we are cautioned:

> We know that the law is spiritual; but I am unspiritual, sold as a slave to sin. I do not understand what I do. For what I want to do I do not do, but what I hate I do. And if I do what I do not want to do, I agree that the law is good. . . . I know that nothing good lives in me,

184

that is, in my sinful nature. For I have the desire to do what is good, but I cannot carry it out. For what I do is not the good I want to do; no, the evil I do not want to do—this I keep on doing. . . . What a wretched man I am! Who will rescue me from this body of death? Thanks be to God—through Jesus Christ our Lord!

—ROMANS 7:14–25

The law of God is holy, righteous, and good, but we are none of those, even as believers. We are still selfish, demanding, unholy, ungrateful, and rebellious. In spite of the fact that we have laid down our arms in our war against God, we are still capable of treachery. Although we are sons and heirs, we continue to require God's fatherly discipline. Although we have been crucified to the world, we are still worldly in our attitudes and actions.

Some escape such realistic biblical language by creating a two-level scheme in which superior Christians may live the perfectionistic life by "using" the Holy Spirit, while the rest are allowed to experience defeat. Since it is either one or the other according to perfectionism—either total victory or total defeat—it is quite impossible for these believers to accept partial victory, as Paul clearly does. Whenever Paul looks within, he is depressed, but when he looks outside himself, as he does at the end of the passage, he is encouraged. Finally, the hard realities of Romans chapter 7 are followed by a matchless, victorious announcement: "Therefore, there is now no condemnation for those who are in Christ Jesus. . . ." (Rom. 8:1).

The life of the Christian under the cross, then, is unquestionably imperfect. It is a mixture of faith and doubt, obedience and disobedience, health and sickness, ease and distress, pleasures and pain, plenty and poverty. But in all of this, whether good or ill, it is the cross of Christ, not the circumstances of life, that determine the believer's security and hope. As patience is missing in much of contemporary spirituality, so too is the notion of hope. We cannot wait for God to make all things new: we must legislate heaven on earth, or name and claim our own personal happiness, or claim our victory over all known sin. And yet, Paul cautions us to persevere in hope:

The creation waits in eager expectation for the sons of God to be revealed. For the creation was subjected to frustration, not by its own choice, but by the will of the one who subjected it, in hope that the creation itself will be liberated from its bondage to decay and brought into the glorious freedom of the children of God. We know that the whole creation has been groaning as in the pains of childbirth right up to the present time. Not only so, but we ourselves, who have the firstfruits of the Spirit, groan inwardly as we wait eagerly for our adoption as sons, the redemption of our bodies. For in this hope we were saved. But hope that is seen is no hope at all. Who hopes for what he already has? But if we hope for what we do not yet have, we wait for it patiently.

—ROMANS 8:19–25

There is an anti-gnostic thrust in this passage. First, the believer's final redemption is tied up with the whole of creation. It is not only the redemption of our bodies but of "the whole creation" which participates in our groaning, the cry for final liberation from all suffering, pain, sickness, poverty, war, and sin. Where is this cry, this longing, this hope in our circles today? From God's perspective, it is true: We still have not found what we are looking for on this side of the Jordan. Paul's point hits the mark— "Who hopes for what he already has?"

Some may chide us for contenting ourselves with "less than God's best." But when suffering, doubt, and temptation really hit us, only this biblical vision will anchor us to the Rock. We may be accused of not living in "victory," but we will fight on, knowing that our sword will fall from our weary grip only when we lie down in death. Martin Luther expressed it this way:

> That may be called the Christian life that is never at perfect rest, and has not so far as attained as to feel no sin, provided that sin be felt, indeed, but not favored. . . . While flesh and blood continue, so long sin remains; wherefore it is ever to be struggled against. Whoever has not learned this by his own experience, must not boast that he is a Christian.[12]

Celestial existence awaits us in the celestial city, but here, like Bunyan's Pilgrim, we are faced with unending opposition and find ourselves often overwhelmed. It is in these moments that the theology of glory will tell us to step up to the higher plane. But Scripture calls us to look to Christ in the middle of it all, right where we are. While the theology of glory will meet spiritual depression and "the sin that so easily entangles" (Heb. 12:1) by directing us to what is happening within us, the theology of the cross will point us in a different direction: "Let us fix our eyes on Jesus, the author and perfecter of our faith, who for the joy set before him endured the cross, scorning its shame, and sat down at the right hand of the throne of God" (v. 2).

SUFFERING—A WAY TO FREEDOM

Few of us will experience the torment of Dietrich Bonhoeffer, the young German pastor who was executed by the Nazis in 1945, and yet this theology of the cross was his bread of life. In his *Letters and Papers from Prison*, he tells us, "We ought to find and love God in what he actually gives us; if it pleases him to allow us to enjoy some overwhelming earthly happiness, we mustn't try to be more pious than God himself," failing to appreciate God's many gifts. And yet, "It's presumptuous to want to have everything at once—matrimonial bliss, the cross, and the heavenly Jerusalem. . . ."[3]

Christ endured not only the physical suffering, but the anguish of God's wrath against us in our place. How can we complain as if we suffered more than he? Bonhoeffer had no patience for the individualistic view of salvation, which made everything revolve around "me and my own personal happiness," in "the anthropocentric [human-centered] sense of liberal, mystic pietistic, ethical theology," preferring to ground his hopes in "the creation and the incarnation, crucifixion, and resurrection of Jesus Christ."[14]

To a friend he insisted that the message of the cross in connection with our suffering is found not only in the New Testament, but in the Old. To see the cross merely as something that gives us health, wealth, and happiness is to miss its richness,

> . . . and that is just what gives rise to an unhealthy methodism, which deprives suffering of its element of contingency as a divine ordinance. . . . Indeed, the only difference between the Old and New Testaments in this respect is that in the Old the blessing includes the cross, and in the New the cross includes the blessing. To run to a different point: not only our actions, but also suffering is a way to freedom. In suffering, the deliverance consists in our being allowed to put the matter out of our own hands into God's hands. In this sense death is the crowning of human freedom. . . . I think that is very important and very comforting.[15]

While Bonhoeffer's theology, like Barth's, was less than orthodox at certain important points sense, his use of the theology of the cross is instructive for us: "The church is the church only when it exists for others," as Jesus, "the crucified" was "the man for others."[16] As Christopher Lasch pointed out, "Unable to conceive of a God who does not regard human happiness as the be-all and end-all of creation, the practitioners of 'I'm okay, You're okay' spirituality cannot accept the central paradox of religious faith: that the secret of happiness lies in renouncing the right to be happy."[17]

Those who promise the world health, wealth, and happiness, or total victory over sin in this life, are false prophets who refuse to accept individual redemption with the redemption of the whole creation at the end of history. Their message of glory is selfish, and that which biblical religion calls sin (i.e., being curved in on ourselves) they call the gospel. They promise individual, spiritualized escape from the world, not the future redemption of the world in all of its comprehensiveness and materiality.

Gnosticism promises the salvation of the spirit immediately from its supposedly fleshly exile, not the salvation of the whole created order in the future. If we are to be faithful to Scripture, we must be willing to embrace the cross in this life, and to groan with the rest of creation. It will be a foolish way to live, in the eyes of the world. And worldly Christians will tell us that it is hopelessly inadequate as a way of attracting "seekers" by appealing to their felt needs. "But for those who are being saved, it is the power of God and the wisdom of God" (1 Cor. 1:24).

TRUE LOVE AND THE WAY OF THE CROSS

Paul says that the preaching of the cross is foolishness to Greeks because they seek wisdom. The word Scripture uses for wisdom is this *gnosis*—from which, as we have already seen, we get the term "Gnosticism." It is not wisdom or knowledge in the biblical sense, but the "higher knowledge" that is mystical and direct.

In 1 Corinthians 13, Paul contrasts love with *gnosis*. Many have used this passage to argue for the superiority of religious emotion over intellectual reflection, since Paul says that knowledge *(gnosis)* will pass away, while love will remain. However, this was far from Paul's intention. In fact, it was the gnostic who made this sort of case, as the Greek concept of *eros* (from which we get "erotic") love was basically identical to *gnosis*— "higher knowledge" or mystical intuition.

In contrast, Paul not only pits love against *gnosis* (translated "knowledge"), but *agape* against *eros*. This is an important point as we try to work through the meaning of this theology of the cross for our own lives. By understanding what the first-century hearer might have thought when this letter was read to the congregation, we can see more clearly how our own understanding is more gnostic than Christian in some respects.

Swedish theologian Anders Nygren's influential work, *Agape and Eros* (published first in 1932), demonstrated that the New Testament, especially Paul's letters, set up *agape* against the Greek *eros* throughout. The two types of love can be easily contrasted, Nygren argues. *Agape* is God's love for those who offer him nothing in return and initiates fellowship. Especially for Paul, the idea is linked to the cross; in fact, Nygren calls it "Paul's theology of the cross." Nygren observes,

> The cross of Christ undeniably stands at the centre of his preaching.
> . . . Anything that might come alongside this and in any way displace it,
> he carefully avoids, 'lest the cross of Christ should be made void'[18]

The cross is not only the way in which we can define *agape* (1 John 3:16); it is God's realization of his *agape* purposes for his people. Love, then, is not an idea, as in Greek thought, but an action of God. It is not a relationship based on our works, but on God's grace; not on human emotion or ascent, but on divine initiative. Paul calls Yahweh, "the God of *agape*" (2 Cor. 13:11), and the readers would have regarded this as a direct snipe at the gnostic preference for *eros*.

Then what is *eros*, and why does it differ so radically from *agape?* According to Nygren, after careful study of the gnostic texts that drew heavily on Plato and Neoplatonic developments, *eros* can be described under three headings: "Acquisitive Love," "Man's Way to the Divine," and "Egocentric Love." In the *Phaedrus*, Plato states the myth of *Eros* that undergirded much of Greek mysticism: the soul, in its pre-existent state, experienced the "ideal" spiritual realm—the vision of the true, the good, and the beautiful. But the soul fell and became entombed within a body. It is now the struggle of the soul to remember these ideas, these precious visions of the spiritual realm. "This upward attraction of the soul is *eros*," says Nygren.[19]

Eros directs our attention from the physical to the spiritual, from the temporal to the eternal. When Plato and the Greeks speak of "love," then, they are not talking about love for God, God's love for us, or our love for neighbor, but rather the love for the realm of Spirit, the vision of glory.

In his *Symposium*, Plato draws the picture of a heavenly ladder. The mystic must climb this ladder, says Plato, "from beautiful bodies to beautiful actions, and from beautiful actions to beautiful forms of knowledge, until at length one reaches that knowledge which is the knowledge of nothing other than Absolute Beauty, and so knows at last what Beauty really is. It is then, if ever, that life is worth living for man, when he beholds Beauty itself."[20] The ancient gnostics appropriated Plato's vision, the medieval mystics and philosophers perfected it (Aquinas called the highest stage in the monk's ascent, "The Beatific Vision"), and modern Christians—liberal, conservative, Quaker, Roman Catholic, charismatic, and pietist—continue to enjoy this mystical and erotic vision of individualism, inwardness, and experience.

Eros is an acquisitive love because it is centered on obtaining something rather than on simply loving, enjoying, and serving a person for his own sake. "The most obvious thing about *eros* is that it is a desire, a longing, a striving," says Nygren. "Hence love, as Plato sees it, has two main characteristics: the consciousness of a present need and the effort to find satisfaction for it in a higher and happier state."[21] *Felt needs* might be a more contemporary way of describing it. It is demanding and never satisfied.

Second, *eros* is "man's way to the Divine." The only communication humans have with gods, says Plato, is *eros*, the constant striving for perfection. Nygren observes, "*Eros* is the way by which man mounts up to the Divine, not the way by which the Divine stoops down to man."[22] Third, *eros* is "Egocentric Love." "Everything centres on the individual self and its destiny. All that matters from first to last is the soul that is aflame with *eros*—its Divine nature, its present straits while it is in bondage to the body, its gradual ascent to the world above, its blessed vision of the ideas in their unveiled glory."[23]

It not only seeks to acquire for itself and to make its way up to God (making it already self-centered), it is preoccupied with self-love. As Plato put it, "It is by the acquisition of good things that the happy are made happy."[24] The modern parallels are as fascinating, of course, as they are obvious.

All of this stands in the foreground as Paul regularly mounts his attack on the Gnosticism that threatened to undermine his church plants. It is why he pits the theology of the cross *(agape)* against *gnosis (eros)*, which is a theology of glory, in 1 Corinthians 1 and 2. *Agape* is a love that conde-

scends from heaven to earth to save out of sheer freedom and mercy, not a love that reaches upward to acquire, consume, ascend, and experience. *Agape* sacrifices rather than demands. It bears its suffering for the good of someone else rather than escaping into some super-spiritual realm where one's felt needs are finally assuaged.

The theology of the cross not only tells us how sinners are reconciled to a holy God; it establishes the road on which believers are to walk for the rest of their lives. It is by God's *agape*, not the believer's, that one is actually saved. But it then becomes the justified believer's responsibility to imitate this kind of love, a love that could never have been known or identified apart from the reality of Christ's cross. It is neither the believer's idea of love, nor his or her experience of love, but God's selfless act of love in the cross of Christ that defines *agape* in opposition to every pagan version.

Eros, however, can never really satisfy. The hedonist who seeks his own satisfaction and determines to find God one-on-one, on his own terms, will be forever dissatisfied in this life, and will be eternally miserable in the next. This is why Jesus insisted that we lose our life in our to gain it, dying in order to live.

FAITH, HOPE, AND LOVE

Many have regarded love as the supreme virtue among the triad, "Faith, Hope, and Love," on the basis of Paul's declaration that prophecies, tongues, and knowledge "will pass away," while love will remain (v. 8). But as W. Robert Godfrey has pointed out, the apostle here distinguishes love not in terms of its excellence, but in terms of its duration.

Prophecy, whether God's self-disclosure in Scripture or in preaching, assumes that there are fallen sinners who must be reconciled to God and instructed in the essentials of genuine faith and practice. Faith, similarly, presupposes the need to trust Someone outside of oneself for redemption from sin and judgment. It is "the assurance of things hoped for" (Heb. 11:1).

In heaven, however, the sinner who on earth had already passed from being "dead in trespasses and sins" (Eph. 2:1), to being "alive together with Christ" (v. 5) and justified by grace alone through faith alone unto good works (vv. 8–10), is finally glorified. In this life, sanctification is incomplete and imperfect. Faith wavers, the understanding is clouded—even though God has clearly revealed himself in his Word, which proclaim his redemptive acts. We

are sometimes shaken in our assurance, and must constantly return to Word and sacrament for renewed hope.

But in heaven, we are instantaneously glorified. Our sanctification immediately catches up with our justification. In glorification, God removes not only sin's guilt and power, but its presence, from the life of every believer, so that full and instant perfection in righteousness is given in one moment. We no longer require faith and hope when we are finally glorified, as there will be no more promises—only fulfillment—but love will go on throughout eternity.

Paul goes on to say in 1 Corinthians 13, "For we know in part and we prophesy in part, but when perfection comes, the imperfect disappears. When I was a child, I talked like a child, I thought like a child, I reasoned like a child. When I became a man, I put childish ways behind me. Now we see but a poor reflection as in a mirror; then we shall see face to face. Now I know in part; then I shall know fully, even as I am fully known" (vv. 11–12).

Love remains, even after prophecy and knowledge, because in heaven our knowledge of God will finally be direct and immediate. That for which the mystics seek so enthusiastically will be finally given, not here, but there; not now, but then. It will not be attained by human eros, but will be freely given, as everything else, by divine *agape*.

Those who seek God immediately and directly here and now are too ready to dispense with the scaffolding of faith and knowledge, doctrine and Scripture, preaching and sacraments, as if they had outgrown childhood supports. Advanced beyond their age, they feel themselves to be in God's immediate presence as if they were now already glorified saints. Because they are "in the Spirit," they do not need inferior human language, words, doctrines, and rituals. But this is not Paul's teaching: "Now we see but a poor reflection as in a mirror; then we shall see face to face. Now I know in part; then I shall know fully, even as I am fully known. And now these three remain: faith, hope, and love."

Not only love, but faith and hope, are the abiding links to that which awaits us. In fact, it is faith alone, not love, through which we are justified and guarded. And faith and hope require suffering, perseverance, promise, and a divine encounter through common things that are made sacred vessels of divine grace in God's house.

Words: how fragile and powerless in the face of signs and wonders. And yet, it is the Word of God that created us, sustains us, and redeems us. Water, bread, and wine: how common and boring. And yet, the Holy Spirit uses them to bring us to our Lord and Savior Jesus Christ and to keep us

there, confirmed and established in the promise of the gospel Word. We find God at his greatest strength in the weak things according to the world, the unspectacular, the average things, that God has set aside for sacred use.

"THY LOVE INFLAME IN ME"

One day, we will see God face-to-face just as Peter, John, James, and the other sinners and prostitutes, tax collectors, and thieves saw him so long ago. We will see not only his backward parts, as Moses did, but his face—which in our present frame, no one can see and live. Until then, we must be satisfied with receiving God and enjoying his presence as he has "clothed" himself in flesh, in preaching, in teaching, in sacrament. Here, God hides us behind the rock and allows his glory to be indirectly viewed, as, looking to the cross, we see the Name pass by: "I will have mercy on whom I will have mercy. I Am who I Am." Granted, these are "mirrors," as Paul calls them, seeing God indirectly and through our unfocused and shadowy vision, but they are sufficient for intimate communion with the Triune God until we see him as he is, unveiled for immortal eyes.

We possess eternal life by promise, but in the next life, we will enjoy it in its fullest reality. In this life, our relationship with God is continually mixed with joy and despair, moments of experiencing great nearness to God and other moments experiencing what appears to be total abandonment. And yet, it is in those fearful moments of perceived estrangement that God is nearest. It is just when things seem the most foolish, that God's wisdom breaks through to us. It is just when we are the most powerless that God, using a means that appears equally powerless, is saving, revealing, and loving. Like the cross itself, God is at his best when it looks as if he is at his worst.

War with sin and doubt, guilt and depression, are not signs of defeat, but proof of Christ's victory. After all, those who are not baptized into Christ by the Spirit are at peace with sin and unbelief. The absence of war within is true only of people in one of two states: unregenerate or glorified. The believer is presently in neither. Such conflict is not the evidence that one is a "carnal Christian" but is the genuine experience of every believer throughout the course of this life.

True faith does not run ahead of God's plan as if we were already enjoying paradise. It looks for the crown at the end. Meanwhile, it is willing to fasten the trembling hand to Jesus, who "humbled himself and became obedient to death—even death on a cross!" (Phil. 2:8). In fact, the Christian not only imitates our Lord's humiliation, but is baptized into that historical event.

In Adam, we have the mirror of ourselves trying to confuse ourselves with the Creator, ascending above our created place to share God's glory through a "higher knowledge." In the Second Adam, we see the Creator descending below his eternal rank to become less than the least of all human creatures, opposing Satan with the written Word. It is this message that evokes genuine emotion and piety, melting our heart with the condescending love of the glorious Son of God:

> What love is this of thine, that cannot be
> In thine infinity, O Lord, confined,
> Unless it in thy very person see
> Infinity, and finity, conjoined?
> What? Hath thy Godhead, as not satisfied,
> Married our manhood, making it its bride?
> Oh, matchless love! Filling Heaven to the brim!
> O'er-running it; all running o'er beside
> This world! Nay, overflowing hell, wherein
> For thine elect there rose a mighty tide,
> That there our veins might through thy person bleed
> To quench those flames that else would on us feed!
> Oh, that thy love might overflow my heart,
> To fire the same with love! For love I would.
> But, oh, my straitened breast! My lifeless spark!
> My fireless flame! What, chilly, love, and cold?
> In measure small? In manner chilly? See!
> Lord, blow the coal. Thy love inflame in me.
> —Edward Taylor [1642-1729]
> *Preparatory Meditations Before*
> *My Approach to the Lord's Supper*

The Christian story ends where it began. Humankind's fall began when he tried to attain his own divinity. The story continually repeats the human search for "the naked God." But it is actually man himself who stands naked, a stranger as Camus put it, before God, himself, and others. But he can be clothed and welcomed, if he will accept the Father's robe and the Father's family, graciously provided by the God who is himself clothed in human flesh and delights in calling us his brethren.

194

APPENDIX A

A Perspective on the Spiritual Drift in Hymnody

The average Christian will learn more from hymns than from any systematic theology and the hymns also chart the progression from classic hymns of the seventeenth and eighteenth centuries (especially those of Charles Wesley, Augustus Toplady, John Newton, and William Cowper) to the romantic "songs and choruses" of the nineteenth and twentieth centuries. Below are some classic hymns to contrast with examples that I dragged out of a very (happily) dusty box of music books many of us grew up with in fundamentalist and evangelical churches.

CLASSIC HYMNS

"All People That On Earth Do Dwell," to the tune of the Doxology, is the "Old Hundredth" (Psalm 100), composed by Louis Bourgeois, Calvin's church composer, in 1551. The music actually says the same thing as the words, moving reverently and majestically through this God-centered psalm. And yet these metrical psalms were so joyful that Queen Elizabeth named them "the Geneva jigs." Too often, joy is confused with triviality and exuberant thanksgiving with noise, but here we have an example of worship that possesses gravity, depth, seriousness, and gratitude together.

Who can forget John Newton's "Amazing Grace"? But he also wrote, "Glorious Things of Thee Are Spoken," with the third verse reading,

"Blest inhabitants of Zion, washed in the Redeemer's blood, Jesus, whom their souls rely on, makes them kings and priests to God. 'Tis his love his people raise over self to reign as kings; and as priests, his solemn praises each for a thank-offering brings."

Like the warm orthodoxy of eighteenth-century Lutheran hymns, the Calvinistic hymns of the same period reflect the harmony of awe and joy, thoughtful reflection and jubilant emotion. One actually feels like expressing emotion when the great lines from redemptive history are sung! It is not "Alleluja" sung repeatedly, or "Wow Jesus, you're so neat." These cross-centered hymns contain realistic confessions of sin and reliance on the Atonement that are often missing from the general body of contemporary praise music.

For instance, Newton sings, "Could we bear from one another what he daily bears from us? Yet this glorious Friend and Brother loves us though we treat him thus: Though for good we render ill, he accounts us brethren still." Who can hold back the tears and expressions of joy when singing those lines? One of my favorites is Cowper's "Let Us Love and Sing and Wonder":

"Let us love, and sing, and wonder, let us praise the Saviour's Name! He has hushed the Law's loud thunder. He has quenched Mount Sinai's flame: He has washed us with his blood. He has brought us nigh to God. . . . Let us wonder; grace and justice join, and point to mercy's store; when through grace in Christ our trust is, justice smiles and asks no more."

These classic hymns, just a sampling of the riches contained in hymnals that are now quite difficult to locate except in used theological bookshops, are hardly stiff, cold, and formal. But the passion within the lyrics is linked to truth. There is content, without which the great hymnwriters believed there could be no legitimate, godly emotional response.

THE NINETEENTH-CENTURY ROMANTIC HYMN, OR "SONG"

Like many Puritan poets, from the Elizabethan period onward, Isaac Watts (1674–1748) exploited the imagery of a garden in "The Church the Garden of Christ."

We are a Garden wall'd around,
 Chosen and made peculiar Ground;
A little Spot inclos'd by Grace
Out of the World's wide Wilderness.

The contrast between this earlier appeal to the garden imagery and that of the romantic period is illustrated in the familiar hymn of the early twentieth century, "In the Garden." Rather than the church corporately figured as the garden of Christ, this later hymn declares, "I come to the garden alone." Jesus, the lover, meets his paramour among the dew-soaked roses. Such an experience "none other has ever known." It is such a personal relationship that it is as if no one has enjoyed it besides the individual writing (and presumably singing) this hymn. It is not a hymn of the people of God, but of the self and its lover.

By claiming a direct, immediate, secret, mystical, and indeed unique experience with God, this hymn represents a departure from historic Christian belief. It represents the romantic shift from the objective to the subjective, from the person who is known to the person who is knowing (knowing in the gnostic sense, viz., experiencing). "When I'm with Him" is a far cry from "Crown Him with Many Crowns." The former reads, "When I'm with him, . . . when I'm with him, . . . the fairest pleasures of the world grow dim; . . . and in my heart I feel the thrill of glory, when I'm with him, when I'm with him."

"Since Jesus Came into My Heart" is typical of the romantic hymns in that it is a musical "testimony" of the hymn-writer's own personal experience that is set forth as normative for the worshiper. Jesus is still the central figure, but it is not Jesus as the Lamb of God, but as the lover who indwells the self, that is often in view. As we have argued, it is dangerous to react against this sentimentalism by rejecting the wonderful biblical truth that we are indwelled by the Holy Spirit. Furthermore, Jesus is, in a real sense, our lover whose selfless compassion secured us as his co-heirs. Nevertheless, this metaphor of the lover is not an end in itself. His love cannot be separated from his saving action, and this is where many of the romantic hymns lose touch with the theology of the cross.

"Victory" and perfect peace, perfect joy, perfect surrender are prominent themes in these songs, heavily influenced not only by Romanticism but by the Keswick "Higher Life" movement, which B. B. Warfield characterized as "Protestant mysticism."

Even "Blessed Assurance" offers evidence of this influence of the Higher Life movement on its author, Fanny Crosby: "Perfect submission, all is at rest. I and my Savior am happy and blessed." The God and the Christ outside of us (the Reformation emphasis) is replaced with God and the Christ within the individual's heart (the medieval and gnostic emphasis).

The gnostic disdain for human aspects (body, passions, etc.) appears again and again as we "Fight manfully onward, dark passions to subdue." Heaven is a major theme, but it is seen more in terms of romantic sentimentalism and escape from nature than as glorification and perfect communion with Christ. "Sinner, why not come and join us on our trip to the sky?" one hymn-writer queries. "I'll Do the Best that I Can" was a popular hymn written by the Stamps Quartet.

In "Climbing the Stairway of Love," we read, "I now am climbing the stairway that leads to heav'n above. Each step is guided by God's great hand of love. I'm moving higher and nearer that home up in the sky, and if by faith I keep climbing I'll reach it by and by." Here are some other examples: "Higher yet and higher, out of clouds and night, nearer yet and nearer rising to the light,—Light serene and holy, where my soul may rest, purified and lowly, sanctified and blest."

In the "Living Above" songs and choruses, the first entry is, "I Want to Rise Above the World": "I want to live up in the highest heights where Heaven's radiance glows." At least one could interpret this chorus as looking forward to the future state, but another exults in what is claimed here and now: "I've been on the mountain top and seen his face. . . . Lifted in his arms to heights I tho't could ne'er be mine."

The theme of seeing God's face and experiencing that direct encounter is what Luther meant by the "theology of glory": the desire to see "the naked God" in his majesty. While Newton was singing about the "glorious things" that are spoken of Zion, God's holy church, Ellen Goreh writes of being "In the Secret of His Presence." "Would you like to know the sweetness of the secret of the Lord? Go and hide beneath his shadow: this shall then be your reward; and when-e'er you leave the silence of the happy meeting place, you must mind and bear the image of the Master in your face, of the Master in your face."

Oswald J. Smith's "Deeper and Deeper" expresses a similar idea: "Into the heart of Jesus, deeper and deeper I go. . . . Into the will of Jesus, deeper and deeper I go . . . . Into the cross of Jesus, deeper and deeper I go. . . . Into the joy. . . . Into the love. . . . Rising with soul enraptured far from the world below." Even the mention of the cross here is not a reference to the same cross that stood outside of center-city Jerusalem in 33 A.D., but a metaphor or allegory for one's own personal experience of intimacy with Jesus.

The mystical intimacy between the soul and Jesus (i.e., his Spirit) is represented in, "The Touch of His Hand On Mine." "There are days so dark that I seek in vain for the face of my Friend Divine; but tho' darkness hide, he is there to guide by the touch of his hand on mine." While such authors are often men, most men I know would feel somewhat uncomfortable singing "love songs" to another man, even if he is Jesus Christ. The mystic's love for Jesus is romantic; the orthodox believer's love for Jesus is filial and is always linked to his saving work. We do not love Jesus "just for who you are," for apart from his saving acts we do not have any reason to love him any more than we love any other historical figure.

This theme of the "namelessness" of God is replete in gnostic as well as mystical literature: God cannot be described, or, if he can at all, it is by negation—that is, by saying what he is not. Similarly, the Gaithers write, "There's Just Something about that Name." Well, what? All of the names for God and for Jesus Christ are pregnant with theological meaning, but unless one unpacks that truth, we are left with "just something about that name." In our day especially, nobody seems to know quite what that "something" happens to be, for that would ruin the moment with theological questions. Please understand that these criticisms are in no way intended to charge the authors with heresy, but simply to contrast the two distinct forms of piety engendered by two distinct orientations.

Reviewing many of these songs I grew up with, I was amazed at the extent to which Jesus seems to be conceived of exclusively as a friend and as someone who lives inside of us. I searched in vain to find a single chorus that clearly presented Christ as the One who satisfies the wrath of a holy God, for wrath and judgment are out of keeping with the romantic spirit. It is love, the ineffable (that is, unexplainable) One, the indescribable encounter, that is of interest. One finds very little objective, redemptive, doctrinal content in their works and if that is true for the songs produced during the postwar years to the eighties, it is even a greater problem with the *Maranatha Songbook* and the Vineyard songbooks. Let us limit the discussion to the latter, although we could use a great deal of space on the *Maranatha Songbook*.

Remarkably, written by a husband- and-wife team, "By Your Side" goes like this:

"By your side I would stay, in your arms I would lay. Jesus love of
my soul, nothing from you I withold."

John Barnett writes, "There is a season for faith beyond reason, there is
a time for lovers to cry." Not only is this deeply sentimental; it makes little
sense. Besides advocating anti-intellectualism, it sounds like the advice of
a talk-show therapist or author of a romance novel.

As we have seen, the "theology of glory" characteristic of Gnosticism
and mysticism in general, has as its goal the ascent into the presence of
God to touch him and to see him in all of his glory, even though he has
said that no one can see him and live. "Draw me closer, Lord," goes another Vineyard song. "Draw me closer, dear Lord, so that I might touch
You, so that I might touch You, Lord I want to touch You. Your glory and
Your love, Your glory and Your love, Your glory and Your love, and Your
majesty." This is an invitation to disaster, for apart from Christ (who is
nowhere to be found in this song), "our God is a consuming fire," and to
see him or touch him is to be turned to ash (Heb. 12:29).

"I'm in Love with You" is another "love song to Jesus." Since the rest of
the song does not say much more than the title, we need not quote the
entire piece. A little later in the songbook we are encouraged to "turn t'ward
to kiss Your face." It is difficult to find a single song in the Vineyard
songbooks that actually presents us with a Christ-centered, cross-centered,
doctrinally sound and thoughtful exposition of biblical teaching for use in
praise. Yet we are told in Scripture that our congregational singing is actually part of the teaching of God's Word (Eph. 5:19).

Clearly, the one praising is more central than the one praised: "I Bless
You," "I Have Found," "I Just Want to Praise You," "I Only Want to Love
You," "I'll Seek After You," and on and on we could go. When we are
singing these choruses, we should ask ourselves whether we are really singing praise to ourselves or to God. If the focus is on our activity, rather than
on God's saving work in Christ, then clearly we are worshipping the wrong
person.

After a week of struggling with sin in my life, the last thing I need to
do is enter God's presence exulting in my heart and actions.

"Spirit of God" reads,

"I can almost see your holiness as I look around this place. With
my hands raised up to receive your love, I can see you on each face.

Spirit of God, lift me up, Spirit of God lift me up, fill me again with your love sweet Spirit of God."

Notice the "theology of glory": The worshiper is expected to sing, "I can almost see Your holiness as I look around this place." And yet, Isaiah, when he saw God's holiness, immediately recognized, "I am an unclean man and dwell among a people of unclean lips" (Isa. 6).

Further, "With my hands raised up to receive Your love"? Rather than hands raised out to receive the earthly elements of bread and wine, or to turn the pages of Scripture, it is the hands raised up to the air that become receptacles of divine love for the soul. Finally, can the people really "see [God] on each face"? At its best, it is sentimental mysticism; at its worst, it is gnostic pantheism. Emerson and Thoreau would have appreciated the "spark of divinity" on each face, but it is certainly sub-Christian by any measure.

The famous "Spirit Song," written by John Wimber, reads, "Oh let the Son of God enfold you with his Spirit and his love." Now, how would that first line be rewritten in a more classical Christian vein? Perhaps, "Oh trust the Son of God to redeem you by his flesh and his blood." It even rhymes with the original version.

CONCLUSION

This is not written in order to provoke reaction, but to help us recognize the extent to which popular forms of worship have come to be dominated by gnostic influences. These influences are not calculated by the songwriters, who are, no doubt, sincere and devoted believers, and there are exceptions to the rule I've described. Nor is it to suggest that those who write (or sing) them are heretics, even though some of the content is at least heterodox and in a few cases heretical. One must persist in heresy and refuse correction in order to be an enemy of the Faith, but ignorance is a serious problem that cripples the church and easily accommodates departures from clear biblical teaching. May God grant us a new generation of Bachs, Handels, Newtons, and Topladys who can tune their harps to sing God's praises in a way that sacrifices neither truth nor love.

APPENDIX B

Questions for Further Reflection

1. *Sometimes I experience radical encounters with God in worship and in prayer, life-changing encounters. Are you saying that this is wrong?*

Quite the contrary. The psalmist declared, "My heart is stirred by a noble theme . . . ." (Psalm 45:1). Similarly, the apostles always reached their highest crescendo of praise when they had just spread out again before the sight of themselves and their readers the great jewels of Christian truth.

Paul, for instance, reaches his highest pitch when listing the doctrines of grace. After declaring that we have been predestined, called, justified, and will certainly be glorified, he exclaims, "What, then, shall we say in response to this? If God is for us, who can be against us?" (v. 31). He then begins to unpack the practical implications of this sort of teaching: "Who will bring any charge against those whom God has chosen? It is God who justifies. Who is he that condemns?" (vv. 33–34). It is as if he has reached an Alpine summit, reminded once again of the grandeur of redemption: "Who shall separate us from the love of Christ?" he asks, listing the obstacles that might be thought to undermine the believer's relationship with Christ, but concludes, "No, in all these things we are more than conquerors through him who loved us" (v. 37). No wonder Handel set these words to music in *The Messiah!*

Similarly, in Ephesians 1, the same apostle was so excited about our election, redemption, calling, adoption, and sealing in Christ that he wrote one amazing run-on sentence lasting for thirteen verses! He cannot even take a breath for normal rules of grammar! There is a tomb in Palestine that remains empty because God raised His Son from the dead and seated him at his right hand, where he intercedes for us sinners below, until he returns in glory to judge the living and the dead! How can we keep our hearts from bursting with praise and thanksgiving? But it is the announcement of a truth that evokes that response. It is doctrine that shapes life and experience, and bad doctrine or ignorance will not—cannot—lead to healthy Christian life or experience.

Far from being afraid of experience, we should be delighted when a truth so takes hold of our heads and our hearts that we are constrained to respond in gratitude and exuberant joy. But our experience must always conform to God's Word, never vice versa. The biblical approach is to address the whole person—not merely the mind, or the heart, or the will. This is, after all, what is required in the exercise of saving faith itself: *knowledge* (the intellect), *assent* (the affections), and *trust* (the will).

We must bear in mind our Lord's sharp rebuke of the Pharisees, quoting Isaiah 29:13: "These people honor me with their lips, but their hearts are far from me. They worship me in vain; their teachings are but rules taught by men" (Matt. 15:8–9). Scripture itself must determine our experience and worship of God, but we should beware of even turning biblical teaching into an end in itself, whereas the goal of sound doctrine is heartfelt gratitude and thankful obedience. Note that neither Jesus nor Isaiah was saying that it is wrong for us to honor God with our lips (the reference here is to formal, liturgical worship in Israel), but that there must be a connection between the lips and the lives, through the heart.

Our intellect has priority because "faith comes from hearing the message" (Rom. 10:17), and this is a task that requires first that we comprehend what we are hearing and then respond to it emotionally, volitionally, and physically. When I find people who claim to believe in the great doctrines of the Faith, and yet do not seem terribly moved by those truths, my first inclination is not to assume that they "have the right doctrine, but the wrong heart-attitude," but that they do not really grasp the implications of the doctrine in the first place. To put it another way, we must always beware of stopping short at possessing the truth; the goal is for the truth to possess us.

We can expect people only to grow as they (a) understand the truths of God's Word, (b) experience the joy and comfort that comes from those truths, and (c) seek to put "feet" to those truths in everyday life. This is why, for instance, the Heidelberg Catechism not only spells out the doctrines of Scripture, but asks, "How does this comfort you?" It is our duty as preachers and teachers to not only lay out the doctrine, but to help people to process the message, internalize it, and work through the implications in terms of action. But as J. Gresham Machen warned of liberalism, so too we must warn evangelicalism today, that in order to have a practical, applied Christianity, there must first be a Christianity to apply! We experience God in truth, not in experience itself. It is because he reveals himself so magnificently in his Word that genuine experience has any chance of emerging.

2. What would a genuine experience with God look like on a Sunday morning?

In Acts 2, we have the familiar pattern of worship laid out for us. The early Christians gathered regularly to hear the apostolic preaching and teaching, to receive Holy Communion, and to participate in fellowship and prayer together in community. This regular communal fellowship with the risen Christ is the sustenance of the Christian community, the only way in which individuals or the church in general can grow and become witnesses to Christ.

If we used this, then, as a pattern, we would shape our service around the ministry of Word and sacrament. Everything would have to relate directly to these means of grace and serve to give them prominence. So let's take these each one at a time. First, there is the preaching and teaching. How much time and energy is devoted to preparing sermons and lessons? Is the church more committed to programs than to teaching? Is the sermon a concentrated proclamation of the biblical text, or a casual pep talk that requires little study? Or, on the other end, is the sermon a lecture on the meaning of Greek words? Or, is it mere moral exhortation? We call all of this "preaching," but our Lord himself warns us, as he did the Pharisees, that any form of preaching or reading the Bible that misses Christ at the center is not genuine preaching or reading of Scripture.

One reason that many come away from preaching concluding that the Word is insufficient to produce true life and experience is that it is not law-and-gospel preaching, raising the snake on the pole in the wilderness to cheer the hearts of sinners. Are the sermons long enough and substantive enough to actually communicate God's Word to his people in this time and place? Or do we turn first to the sermon when we are looking for time to pare off for "special music" or a visiting drama troupe?

Second, there is communion. Evidently, this was as regular a practice as the sermon itself in the early church, and we learn this not only from Acts 2 and elsewhere, but in the earliest documents of the church and its liturgy. Is communion a regular and integral part of our communal life as the body of Christ? It was for the apostles, and that is why Paul had so much to say about its importance in 1 Corinthians 10 and 11. Interestingly, one of the criticisms that the Reformers had of the medieval church was that the faithful did not receive both the bread and the wine in communion and that they participated in the sacrament so infrequently. Calvin, in fact, thought that it should be offered every time the Word was preached, as seems to have been the custom of the first Christians.

Third, Acts 2 mentions fellowship and prayer. Very often we assume that fellowship is, first of all, horizontal. That is, it is really a spiritual way of "socializing." But that is not the primary meaning of *koinonia* in the New Testament. It is not so much our fellowship with each other, but our corporate fellowship with Christ that is in view. We are all one body not because we have all decided to voluntarily sign up for this or that particular church, but because the Holy Spirit has grafted us into the Vine. Is our fellowship characterized by a common confession of sin and a confession of faith—a common creed? Or do we see ourselves primarily as individuals who happen to be gathered together in a building, as spectators at a football game? Is God doing something for us and with us together, or are we doing something for ourselves and with each other? This is an important question in terms of focus.

Prayer is also mentioned. One thing that has fallen sharply in many evangelical churches today is the time given to prayer. In the older liturgies (forms of worship), whether Orthodox, Roman Catholic, or Protestant, prayer is so important that the service is sometimes even referred to as "Morning Prayer" or "Evening Prayer." The Anglican book of worship, in fact, is called, *The Prayer Book*. It was Jesus himself, raised with a prayer book in the synagogue, who taught his disciples a form of prayer when they asked him, "Teach us to pray." It was not simply a spontaneous, informal prayer that they had in mind, for it was common for rabbis to teach their disciples how to pray with written prayers. Whether formal written prayers or informal extemporaneous prayers (hopefully there will be a good mix), we must recover extended periods of time in regular worship for addressing our God and Savior who meets with us.

I fear that we are simply jettisoning from the regular worship service everything that does not somehow keep the tempo going and sufficiently excite the seeker. Television, with its quick pace, seems to set the standard. This will always lead us to cut out that which we consider "boring"—such as long prayers of intercession, especially those in which particular individuals are mentioned by name. Should we really spend so much time in the service praying corporately for Betsy Miller's recovery from surgery? If entertainment is our goal, this will be easily excised from the service, but if our goal is fellowship in Word and sacrament, in prayer and mutual encouragement, we cannot be so bold.

If the Spirit is especially present where his people are gathered in fellowship around Christ, should we deprive our fellow-Christians from our intercession, when God promises to answer prayer? Paul stated, "I urge, then, first of all, that requests, prayers, intercession and thanksgiving be made for everyone," including the government, including non-Christian officials (1 Tim. 2:1).

In practical terms, this means that we should reassess our view of music in worship as well. Is it supportive or central? Here is where things get really tricky, and this may reveal that we have almost made an idol out of music. Is the choir too prominent and is more time given to the worship band than to these other aspects of worship that are actually commanded in Scripture? Does the music lead the congregation in worship or does it tend to become an end in itself?

The Reformation refused to throw the baby out with the bathwater, retaining those basic elements that had characterized Christian worship, while purging the service of human innovations. The idea of "starting from scratch" was inconceivable—not merely because the Protestants were slaves to tradition, but because they had an acute sense that they were sinful, and sinful people who ignore the wisdom of the ages are always reinventing a broken wheel that will have to be constantly corrected by successive generations.

We have already seen the biblical justification for the elements in the service from Acts 2. Studying the biblical passages that provide us with glimpses of normal worship, we can discover the following elements, most of which followed the pattern of Jewish synagogue worship, with baptism replacing circumcision and the supper replacing Passover. We have the call to worship or benediction (Num. 6:24–27; Rom. 1:7; 15:33; 1 Cor. 1:3; 16:23–24; Heb. 13:20–21); public reading of Scripture (Luke 4:17–19;

Col. 4:16; 2 Thes. 3:14); the sermon (Acts 20:7–12; 1 Cor. 14:26); the Lord's Supper (1 Cor. 11:17–34). As we have also seen above, Paul called for public prayers of petition and thanksgiving.

For these reasons, the evangelical worship service that emerged out of the Reformation, with some variations, included: an opening invocation of benediction in which God's blessing was conferred on the people; the reading of the law, followed by confession of sin. After the corporate acknowledgment of sin and the need for forgiveness, and the acceptance of that forgiveness in Christ, the minister declares the assurance of pardon in Christ's name. Notice how evangelistic this service is designed to be, for Christian and non-Christian alike! After all, they believed that Christians needed to hear the gospel as badly as unbelievers. Some sort of expression of joyful thanksgiving should follow this announcement, followed by the confession of faith (usually the Apostle's or Nicene Creed, joining with fellow-believers through the ages), the prayers, Scripture reading, the sermon and, depending on frequency, the Lord's Supper. A closing benediction sends the people on their way as the Savior himself gives them His parting grace as they go back out into the world.

Observing the intensely vertical direction of this order of worship, we can easily see how this dimension is often lost in seeker-driven worship today. This classic form of worship, drawn from the Scriptures rather than from our own cleverness or taste, balances form and freedom so that each week we can be confident that the whole congregation will be reevangelized and sent out to be "salt" and "light" in the coming week.

3. *What's wrong with contemporary "praise and worship" services and how do you justify the suggestion that there is only one biblical way to worship? Isn't style neutral?*

An age-old debate throughout church history, the struggle to define the extent to which our services must conform to the Bible has obtained fresh relevance. The Protestant Reformers were concerned that the medieval church had been too "creative," too innovative, in adding ceremonies and worship activities. The result was a fresh look at the ancient worship of the church and the biblical commands, preserving that which had apostolic warrant (the prayers, the forms for worship, minus idolatry and superstition). Their goal was not to reject everything in tradition, but to evaluate everything in the light of Scripture. It had to conform to the pattern described above and the ceremonies, exciting as they might have been for those attending medieval services, had pushed the Word into the shadows.

The Reformers' critique of the medieval church as "innovation" in worship can be made of contemporary evangelicalism, where the zeal for the "new and improved" in popular American culture is shared by many Christians. God does not want us to be creative and exciting in our worship. He has given us our guidelines, so that we need not consult the Philistines and Canaanites as to how we should come into God's presence. "God is spirit, and his worshipers must worship in spirit and in truth" (John 4:24). Our imaginations, our emotions, our clever minds, are "idol factories," as Calvin said, and they will always lead us away from God unless we are constantly judging our worship by the Word. While tradition can err, it does not err quite as easily as individuals.

C. S. Lewis spoke of "chronological snobbery," an epidemic of our age, which leads moderns to look down their noses at past ages. If it is new, it must be wiser. After all, did we not put a man on the moon? But wisdom and know-how are not the same. Every new, fresh, creative idea I have ever had for worship, it turns out, has some antecedent in church history, often rejected for good reason. Some debate hashed out all of the ramifications. Now, I might still disagree with the way things were settled at the end of the day, but would I not be foolish if I failed to make use of the arguments each side set forth? Why should I try to reinvent the wheel? It would be like a lawyer preparing for an important case without reading anything about past cases of a related nature.

Contemporary worship is not merely a matter of the period. We are all engaged in contemporary worship in that sense, since we are alive now in this time and place and not in another. But, like contemporary Christian music, which in many ways has shaped contemporary praise and worship, we are now talking about a distinct style, a unique genre that is inherently iconoclastic and often deeply influenced by the gnostic spirit of individualism, subjectivism, mysticism, and a deep suspicion of institutional authority in the form of creeds, confessions, church discipline, and the like. In short, this style of music is shaped by popular culture, and one has to ask, it seems to me, whether popular culture is more suited to carrying the virus of worldliness than cultural expressions that were at least more self-consciously attuned to Christian concerns. Bach, Handel, or, for that matter, Watts, Toplady, and Wesley, were far more biblically literate and saturated with the God-centered theology of their Reformation communions than those of us living today. While we should not fail to notice the great composers and writers in our midst who are both artists and students of Scripture, we should not expect a great revival of church music to be produced by a religious subculture that is driven by the marketplace.

In the "Arts" section of *Newsweek*, May 30, 1994, an article on contemporary Christian music appeared, occasioned by—you guessed it—a sexual scandal. *Newsweek* writer Paul O'Donnell observed that the form is almost exclusively "modeled on the seventies' soft rock of Carole King and James Taylor." "It's sappy-sweet and never sad," he notes. As Christian artists moved further into the mainstream of pop music, "The object of the singers' love grew vaguer; videos got gaudier." It's a far cry from "quartets humming 'blood-and-cross' hymns.'" While some of the earlier leaders in the contemporary Christian music scene express concern over the fact that Warner, EMI, and other secular conglomerates have now moved into the market, many of them assuage their consciences with the thought, *At least it's better than the alternative: secular pop*. But is it better, especially if a secular news magazine can spot the shallowness and the absence of the cross?

In the 1920s, J. Gresham Machen, an orthodox Presbyterian professor who opposed the liberal drift of his church and seminary (Princeton), warned against Bible reading in public schools on the grounds that the core message of Scripture—sin and redemption—would be scuttled. In order to appeal to a broad public consensus, the state would be imposing a new religion of human morality in the place of Christ's saving work, and this would be a disaster for church and state alike. Could we not make a similar argument in this case? Free enterprise capitalism means that the marketplace rules and whatever other objectives various artists might have for their music, Christian pop—if it is successful in the marketplace— must jettison any sharp edges that might restrict the sales share. The result of capitalism and contemporary popular music merging with the evangelical ghetto becomes painfully clear: a banal, spiritually, and intellectually benign genre of mass consumption.

Just as Machen's critics insisted that exposing the nation's children to biblical morality would be better than nothing, so advocates of contemporary Christian music defend the industry on this rather pragmatic basis. However, if Christianity is true and preaching another gospel, which is no gospel, is taken as seriously as the New Testament indicates, how could it be preferable to a clear-cut secular alternative? At least Madonna has a reputation for immorality and greed, but who will protect our Christian children from the doctrinal confusion of so much contemporary Christian music? In this respect, one should be far less worried about Clapton than about Carman. (Besides, ironically, Clapton at least has a song, "Lord, Have Mercy," while Carman advocates the prosperity gospel and a curious *Star Wars* theology.)

There are some outstanding exceptions of which I am aware, but many in this industry view themselves as free spirits that soar above the clutches of church authority. Unlike composers such as Bach and Handel and writers Toplady and Newton, these do not see themselves as accountable to the church for their music, but as accountable to a profit-making company. The question is, What factors and influences shape this style? Quite clearly, it is popular music—a style that is closest to commercial culture. When the psalmist exclaims, "My heart is stirred by a noble theme" (Psalm 45:1), it is difficult to conceive of him composing a tune that sounds remarkably like a familiar jingle for an airline or automobile advertisement.

Style is not neutral; it is the "incarnation" of the message. As flesh is to the soul, style is to the message. "Amazing Grace" to the tune of "Gilligan's Island" is not merely bringing God closer, but is a trivialization of the content, rendering the god who is finally brought nearer not much of a god worth worshipping after all. The upbeat, "pop" orientation of so much of contemporary worship reflects the imbalance of current evangelical spirituality, where shallow "don't worry, be happy" sentiment replaces mature discipleship and the fear of God that leads to wisdom (Psalm 111:10).

Theology is never divorced from the forms in which it is expressed. Furthermore, the contemporary Christian music industry, which is responsible for much of the new praise music, is not answerable to any official ecclesiastical body, in sharp contrast to the practice of church bodies through the early part of this century. For instance, hymns published in the Presbyterian hymnal of the last century bore the benediction, "Approved for worship by the General Assembly." At the very least, ministers and elders should carefully analyze the music rather than leaving it to musicians and music directors who may not have a trained eye for spotting weak or misleading theology.

The fact of the matter is that the classic hymns (generally speaking, before the nineteenth century) were written by pastors or well-informed laypeople who were deeply immersed in the great truths of Scripture. By contrast, we are living at a time when there is a crisis of truth even in the evangelical churches. Shallowness, doctrinal ignorance, and spiritual apathy are too often tolerated in the name of love and unity. In this kind of situation, it is quite predictable that an inferior quality of hymns and worship music will dominate. Like the Reformation, which gave us Bach, Handel, congregational singing, and the now-forgotten tradition of psalm-singing, we need another theological and spiritual reformation that will create a new wave of church music.

Yale's George Lindbeck and Duke's William Willimon are among a growing chorus calling us to recover our own language as Christians. We are so eager to win the culture, it seems, that we have forgotten our own identity. The result is that we are constantly aping the culture, expecting a secular, market-driven society to give us our melody and often the message itself. Church music is unlike rap music or country music or even contemporary Christian music. It is not even "classical music," although that assumption is often made. Bach's "Sheep May Safely Graze" is, strictly speaking, church music rather than classical music, while his "Brandenberg Concertos" fall into the latter category. Church music is its own genre, its own distinctive class of congregational "folk music," part of Zion's heritage, and just as we must never give up words such as "sin" and "redemption" simply because they are not considered in vogue, we must not give up the rich heritage of hymns and psalms simply because unbelievers have never heard them.

On another level, this failure to sing as well as speak our own language of Scripture is not only undermining the community of faith; it fails to really attract the unchurched. Reports are coming in from various quarters now, telling us that the number of converts to evangelical faith is steadily decreasing for the first time in this century—at the very time when we are boasting in our success. Could it be, at least in part, because "seekers" would not bother with church unless it offered something different from what they could get somewhere else? Not long ago, I was talking to an unbeliever who said that she had attended an Orthodox Jewish synagogue recently. She was still deeply affected by the strangeness of it all, the centuries-old forms that seemed to provide the people there of all ages, including the friend who brought her, with a sense of relatedness that was lacking in her own rootless life. Could this be why many younger evangelicals are turning to Rome and Eastern Orthodoxy just as many of their own leaders are handing the churches over to popular culture? Is there nowhere to escape from the banality, glitz, and self-centeredness of talk-shows, sit-coms, and rock concerts?

It is a disappointing measure of the state of affairs today that one must visit a secular music store to find church music recordings because the Christian gift stores do not stock them. It is a most remarkable irony that in our day it is those music stores that stock Madonna rather than Carman that continue to make our church music available, and that the music that was written for congregations to sing in worship down through the ages must now be heard almost exclusively in secular concerts. The world preserving church music: Who would have ever thought?

4. *How can you be opposed to contemporary praise and worship services on biblical grounds if the songs are taken directly from the Psalms?*

On the surface, it does look like an audacious criticism: Who can criticize God? But one need only scan the various collections of praise choruses out there to notice that there is a something strikingly absent: the "meaty" portion of the biblical passage. Take the Psalms, for instance. Most are divided into two sections: doctrine and application, or, the record of divine activity and the call for response.

Let's look at Psalm 106, for example. It begins with a call to worship: "Give thanks to the LORD, for he is good; his love endures forever." Even in the opening call, there is a reason for giving thanks: he is good and his love endures forever. Then, from verses 2 to 46, the song describes the faithlessness of Israel and the faithfulness of God in spite of it. The psalmist even includes himself as part of the sinful nation. It is a historical narrative, recounting disobedience after disobedience and God's recurring, never-failing redemption. It is the people of God telling the story around the campfire, a story of God's faithfulness in spite of everything stupid and sinful they have done. Only in the last two verses of this hymn does the psalmist call for response again and even here it is a call for God to act: "Save us, O LORD our God, and gather us from the nations, that we may give thanks to your holy name and glory in your praise. Praise be to the LORD, the God of Israel, from everlasting to everlasting. Let all the people say, 'Amen!' Praise the LORD."

My suspicion would be that if this psalm, one of the richest, were included in a contemporary chorus book, it may well suffer severe editing, leaving it with perhaps only the first and last verse! Many of these praise choruses focus on the worshiper rather than on the one who is being worshipped. The reader would do well to go through one of these collections of modern praise choruses and note the references to "I," "My", and occasionally "We." Too often, we are singing our own praises, celebrating our own celebrating! Where is the content? Why should I praise the Lord? Tell me something about him that will stir my heart to sing his praises. Do not simply tell me what I should be doing right now; tell me what God has done. Recount his activity, his saving purpose, his wonderful and unfailing promises. My love, devotion, praise, and zeal are fleeting and fickle, but his are from everlasting to everlasting. Contrast, "I keep falling in love with you, over and over, and over and over again," repeated, with that second line from "Rock of Ages": "Could my zeal no respite know, could my tears forever flow, nought for sin could these atone. Thou must save, and thou alone."

The biblical text never gives us the subjective (my experience or my offering of praise or obedience) apart from the objective (God's saving work in Christ). To put it another way, it never concentrates on what we are to do before first establishing what God has already done. Much of contemporary praise music fails to set God and his redemptive acts clearly before our eyes so that we will have something to motivate heartfelt gratitude. To be sure, the psalmist rarely fails to direct the people to praise God in response, but it is always linked to something that has gone before it. That initial part, the recounting of God's acts, is often missing, even in contemporary choruses that rely directly on the psalmist's text.

Another point should be made in this connection. Not only are the doctrinal or historical sections often ignored, but the less "happy" psalms are avoided as well. A friend recently pointed this out to me in connection with Psalm 5. Many of us are familiar with the praise chorus taken from the first three verses, beginning, "Give ear to my words, O Lord, consider my meditation. Hearken unto the voice of my cry. My voice shalt thou hear in the morning. O Lord, in the morning, will I direct my prayer, unto thee, and will look up" (vv. 1–4). But that is not where the psalm finishes. The very next verses read, "You are not a God who takes pleasure in evil; with you the wicked cannot dwell. The arrogant cannot stand in your presence; you hate all who do wrong. You destroy those who tell lies; bloodthirsty and deceitful men the Lord abhors" (vv. 5–6). It is a little difficult to sing these lines with rapturous delight, and, no doubt, the psalmist did not intend it to be sung in that fashion. Nevertheless, it was sung. It was part of the whole story.

This, clearly, is the "law" portion of the psalm, driving us to despair of our own righteousness, so that the next section of the psalm (the gospel) will make sense: "But I, by your great mercy, will come into your house; in reverence I will bow down toward your holy temple. Lead me, O Lord, in your righteousness because of my enemies—make straight your way before me" (vv. 7–8). Unbelievers are under God's judgment (v. 10), "but let all who take refuge in you be glad; let them sing for joy" (v. 11).

5. *If the focus of corporate worship is on what God has done and is doing rather than on what we have done and are doing, what is the place for singing?*

In this book, I've argued that we have raised singing and praise to a sacrament, where we believe that God comes to us and embraces us as we engage in musical celebration. Does this mean that we should abolish singing altogether and exclude music? Hardly! I am with Luther in his suggestion that music is second only to theology as a servant of God. In fact, I would argue that congregational singing is part of the Word of God. We are singing truth, teaching one another and forming our weak speech to at least attempt to give God his due.

We must be careful in this matter of what we sing not because music is unimportant, but precisely because it is so vital. Just as we would want to be sure that the preacher handled the text accurately, we should expect nothing less of the musicians or the congregation singing the text provided for them. We are singing not only to God and for God, but to and for each other as priests. We are declaring God's Word in song rather than sermon, but it is still the Word. This is why we must be so careful with our selection of music.

God's Word does bring Christ to us in the singing and in the other parts of the service where it is proclaimed, read and affirmed, but chiefly in the proclamation of the Word in the form of the sermon. But the purpose of congregational singing is to call upon the name of the Lord and then to thank him for hearing and answering that prayer. What happens in the middle of all of that—the central focus of worship—is God's action in Word and sacrament, as his Spirit links us to Christ's saving life, death, resurrection, and present intercession.

Therefore, singing should never be seen as the point of the service. It is the response to these divine activities. Changing the name from "worship" to "celebration" often reflects a deeper shift from a service that is God-centered to a service that is human-centered, focused on our celebration rather than on the One who is worthy of our fear and praise, adoration and thanksgiving. But in the biblical view, the worship service is not primarily our offering to God, but his offering to us. It is his coming again and again into our lives, judging, justifying; condemning, delivering; crushing, restoring. Our response must accommodate all of these divine actions.

We must always beware of the temptation to invent new sacraments, and especially in viewing praise as a magical technique for conjuring up the presence of God. He is present by his Spirit through Word and sacrament and links us to Christ in an intimate fellowship even if there were no music during the entire service. We must not suppose that God can be brought down to earth and experienced more deeply to the degree that we praise him. He sends his Spirit on his terms, through his appointed means.

6. *You almost make it sound as if God is only involved with our lives through Word and sacrament and if that's true, doesn't that restrict God's personal activity to the church hour? Doesn't this simply promote a deistic religion, where God is not really involved in our daily lives?*

There are these twin dangers, often attractive even to the same person: either to see God's grace as unmediated (that is, not requiring any material means, since it is spiritual) or to see it as mediated through *everything*. If Word and sacrament do not limit the means through which God reveals himself and dispenses his saving promise, we will see nearly every human activity as "sacramental." Not only do we find it especially easy in our age, filled with idols of the imagination, to see God's grace in this way; it is related to the opposite poles mentioned at the beginning of this book *immanence* (nearness) and *transcendence* (distance).

To be sure, God is everywhere and is not to be seen as confined to space which he himself has created. But it is not primarily physical distance we are talking about here. It is holiness, a sense of moral and ontological distance. That is, God is rather different from me, because I am a creature and a sinful creature at that.

There is a great attraction in our day, even on the parts of some evangelicals, to eradicate the distinction between Creator and creature. It is as if the very idea of God's transcendence is itself erroneous. How could we have a personal relationship with a God who was distant? But that is just where the incarnation comes in, right at the point where we begin to think that having a personal relationship with God means either that one does not need physical means or that everything is capable of serving as a means of God's self-disclosure and redemption.

These opposite tendencies, then, come from the same source. Whether we deny sacraments as means of grace or affirm more than Word and sacrament as means of grace, we are saying the same thing. We are saying that God comes to us in ways that are apart from or beyond Word and sacrament. Both anti-sacramentalism and hyper-sacramentalism make the same point: God is entirely immanent, either directly or through nearly every common daily experience of life.

But is God not involved with our daily lives? Does he merely break in or intrude on our lives when we are sitting inside a church building, hearing a sermon and receiving bread and wine? No, that is not what is being argued. Our point is that there are two ways of speaking of God's activity or involvement: providence and miracle. When God provided for the children of Israel in the wilderness by sending showers of bread and quail, it was a miraculous provision. When he provided for Israel after the nation had arrived in the land, by sending rain and bountiful harvests, he was no less involved in the lives of his people, but it was a providential rather than miraculous involvement.

If we fail to see this distinction between providence and miracle, we will end up either failing to see God as intimately involved with the great majority of our lives, or trying to turn everything into a miracle. Those who are suspicious of God's providential activity or are not content with his involvement through natural processes and ordinary means actually call into question the belief that God is the Creator and Lord of nature. We have seen that this is a gnostic dualism between creation and redemption, nature and grace. We need not resort to either deism (entrusting the better part of our lives to materialistic, natural forces) or superstition (rejecting God's use of natural means to bring about his purposes in our lives).

God is involved with our lives when we are having children and raising them in his care and keeping; nevertheless, conception and childbirth are not miraculous, but providential. When, however, God became a zygote in the uterus of a Jewish virgin, God's involvement in this business of conception was indeed miraculous. And while God is indeed interested in and involved with our lives when we are at our work, fixing our car, listening to a symphony, or playing with our kids in the park, this is a providential involvement. He is just as involved in those activities as he was in creating the world at the beginning of time. But God is involved with even atheists to this extent, whether they know it or not (Matt. 5:45; Acts 17:25–28).

This is why we do not need to be afraid of the natural realm, as many Christians influenced by gnostic tendencies seem to be these days. We do not have to "Christianize" the natural world; God created it. There is nothing unspiritual about thanking God for healing us through a skillful surgeon and the pharmaceuticals he imbedded into trees and plants. Our recovery does not have to be miraculous for it to be credited to God. Similarly, we do not have to abandon secular callings, pursuits, and environments simply because they are not "Christian" ministries, activities, or environments.

Creation is not evil because it is creation; rather, both secular and sacred realms are evil because men and women have voluntarily chosen to rebel against the good Creator. We do not have to justify creation by making it in some sense "sacramental"—a means of God's coming to us in ordinary events. He already does come to us, and to everyone, through the natural creation—but as Creator, not as Redeemer (Rom. 1 and 2). It is only in Christ that one finds God a gracious Father and Savior. And it is only through his ordained means that one finds Christ offered and given for salvation. So when the Holy Spirit grafts us into Christ through faith, given and strengthened through Word and sacrament, this is miraculous involvement, a miraculous participation in our lives and it is, in that sense, unique. Just as the miracles recorded in redemptive history were unique, one-of-a-kind "intrusions" of God as he worked in extraordinary ways, so our miraculous moments with God are unique.

God is always involved, but is miraculously involved—overcoming our sin and unbelief, turning our hearts of stone into hearts of flesh—in our lives through his ordained means of grace. God is involved in this "holy time," not in an ordinary (i.e., providential) but in an extraordinary (i.e., miraculous) manner.

Some will say that this is the typical Enlightenment "dualism" that led to the separation of God from this world in the first place. But deism is not the argument presented here, since we have said clearly that God is involved providentially in every facet of human life—of unbelievers as well as Christians. But pantheism (i.e., perceiving God a part of the creation itself) is no better alternative than secular deism (removing God from involvement with daily life).

Perhaps one difficulty here is the definition of "sacrament." When some feel it necessary to justify God's involvement in daily, ordinary events by christening it "sacramental," they are usually thinking of nothing more than God's personal presence. To say that a trip to Yellowstone is "sacramental," for instance, is usually intended to mean little more than that God's creative power and majesty were clearly seen in the things that have been made (Rom. 1:20). According to Romans 1 and 2, even the unbeliever comes into contact with God in creation, but that is not a saving contact. In fact, it only condemns him for not believing even when God reveals himself so clearly as Creator.

A sacrament serves a much greater purpose. It not only discloses God as Creator, but as Redeemer, and not only as the Redeemer of people in general, but as *my* Redeemer. Furthermore, a sacrament not only reveals; it confers. Through Word and sacrament, God actually gives that which he promises in his gospel—forgiveness of sins, freedom from the tyranny of sin, and eternal life. The sacraments not only testify to or signify divine activity in salvation, but are part of that divine redemptive activity. We do not need a sacrament for the bestowal of life, health, marriage, a calling, and friendship. God gives these things to Christian and non-Christian alike, simply as a faithful Creator—even though the unbeliever holds him in contempt and stands judged.

A sacrament is a means of saving rather than common grace. Just as there can be no salvation apart from a miraculous new birth (John 3:3), so there can be no impartation of the new birth apart from the Spirit working through ordained means (Tit. 3:5). Unlike a trip to Yellowstone, a sacrament is not a means of common grace, but of saving grace. It does not simply impart wonder at God's involvement in creation, but proclaims and seals divine forgiveness, reconciliation, adoption, justification, and sanctification. Nothing other than the Word, baptism, and the Lord's Supper are given this place by God as a means of grace. So we must remember these two rules: Never confuse nature and grace and never oppose them to each other. God is present everywhere and always in providence, but is present in salvation only as he "clothes" himself in Christ and his ministry.

7. *Does Baptism actually save? Why do so many baptized people never exercise saving faith?*

In the face of super-spirituality, it is always necessary to stress God's objective, ordained and formal means of bringing us into fellowship with himself.

Nevertheless, even the biblical sacraments cannot be viewed magically, as if God were *bound* to means. It is true that he does not work outside these means, but it is equally true that he does not *have* to work through them.

God's freedom is upheld in his insistence, "I will have mercy upon whomever I will have mercy and I will show compassion on whomever I will show compassion" (Rom. 9:15). In fact, when Moses wanted God to show him his glory, this was the revelation God gave him (Exod. 33:19). Since baptism is the New Testament equivalent of circumcision in the Old Testament, some parallels may be helpful on this score. In the parables, our Lord warns that it is not enough to simply be a Jew by ancestry. When those who had been following Jesus heard him say that they were slaves, they were enraged: "We are Abraham's descendants and have never been slaves of anyone. How can you say that we shall be set free?' Jesus replied, 'I tell you the truth, everyone who sins is a slave to sin'" (John 8:33–34).

In Matthew's Gospel we see John the Baptist issuing a similar response: "And do not think you can say to yourselves, 'We have Abraham as our father.' I tell you that out of these stones God can raise up children for Abraham. The ax is already at the root of the trees, and every tree that does not produce good fruit will be cut down and thrown into the fire" (Matt. 3:9–10).

Paul follows this line of argument by declaring, "It is not as though God's Word had failed. For not all who are descended from Israel are Israel. Nor because they are his descendants are they all Abraham's children" (Rom. 9:6–7). This is where Paul launches into his defense of God's prerogative to choose whom he will to be saved. Finally, we arrive at Hebrews 4, where the writer warns the readers of going back to Judaism once they have embraced Christ. He does this by reminding them of what happened to the Israelites in the wilderness, when they doubted the promise. "For we also have had the gospel preached to us, just as they did; but the message they heard was of no value to them, because those who heard did not combine it with faith" (Heb. 4:2). Those who believe, Jew or Gentile, enter into God's promised land of rest (v. 3). The rest, even though they are in the covenant and hear the preached gospel, reject it for themselves.

Did this mean that circumcision was an invalid sacrament? Hardly. After all, it was through this sign and seal of God's covenant of grace that the believing Israelites were incorporated into one redeemed people. We speak of a "chosen people," even though the Bible itself testifies to the sad truth that many within this covenant community were not elect. The same is true in the New Testament. Just as God's Word has not failed because some reject it (Rom. 9:6), so too his sacrament of baptism has not failed because some embrace the promise that baptism gives.

God works through his ordained means, but is under no obligation to save everyone who hears the Word or is baptized. We do not know the secret will and operations of God, and that is none of our business—so we bring our children to the Lord believing that they are as entitled to the promises as we are because of God's gracious offer to us and to our children (Acts 2:39). Just as we are to preach the gospel to all people, not knowing who is among the elect, we are to mark our children with the sign and seal of grace. It is God's promise that requires us to obey him in this matter.

Does Baptism actually save, then, if so many who are baptized fail to believe? If the sacraments serve the same purpose as the Word—that is, if they are means of grace—then we can ask the same question of the Word: Does the preached Word actually save, if so many fail to believe? Most of us have no hesitation in answering, "Of course not. God offers eternal life—but if we reject it, we have no one to blame but ourselves. If we accept it, we have no one to praise but God." The same is true of baptism. If God offers eternal life to everyone, even to those outside the covenant of grace, then how much more will he hold us responsible for rejecting his saving grace sealed to us by his Spirit through the Word and baptism?

Those who are reconciled to God are saved through his saving announcement in *word* (preaching) and *deed* (Baptism). Those who reject that saving announcement even though they are covenant heirs are among those to whom the writer to the Hebrews declares, "It still remains that some will enter that rest, and those who formerly had the gospel preached to them did not go in, because of their disobedience. Therefore, God again set a certain day, calling it *today*, when a long time later he spoke through David, as was said before: 'Today, if you hear his voice, do not harden your hearts'" (Heb. 4:6–7).

8. *What should I be thinking about at Communion?*

A practical question some may have after reading the material on Holy Communion relates to the attitude, or frame of mind, when we are participating in this sacred meal. Should we be remembering Christ's physical agony on the cross? Should we be concentrating on our attitude and our response to Christ's death for us?

If the purpose of communion is to be a means of grace, then it is not a matter of remembering or reflecting, but of God giving. God is not asking us to pretend that we were there two thousand years ago and meditation of this kind often depends on the degree of one's imaginative skills. In communion, God is not simply asking me to remember what was done so long ago, but he is actually, by his Spirit, linking me to that historical event. He is giving to me, in my empty hands, eternal life. It is not that the bread and wine are magically transformed into eternal life any more than they become Christ's physical body and blood. Rather, it is through them that God meets me and distributes Christ's heavenly life. We feed on Christ by faith through the Word and through the communion with his body and blood.

What Christ did for us two thousand years ago, he gives to us here and now. It is not just a past event to remember, but a present action of God, that is in view. Therefore, we should be thinking about the Word's announcement of forgiveness, sealed to us in communion. It is God, not we, who make it effective, and that is Good News! Remember, it is not about piety, zeal, the degree of faith, or growth in sanctification. Communion is given to increase our faith and obedience, not as a reward for our faith and obedience. It is God's earnestness, not ours, that is center-stage in this divine act.

9. *How do I get the most out of the sermon, especially if it is the primary means of grace?*

I hesitate to quote someone who himself wrote some disturbing things about God's Word and sacraments, but Karl Barth's insights on this point are quite helpful. He told his students that everyone would get more out of the sermons if (a) the minister treated his sermon as the very Word of God and (b) if the congregation listened to it in that manner. "If we expected to hear God's Word more," he said, "we would hear it more even in weak and perverted sermons. The statement that there was nothing in it for me should often read that I was not ready to let anything be said to me. What is needed here is repentance by both pastors and congregations." The Puritans also had a great deal to say about getting the most out of the sermon, and theirs would hardly ever fall short of an hour and a half, followed by a break and then another sermon! They also enjoyed afternoon discussions of the sermon, and this can be an effective way of working out the implications of the text. Questions may be raised, applications discussed, and appropriate actions pondered.

Above all, we must all come prepared to hear God. Pastors should not give the impression that it is the preacher's own word, his own reflections on life and spiritual growth, or his own experiences and exhortations. This is why the preached Word has traditionally occupied a physical height through a raised pulpit, to accent the divine activity it represents. If the minister is casually roaming the stage, the congregation will be inclined to treat the message in a similar manner. We are, after all, easily directed by impressions. Similarly, the congregation should not come ready to grade the sermon on a scale of one to ten, but should come prepared to be confronted and comforted by God as he meets us through his ambassador.

10. *How should we view our ministers?*

If these worship activities are our standard, then we have to ask ourselves some difficult questions. First, as ministers, how much time and energy do we put into preaching and teaching? This is not a question for pastors and teachers only, but for the whole church. That is because the pastor today is increasingly expected to serve the role of a chief executive officer. While there are many reasons for this, at least one practical reason is the fact that lay church officers are often chosen for worldly rather than for biblical reasons. In 1 Timothy 2 and 3, Paul outlines the requirements for worship and also for church officers. An elder "must be above reproach" in his character and conduct, with his own household (which Luther called "the little parish") in good order. "He must not be a recent convert, or he may become conceited and fall under the same judgment as the devil," Paul says (3:6).

Elders are especially concerned with the spiritual government of the church. It is not their task to administrate the financial and bureaucratic affairs of the church, but to visit the sick and the widow, to regularly visit the members of the church in their homes, and to encourage, exhort, and admonish. They are to make sure that the fathers especially are being priests of their own homes, teaching the children and leading them in the Faith. If their own homes are in disarray, they cannot fulfill this responsibility with integrity. "The elders who direct the affairs of the church well are worthy of double honor, especially those whose work is preaching and teaching," and Paul takes this to include satisfactory wages (5:17–18).

Deacons serve the church by looking after the financial and administrative affairs, especially in terms of charity. But then even deacons must not only have personal integrity, but "must keep hold of the deep truths of the faith with a clear conscience" (3:9). They cannot simply be chosen on the basis of their social standing in the community or their business experience. "They must first be tested," and only then can they serve, Paul insists (v. 10).

In the early life of the church, the administration of charity was becoming a major task, as the apostles required the care of the poor saints (especially widows and orphans) to have a high priority. However, the burden of administrating this project began to occupy the time and energy of the apostles themselves. "So the twelve gathered all the disciples together and said, 'It would not be right for us to neglect the ministry of the word of God in order to wait on tables. Brothers, choose seven men among you who are known to be full of the Spirit and wisdom. We will turn this responsibility over to them and will give our attention to prayer and the ministry of the word'" (Acts 6:1–5). Stephen and six others received the laying on of hands as they were chosen to become the church's first deacons. As a result, "The word of God spread. The number of disciples in Jerusalem increased rapidly, and a large number of priests became obedient to the faith" (v. 7).

There was simple correlation between freeing up the ministers from their administrative "busy-work" so that they could study and pray, and the success of the church in reaching Jerusalem with the Word of God. I am convinced that one of the reasons for the state of the church today is that we expect our pastors to function as managers in a corporate firm. One of the most common things I hear from pastors today is that they do not have time to read, to study, and to pray. Their own personal spiritual health suffers because they have enormous burdens to "run the church." It is not their responsibility to run the church! That is why there are elders and deacons. We must remove the administrative fetters from our pastors and teachers, so they can be free to learn in order to teach, to pray in order to have something from God for the rest of us.

It is the ministry of Word and sacrament that is most important, not the myriad of "ministries" that we have invented for building successful churches on corporate business models. And after the ministry of Word and sacrament comes the ministry of spiritual guidance (the elders) and the ministry of charity (the deacons). If there is any time left over for other ministries, only then should we consider broadening the activities of the church. Let us have the courage to turn our pastors' offices into pastors' studies again.

11. *What is a true church? What are its marks?*

We see the marks of a true church in Acts 2. From this and a host of related passages, the Reformers narrowed the biblical marks down to two essential points: the Word rightly preached, and the sacraments rightly administered. The Reformers added church discipline as a third mark.

First, the Word must be preached correctly. This does not mean that we will always see eye-to-eye with every sermon. In fact, there may be some areas where we are deeply convinced that the pastor is confused. It might even be an important point, but so long as the essential message of the law and the gospel is in tact, the Word is "rightly preached." That is what it meant for the apostles and for the Reformers. We do not leave a church simply because we disagree over his view of the end times, or because he holds a different view regarding the age of the earth.

Furthermore, "the church" was not merely defined by individual congregations, but by the larger body of which these local expressions were a part. Therefore, the Reformers even believed that Rome was part of the true church, though marred and effaced—that is, until the Church of Rome officially pronounced the gospel of justification by grace alone through faith alone "anathema." Then it ceased to be a place where "the Word was rightly preached." That is, it ceased to be a true church.

Second, the sacraments must be rightly administered. This is even more delicate. For instance, if we take this seriously, it means that if we are convinced that scriptural baptism includes the children of believers, we must insist that those churches that deprive their children of this sacrament are not "rightly administering the sacraments." The same would be true of those churches that deny that Christ is truly present in communion and the benefits of his saving work given to believers through the bread and the wine.

This does not mean, however, that one would not regard the members of these other bodies as true Christians, for a distinction has been in the church's historical understanding of scripture on this point. It is the distinction between the "visible" and the "invisible" church. The organization

I serve in Anaheim, in its leadership, is represented by Reformed, Presbyterians, Lutherans, Episcopalians, and Baptists. We are all well aware of these historical "marks of the church," and there are sometimes healthy discussions about this matter. Sometimes the Baptists will tell us that our Reformed and Lutheran churches are not true churches because they do not rightly administer the sacraments by retaining infant baptism, while the Reformed and Lutheran brethren offer the same argument in reverse. Is this simply hair-splitting divisiveness within Christ's body? Not at all. I am grateful that these people take God's Word so seriously that they are willing to stand up for things upon which the Bible places a great deal of weight. But one thing that we all agree upon is the conviction that we are all equally brothers and sisters in Christ. The question of whether this or that church, whether a denomination or a local assembly, is a true church is a matter of formal definition. It is not an assessment of whether a person is truly related to Christ.

Further, we need to ask whether church discipline and good order are maintained, as this was no small matter to the apostles. We must exercise charity in our assessments and we must never conclude that a church is not a true church by ourselves. Here we must ourselves follow proper discipline and leave not only the discipline of ourselves within our own churches to the duly elected elders, but the assessment of other churches to the officers as well. In our day, scandals appear to be epidemic and the gossip, back-biting, and strife that follow in their wake can do more damage than the initial wrong itself. Church discipline means that individual members cannot take matters into their own hands and make judgments about the spiritual affairs of their brothers and sisters. This is left to the officers, who must give an account to God. Thus, at least in theory, such scandals are handled appropriately and behind closed doors.

Public sins require public repentance and private sins are not to become public. If churches followed this rule, as well as the requirements for biblical officers in the New Testament, perhaps ministry would not be so frequently undermined and interrupted. Just as the gnostic tendencies of our age will make it difficult to accept such a high view of God's activity through ordained means, we will also find ourselves opposed when arguing for a high view of order and authority in Christ's church. It is not simply an association of people who have decided to follow Jesus, but a body, an institution, formed by the Spirit for mutual fellowship, love, and accountability.

13. *If true spirituality is communal rather than individualistic, what is the place of "quiet time" and private prayer?*

We have seen how ancient Gnosticism and its modern equivalents are given to private, individualistic spirituality. Does this mean that there is no place for private devotions? Not at all.

The point we do have to bear in mind is that the bulk of biblical examples is concerned with the corporate aspect. While this does not mean that we must never relate our own experiences, it does make the point that the important thing is what happened in the life and times of Christ when he came to save us. More than that, we were created for community, and it was the Fall that interrupted this perfect arrangement so that the most basic form of community—the marriage of husband and wife—became stressful. Cain broke up the familial community by murdering his brother.

Redemption involves the restoration of this communal aspect, so that God willed to form a body, not a collection of fragments. Just a cursory analysis of the biblical metaphors will suffice to make this point: "the nation," "God's people," "Israel," "the Body of Christ," "the church," "the Bride," "the sheep," "the elect," "the redeemed," "the communion of saints," and so forth.

Among the many reasons for giving the communal priority over the individual is the fact that the gospel is not within us by nature, as is the law. By nature, we know the law, but the gospel comes to us as foolishness. An atheist mother teaches her children to stop hitting each other and share their toys, but she does not raise them in the saving knowledge of the Lord. Thus, we will never discover the gospel within and if we were left to ourselves on a desert island, it would be much easier to stray from the clear teaching of the gospel than if we had someone else on the island who could preach the biblical text to us.

This is not to suggest that no transformation can occur when a believer is alone, reading the Scriptures and meditating on its truths. We have all experienced the great depths of liberation known to the psalmist in his meditations. Private devotion is essential for constantly refocusing our faith on Christ and biblical teaching as well as for reminding us of our duty as believers. While it is not the public gathering of the church, it is no less God's voice that we hear in Scripture. And yet, if private devotions were just as sacred a moment as public worship, why would Jesus say, "For where two or three come together in my name, there am I with them"

(Matt. 18:20)? He is forming a people and wills to knit us into his body, not to simply inculcate a personal relationship by ourselves.

14. *Doesn't the Bible itself refer to God as our friend with whom we can experience an intimate relationship? Isn't there a danger of so reacting against a casual view of God that we lose this relational and intimate dimension?*

One of the points I have tried to insist upon in this book is the fact that our distance from God is bridged finally and fully by the God-Man, in his incarnation, life, death, resurrection, and ascension. He has removed the legal obstacles to our fellowship with God and has even stepped across the barricades of time. Not only did he become a figure in human history, he comes to each of us at a particular moment in our own personal history to call us to himself. We are actually united to him through faith in his finished work.

This theology of the cross that so underscores the truth that God loved us while we were yet enemies and still sinners, and that he justifies us even while we are still ungodly, actually gives more place to intimacy than sloppy, sentimental approaches. Here is a God who has not been less than God in loving us. He has satisfied his holiness. It is a holy, just, and righteous love with which he embraces us, not simply a tolerant wink that overlooks our guilt. Furthermore, he does not leave it up to us as to whether we can stir up enough passion in our souls to form a personal relationship. He comes to us and establishes it on the firm rock of his objective Word and sacraments.

Do we want to touch, hear, and see God as John said concerning his own experience of Christ? It will not be by singing about it or imagining that we are touching him. Nevertheless, here he is, given to us as truly as he was laid in the arms of Mary. Do we thirst for the water of life, do we hunger for the bread of life? "Taste and see that the Lord is good" (Psalm 34:8), as you eat the bread and drink the cup. Are you looking for certainty of his love and affection toward you? Do not look within; receive his assurance of pardon by eating and drinking the promise of eternal life.

Those who seek to hear, see, and touch God in their own inner experience find themselves chasing shadows, chimeras, and mirages that dazzle for a moment, only to disappoint. But those who take God up on his promise to give us Christ's body and blood through the Word, baptism, and bread and wine will never be disappointed. "Whoever eats my flesh and drinks my blood has eternal life, and I will raise him up at the last day. For my flesh is real food and my blood is real drink. Whoever eats my flesh and drinks my blood remains in me, and I in him" (John 6:54–56). The reasoning is very simple, objective, and direct: Do I receive Christ, as he offers himself in Word and sacrament? Then I have Christ's own promise, sealed with his own blood, that I remain in him and he remains in me, and I will be raised on the last day.

15. *If the pursuit of "signs and wonders" represents a theology of glory, why did Jesus and the apostles perform them?*

Like the miracles of the prophets, those of our Lord's ministry were signposts of his kingdom. They were not performed primarily for the good of the person healed, nor primarily to attract attention. In fact, again and again we find Jesus restraining his miraculous signs for precisely this reason. For instance, his raising of Lazerus is directly related to his announcement that he is the Resurrection and the Life. His healing on the Sabbath was likewise a sign pointing to a reality far greater than the miracle itself that He was the Sabbath incarnate: "Come unto me, all you who labor and are burdened under, and I will give you rest."

If Jesus viewed his ministry of miracles in terms of a theology of glory, as modern faith-healers, he would hardly have warned people of following him because of the miracles. Is that not the purpose of such "power encounters"? No, Jesus says. "Then some of the Pharisees and teachers of the law said to him, 'Teacher, we want to see a miraculous sign from you'" (Matt. 12:38). Now, for a theologian of glory, this would actually have been a sign of faith. They had come to the show, presenting themselves for the display of divine glory and power. But Jesus replied, "A wicked and adulterous generation asks for a miraculous sign" (v. 39). In Matthew 16:1, we read, "The Pharisees and Sadducees came to Jesus and tested him by asking him to show them a sign from heaven." Jesus again refused to perform a miracle, repeating his earlier warning, "A wicked and adulterous generation looks for a miraculous sign" (v. 4).

This sentiment is displayed when a boy with a demon was brought to Jesus. Again, it would seem that this was a great act of faith on the part of those who entrusted their son to Jesus. But were they coming to him in faith, or were they simply using Jesus as a means to the end of their own happiness? "'O unbelieving and perverse generation,' Jesus replied, 'how long shall I stay with you? How long shall I put up with you? Bring the boy here to me'" (Matt. 17:17).

In a similar vein, Paul warns, "Jews demand miraculous signs and Greeks look for wisdom, but we preach Christ crucified. . ." (1 Cor. 1:22–23). Jesus and Paul were both engaged in a ministry of miracles, but they were designed for a different purpose than signs-and-wonders-seeking crowds and theologians of glory demanded. They were signposts of the gospel. That is why Jesus said that his healing of the paralytic was so "you may know that the Son of Man has authority on earth to forgive sins . . ." (Mark 2:11, emphasis added). The miracles were necessary to fulfill the prophecies of the Son of Man, and yet Jesus was often cautioning those healed not to tell anyone. After healing many, the crowds pressed in upon Jesus, declaring him to be the Son of God and begging him to heal them, but Jesus tried to break away from them. "I must preach the good news of the kingdom of God to the other towns also," he told them, "because *that is why I was sent*" (Luke 4:43, emphasis added).

God has placed his seal of approval on this Man who claimed to be the long-awaited Messiah, God incarnate, God-with-Us. He further approved the apostles and stamped their message with the same authority that was signified by our Lord's own miracles. If we seek miracles today, we will be like those in Jesus's day who sought signs instead of Christ, a faithless generation looking for power and glory instead of weakness and the shame of the cross. We must, therefore, be satisfied with the miracles that Jesus and his apostles performed as giving sufficient authority to the message that they preached. It is the message, not the miracles, that is the point of ministry. If Jesus said that he was sent to preach the Good News of the kingdom and not to dazzle the theologians of glory, surely we should seek no higher and more glorious ministry than his. We need no further demonstration. God has already approved his Messiah and his Messiah's Apostles once and for all. It is now for us to proclaim that divinely-approved and certified message through the power of the Holy Spirit.

16. *What should I do if I am dissatisfied with my church?*

Based on the comments above, we must follow good order and church discipline even when we are convinced that a body is no longer bearing the marks of a true church. It is not up to us to decide by ourselves, so we go first to our elders, including the pastor, and make our case in humility and gentleness, willing to be corrected if we can be shown by the Scriptures to be in error. If we still cannot, in good conscience, be a part of the church, we must make these spiritual officers aware of our intentions and transfer our membership as quietly and graciously as possible. Whatever the case, we should never take it upon ourselves to divide the group or to leave it until we are prepared to transfer our membership to another body.

Some may think that this business of the "marks of the church" will lead to division and spiritual pride. In actual fact, it has the opposite tendency. It means that we cannot leave our church simply because we are dissatisfied with the choir, or the preacher's personality, or because we dissent on nonessential doctrinal issues. The issues have to be clear-cut and serious in nature.

END NOTES

Chapter One

1. William Willimon, "Been There, Preached That," in *Leadership* (September 1995), pp. 74–78.
2. R. Alan Coe, *Exodus: An Introduction and Commentary* (Downers Grove: IVP, 1973), p. 213.

Chapter Two

1. Jackson Lears, *No Place for Grace: Antimodernism and the Transformation of American Culture*, 1880–1920 (New York: Parthenon, 1981), pp. 41–47.
2. David F. Wells, *God in the Wasteland* (Grand Rapids: Eerdmans, 1994), p. ?
3. T. S. Eliot, *Collected Poems, 1909–1962* (San Diego: Harcourt Brace Jovanovich, 1988), p. 55.
4. ibid., pp. 79–82.
5. Joesph Sittler, *Gravity and Grace: Reflections and Provocations*, ed. by Linda-Marie Delloff (Minneapolis: Augsburg, 1986), p. 14.
6. Alexis de Tocqueville, *Democracy in America*, (New York: 1898), vol. I, p. 66.
7. David Riesman, *The Lonely Crowd: A Study of the Changing American Character*, 3rd edition (New Haven: Yale, 1969).
8. Anne Douglas, op. cit.
9. Eric Voegelin, op. cit., p. 12.
10. Wade Clark Roof, op. cit., p. 195.
11. James D. Hunter, *American Evangelicalism: Conservative Religion and the Quandry of Modernity* (New Brunswick: Rutgers University Press, 1983), p. 75.

12. Wade Clark Roof, op. cit., p. 195.
13. Philip Lee, op. cit., p. 119.
14. Harvey Cox, *Fire From Heaven* (Reading, Mass.: Addison-Wesley, 1995), p. 57.
15. ibid., pp. 68–70.
16. ibid., p. 87.
17. ibid., p. 201.
18. See *The Agony of Deceit*, ed. Michael Horton (Chicago: Moody Press, 1991).
19. Harold Bloom, *The American Religion: The Emergence of the Post-Christian Nation* (New York: Simon and Schuster, 1993), p. 177.
20. Pat Robertson, "The Holy Spirit In Your Life," cassette tape on file with author.
21. Kenneth Hagin, *Having Faith in Your Faith* (Tulsa: Faith Library, 1980).
22. Pat Robertson, "The Holy Spirit In Your Life," cassette tape on file with author. Also, in his *Answers to 200 of Life's Most Probing Questions* (Nashville: Nelson, 1984), p. 108, he writes that "when it [whatever you want to possess] is already yours in the Spirit, it is also yours in the visible world."
23. ibid.
24. Harvey Cox, op. cit., p. 224.
25. ibid., p. 313.
26. ibid., p. 318.
27. Pat Robertson, *Beyond Belief* (New York: Morrow & Co., 1985), p.108.
28. Pat Robertson, "The Holy Spirit In Your Life," cassette tape on file with author.
29. Pat Robertson, *Answers To Your Questions* (Virginia Beach: CBN Partner's Edition), p. 76.
30. Geddes MacGregor, op. cit., p. 1.
31. Phyllis A. Tickle, *Re-Discovering the Sacred* (New York: Crossroad, 1995), p. 145.
32. ibid., p. 128.
33. ibid., p. 125.
34. Philip Lee, op. cit., pp. 144, 255.
35. Chuck Smith, *New Testament Study Guide* (Costa Mesa: The Word for Today, 1982), p. 113.
36. ibid., p. 78.

37. ibid., p. 193.
38. Thomas a Kempis, *On the Imitation of Christ*, p. 23.
39. Lewis Sperry Chafer, *He That Is Spiritual* (Grand Rapids: Zondervan, date), p. 23.
40. *Orange County Register*, October 26, 1995, "Accent": "Felled by the Holy Spirit," pp. 1, 6.
41. ibid.
42. Pat Robertson, *Beyond Reason*, op. cit., p. 40.
43. Clark Pinnock, *A Wideness in God's Mercy* (Grand Rapids: Zondervan, 1992), p.140.
44. Cited in Philip Lee, op. cit., p. 210.
45. Abraham Kuyper, *The Work of the Holy Spirit* (New York: Funk & Wagnalls, 1900), p. 257.
46. Wade Clark Roof, op. cit., p. 18.
47. ibid., p. 23.
48. ibid.
49. ibid., p. 30.
50. ibid., p. 258.
51. J. I. Packer cites B. B. Warfield's criticisms and concurs, in "'Keswick and the Reformed Doctrine of Sanctification," *The Evangelical Quarterly*, additional information required.
52. Marylin Ferguson, op. cit., p. 18: "By integrating magic and science, art and technology, it will succeed where all the king's horses and all the king's men have failed."
53. Wade Clark Roof, op. cit., p. 67.
54. ibid., p. 70.
55. ibid., p. 105.
56. ibid., p. 256.
57. ibid., p. 84.
58. ibid., p. 85.
59. David F. Wells, op. cit., p. 199.
60. ibid., p. 195.
61. ibid., p. 201.
62. ibid., p. 202.
63. ibid., p. 129.
64. Wade Clark Roof, op. cit., p. 71.
65. ibid., p. 186.
66. ibid., p. 203.

67. Mark Slouka, *War of the Worlds: Cyberspace and the Hi-Tech Assault on Reality* (New York: Basic Books, 1995), p. 12.
68. ibid.
69. ibid., p. 28.
70. ibid., p. 29.
71. ibid.
72. ibid.
73. ibid.
74. Francis Schaeffer, *The New Super-Spirituality* (Downers Grove: IVP, 1972), p. 13.
75. p. 22.
76. p. 16.

Chapter Three

1. *The Los Angeles Times Magazine,* February 1989, p. 174.
2. George Barna, *Marketing the Church,* (Ventura, CA: Regal), pp. 41, 145.
3. *Newsweek,* September 1984, p. 26.
4. Clement of Alexandria, *Excerpta ex Theodoto,* 78.2.
5. See Peter Jones, *The Gnostic Empire Strikes Back* (Philipsburg, NJ: Presbyterian and Reformed, 1994), for an excellent introduction to the gnostic revival in mainline Protestantism.
6. See Eric Voegelin, *Science, Politics, and Gnosticism,* translated by W. J. Fitzpatrick (Chicago: Regnery Gateway, 1968).
7. Philip Lee, *Against the Protestant Gnostics* (Oxford: Oxford University Press, 1987), p. 80.
8. Cited in Wade Clark Roof, *A Generation of Seekers: The Spiritual Journeys of the Baby Boom Generation* (San Francisco: HarperCollins, 1993), p. 76.
9. ibid., p. 75.
10. Hans Jonas, *The Gnostic Religion: The Message of the Alien God and the Beginnings of Christianity,* second edition (Boston: Beacon Press, 1958), pp. 50–75.
11. Calvin, *The Institutes,* edited by F. L. Battles (missing info. here), p. ?
12. Cited in Henry Bettenson, *The Later Christian Fathers* (Oxford: Oxford University Press, 1971), p. 103.
13. Philip Lee, op. cit., p. 102.
14. ibid., p. 158.

15. ibid. See also Peter Jones, op. cit., where he points to *The Apocalypse of Adam*, a gnostic text about a feminine power that becomes lesbian. He also refers there to the Trimorphic Protennoia, found among the Nag Hammadi discoveries: "I am androgynous," relates the divine revealer. This god/goddess is both Mother and Father, "since I [copulate] with myself." "I am the Womb [that gives shape] to the All by giving birth to the Light that [shines in] splendor. I am the Aeon to [come. I am] the fulfillment of the All, that is . . . the glory of the Mother" (cited by Jones, p. 29).

16. ibid., p. 101.

17. Geddes MacGregor, *Gnosis: A Renaissance in Christian Thought* (Wheaton: The Theosophical Publishing House, 1979, p. 54.

18. U. Bianchi, ed., *Le Origini dello Gnosticismo* (Leiden: Brill, 1967), pp. 178–180. For works on ancient Gnosticism, see also Kurt Rudolph, *Gnosis: The Nature and History of Gnosticism* (San Francisco: Harper and Row, 1987); Edwin Yamauchi, *Pre-Christian Gnosticism: A Survey of Proposed Evidences,* revised edition (Grand Rapids: Baker, 1983); Giovanni Filoramo, *A History of Gnosticism* (Oxford: Basil Blackwell, 1990).

19. U. Bianchi, ed., *Le Origini dello Gnosticismo,* op. cit.

20. Giovanni Filoramo, *A History of Gnosticism* (Oxford: Basil Blackwell, 1990), p. xiii.

21. ibid., xix.

22. ibid., xxi.

23. Nikos Kazantzakis, *The Saviors of God: Spiritual Exercises* (N. Y.: Simon and Schuster, 1969), p. 106.

24. Cf. B. B. Warfield, *Perfectionism* (Philipsburg, NJ: Presbyterian and Reformed, 1958).

25. Kim Riddlebarger, "Trichotomy: A Beachhead for Gnostic Influences," *Modern Reformation* (July/August 1995), pp. 22–25.

26. Jerald C. Brauer, ed., *The Westminster Dictionary of Church History* (Philadelphia: The Westminster Press, 1971).

27. Cited in Vernon L. Parrington, *The Romantic Revolution in America,* vol. 2 of *Main Currents in American Thought* (New York: Harcourt, Brace, 1959), pp. 441–2.

28. Emerson, *Journals*, ed E. W. Emerson, vol. 5, p. 288.

29. ibid., vol. 8, p. 316.

30. Cited in Martin Marty, *Context*, vol. 27, number 14, July 15, 1995, p. 1.

31. Philip Lee, op. cit., p. 93.

32. Cf. Whitney R. Cross, *The Burned-Over District: The Social and Intellectual History of Enthusiastic Religion in Western New York,* 1800–1850 (Ithaca: Cornell University Press, 1982).
33. Martin Marty, *The Righteous Empire* (New York: Dial, 1970), pp. 184–7.
34. Adolf Harnack, *What Is Christianity: Lectures Delivered in the University of Berlin* (New York: G. P. Putnam's Sons, 1904), p. 161.
35. ibid.

Chapter Four

1. Lewis Spitz, *The Renaissance and Reformation Movements* (Chicago: Rand McNally, 1971), p. 38.
2. ibid.
3. See Heiko Oberman's reference to Lortz in *Luther: Man Between God and the Devil* (need info.), p. 248.
4. Lewis Spitz, op. cit., p. 38.
5. ibid., p. 40.
6. ibid.
7. ibid.
8. Walther von Loewenich, *Luther's Theology of the Cross* (Minneapolis: Augsburg Publishing House, 1976), pp. 18–20.
9. ibid., p. 20.
10. Alister McGrath, *Luther's Theology of the Cross* (Oxford: Basil Blackwell, 1985), p. 149.
11. ibid., p. 150.
12. ibid., p. 157.
13. J. Gresham Machen, *Education, Christianity, and the State,* pp. 21–22.
14. ibid., p. 167.

Chapter Five

1. Francis Frangipane, *Charisma* magazine, May 1995, p. 20.
2. Harvey Cox, op. cit., p. 292.
3. Cox, p. 283.
4. Cox, p. 284.
5. Cox, p. 285.

Chapter Six

No Notes.

Chapter Seven

1. *Newsweek*, November 28, 1994, p. 62.
2. Patrick Grant, ed., *A Dazzling Darkness: An Anthology of Western Mysticism* (Grand Rapids: Eerdmans, 1985), pp. 119–120.
3. *The Westminster Dictionary of Christian Theology*, op. cit., p. 53.
4. Clark Pinnock, et. al.
5. H. Richard Niebuhr, [need to track down source]
6. Clark Pinnock, *Grace Unlimited*, op. cit., p. 26.

Chapter Eight

1. John Calvin, *The Institutes of the Christian Religion*, op. cit., 3.1.1.
2. Charles Stanley, *The Wonderful Spirit-Filled Life*, p. 5.
3. ibid.
4. Karl Barth, *The Gottingen Dogmatics: Instruction in the Christian Religion*, vol. 1 (Grand Rapids: Eerdmans, 1990), p. 33.
5. Charles Kraft, *Worship Leader* magazine, April-May 1993, p. 7.
6. Lyle Schaller, *Worship Leader* magazine, July-August 1995, p.34.
7. Karl Barth, op. cit., p. 31.
8. ibid., pp. 31–32.
9. Lyle Schaller, op. cit., p. 34.
10. Richard Foster, *Christianity Today*, February 5, 1996, pp. 26–31.

Chapter Nine

1. Cited by John Armstrong, in *Power Religion*, Michael Horton, ed. (Chicago: Moody Press, 1992), p. 76.
2. ibid., p. 73.
3. Lewis Sperry Chafer, *He That Is Spiritual*, p. 23.
4. John Wesley, *A Plain Man's Guide to Holiness* (London: Hodder and Stoughton, 1988), p. 28.
5. ibid., pp. 28–30.
6. ibid., p. 35.
7. ibid., p. 58.
8. ibid., p. 84.
9. ibid., p. 103.
10. Donald MacLeod, in *Modern Reformation* magazine, September-October 1992, pp. 7–11, 26–28.
11. ibid.
12. ibid.

13. ibid. The continued popularity of this Keswick teaching, promoted by R. A. Torrey, is illustrated in the influence that Charles Stanley attributes to this volume of Torrey's, in Stanley's recent book, *The Wonderful Spirit-Filled Life* (Nashville: Thomas Nelson, 1992), p. 25. It is interesting to see non-charismatics and non-pentecostals adopt an essentially Pentecostal-Holiness view of sanctification.
14. ibid.
15. ibid.
16. ibid.
17. ibid.
18. ibid.
19. ibid.
20. ibid.
21. B. B. Warfield, *Perfectionism*, op. cit., [on Finney].
22. Cited in J. I. Packer, *Keswick and the Reformed Doctrine of Sanctification*, op. cit., p. 153, footnote 3.
23. ibid.
24. J. Robertson McQuilkin, "The Keswick Perspective," in *Five Views On Sanctification* (Zondervan, 1987), pp. 151–183.
25. Lewis Sperry Chafer, *Grace: The Glorious Theme* (Grand Rapids: Zondervan, 1950 reprint from 1922 edition), p. 351.
26. ibid.
27. B. B. Warfield, *Perfectionism*, op. cit., p. 271.
28. *Charisma* magazine, May 1995, p. 30.
29. ibid., p. 31.
30. J. Robertson McQuilkin, op. cit., p. 180.
31. Charles Stanley, op. cit., p. 35.
32. Eric Casteel, in *Modern Reformation* magazine (January-February 1994), p. 22.
33. John Calvin, in John C. Olin, ed., *A Reformation Debate* (Grand Rapids: Baker, 1966), p. 58.
34. Abraham Kuyper, *The Work of the Holy Spirit*, op. cit., p. 502.

Chapter Ten

1. *Newsweek*, November 28, 1994, p. 54.
2. ibid., p. 61.
3. ibid., p. 62.

4. Kenneth Copeland, *The Force of Faith* (Fort Worth: Kenneth Copeland Ministries, 1980), p. 6.
5. C. Peter Wagner, *Your Church Can Grow* (Glendale: Regal, 1976), p. 55.
6. Alister McGrath, *Luther's Theology of the Cross*, op. cit., p. 179.
7. ibid., p. 180.
8. ibid., p. 151.
9. Kenneth Copeland, *Believer's Voice of Victory* magazine, March 1982, p. 2.
10. Pat Robertson, *Answers* (Partner's Edition), op. cit., p. 76.
11. J. I. Packer, "'Keswick and the Reformed Doctrine of Sanctification," op. cit., p. 166.
12. Martin Luther, *Commentary on Peter and Jude*, p. 119.
13. Dietrich Bonhoeffer, *Letters and Papers from Prison* (New York: Macmillan, 1971), p. 169.
14. ibid., p. 286.
15. ibid., p. 375.
16. ibid., p. 382.
17. Christopher Lasch, cited in *The Next Progressive*, Winter 1995.
18. Anders Nygren, *Agape and Eros*, translated by Philip S. Watson (London: SPCK, 1982), p. 115.
19. ibid., p. 172.
20. ibid., p. 174.
21. ibid., pp. 175–6.
22. ibid., p. 178.
23. ibid., p. 180.
24. ibid.

WHAT IS CURE?

CURE is Christians United for Reformation, a nonprofit, tax-exempt organization communicating insights gained from the sixteenth-century Reformation to the contemporary church and society. CURE believes not only that Christians today face a church that in many ways parallels its medieval counterpart, but also that the solutions forged by the reformers are applicable today. CURE's message therefore models that of the reformers, who challenged their church to base its teachings on biblical principles alone. Their rallying cries were "Scripture Alone," "Christ Alone," "Grace Alone," "Faith Alone," "To God Alone Be Glory," and "The Priesthood of All Believers."

SCRIPTURE ALONE

The religious leaders of the reformers' day held Scripture in high regard. The problem was that they believed it wasn't the only source of God's truth. So they elevated extrabiblical teachings and traditions above it.

Today, although most evangelicals would say they believe in the Bible as the sole source of God's truth, the voices of the modern world—consumerism, pragmatism, and the therapeutic and managerial models—are often heard above the voice of Scripture. Instead of objective biblical truth, subjective hunches and intuition abound, with doctrinal and ethical issues frequently settled not by an appeal to the Scriptures but by quoting whatever a popular Christian personality has said. Some evangelicals and fundamentalists add to Scripture their own rules and rituals. In the face of all of this, CURE reissues the cry, "Scripture alone!"

CHRIST ALONE

Today, the Bible is often preached as a handbook for daily living, providing practical principles for leading a happy and successful life. Biblical characters are presented as nothing more than moral examples for believers to emulate. Much like a Christianized *Aesop's Fables,* the story of David and Goliath becomes a source of inspiration for believers to "slay the giants in their lives," and Joshua is a guide to wisdom for business and leadership principles.

But is this really the purpose of the Bible? Jesus confronted the Pharisees, a Jewish religious group specializing in making the Scriptures "practical," with this rebuke: "You diligently study the Scriptures because you think that by them you possess eternal life. These are the Scriptures that testify about me, yet you refuse to come to me to have life" (John 5:39–40). The whole Bible focuses on Christ, yet church growth, self-esteem, political activism, co-dependency, and a host of other "practical" applications often replace the preaching of Christ and him crucified. "Christ Alone!"

GRACE ALONE

"God will not deny his grace to those who do what lies within their power," asserted a popular medieval slogan. A modern equivalent, "God helps those who help themselves," is endorsed by 86 percent of American evangelicals.

Most evangelicals today can quote Ephesians 2:8–9 from memory: "For it is by grace you have been saved, through faith—and this is not from your selves, it is the gift of God—not by works, so that no one can boast." Nevertheless, there is very little understanding today of just what grace means. The doctrines surrounding this central biblical teaching—total depravity, election, justification, faith as the gift of God rather than the contribution of a free will, and the perseverance of the elect in faith—are not part of the spiritual diet in most churches. With only a vague notion of grace and a few memorized slogans, many fail to enjoy the deep and solid assurance and spiritual rest that comes from an understanding of "Grace Alone!"

Faith Alone

The doctrine of justification by grace alone through faith alone was so important to the reformers that they called this the doctrine "upon which the church stands or falls."

But most Christians today cannot define this central tenet of their faith. Like their counterparts in the medieval church, many contemporary Christians believe that being forgiven by God is the result of a life-long process of cooperating with the Spirit in cleaning up their lives. They hope that in the end their virtues will outweigh their vices. But for the reformers, one was declared right with God the moment the Spirit gave the person faith to trust in Christ alone as his or her righteousness. Righteousness is not obtained by working for it, but by receiving by faith the perfect righteousness of Christ. Ever wonder if God really accepts you even though you aren't living the "Victorious Christian Life?" He does. "Faith Alone!"

To God Alone Be Glory

This phrase from the Reformation was found on public buildings, in taverns and music halls, as well as in churches. J. S. Bach signed his compositions with it and even had it etched into the organ at Leipzig! Because of this truth, even the cobbler and the milkmaid were able to understand that their daily tasks were opportunities to bring acclaim to God's name. All of life, not just religion, became the "glorious theater of God's activity," as Calvin put it.

At a time when evangelicalism is so human-centered, seemingly preoccupied with the happiness of glory itself, and in which nonbelievers often view the church in America as little more than a personality cult, this message needs to be proclaimed once again. "To God Alone Be Glory!"

The Priesthood of All Believers

Medieval Christians who really wanted to be "sold out" for the Lord joined a monastery; the others, who were viewed as being less spiritual, simply made money and lived for this world in their secular vocations. The reformers, however, challenged this sacred/secular antithesis by asserting that all Christians—whether farmers, bakers, or milkmaids—were priests in their individual callings (see 1 Pet. 2:9).

Today, Christians engaged in full-time ministry are often viewed as "first-class" Christians, while the rest simply have a job. But the Bible teaches that one can serve God just as faithfully by being a homemaker, artist, doctor, or waiter as by being a missionary or pastor. Not only so, but being a "priest" in the business world means more than working only for a "Christian" company or only producing "Christian" products. The whole world belongs to God. It's time to return to an understanding of "the Priesthood of All Believers."

CHRISTIANS UNITED FOR REFORMATION
2034 East Lincoln Avenue #350
Anaheim, California 92806
(714) 956-2873
(714) 956-5111 (fax)
E-mail: CUREInc@netcom.com or CUREInc@aol.com